LETTERS OF
CHARLES ELIOT NORTON

IN TWO VOLUMES

VOLUME II

Victor D. Brenner, fecit 1906

LETTERS OF
CHARLES ELIOT NORTON

WITH BIOGRAPHICAL COMMENT

BY

HIS DAUGHTER SARA NORTON

AND

M. A. DeWOLFE HOWE

ILLUSTRATED

VOLUME II

BOSTON AND NEW YORK
HOUGHTON MIFFLIN COMPANY
The Riverside Press Cambridge

CONTENTS

ILLUSTRATIONS

LETTERS OF
CHARLES ELIOT NORTON

VOLUME II

Les écrivains illustres, les grands poëtes, n'existent guère sans qu'il y ait autour d'eux de ces hommes plutôt encore essentiels que secondaires, grands dans leur incomplet, les égaux au dedans par la pensée de ceux qu'ils aiment, qu' ils servent, et qui sont rois par l'art.

SAINTE-BEUVE.

As each man has a conscience, a moral mentor which assures him what is truly best for him to do — so has every state a class, which, by its very character, is dedicated to eternal and not to temporary interests. . . . This is the class of scholars. This elevation and correction of public sentiment is the scholar's office in the state. . . . [He] is the representative of thought among men, and his duty to society is the effort to introduce thought and the sense of justice into human affairs.

G. W. CURTIS.

LETTERS OF
CHARLES ELIOT NORTON

CHAPTER IX

THE TEACHER

(1873–1879)

WHEN Norton returned from England in 1873, forty-six years old, the work with which his name is most closely associated — the work of a teacher — lay all before him. His preparation for it was obviously richer than it could have been had he pursued the usual academic course and begun the routine of instruction in early life: he came to his work not as a pedagogue, but as a man of letters and of the world. It was to one so equipped that Norton's cousin, President Eliot — still in the early stages of converting the small college into a great university — committed the task of instructing its youth in regard to the Fine Arts. This commission first took the form of a lectureship on the History of Art. In the academic year of 1874, Norton announced and delivered a course on the History of the Fine Arts and their Relations to Literature. In 1875 he was appointed Professor of the History of Art in Harvard University, and for twenty-three years performed the full duties of that office. In 1898 he became Professor Emeritus, and for the ten remaining years of his life held a place of recognized leadership in the intellectual, artistic and social interests of his community.

It is perhaps worth while here to record what the actual situation in regard to the study of the Fine Arts in our universities was in 1874. Writing to Norton in January, 1874, E. W. Gurney, then "University Professor" of History at Harvard, said: —

"I suggested a plan like this [the establishment of the chair of Fine Arts] to Eliot, last year, as the best means by which to secure your services to the College, and at the same time to provide that the study of History should be recognized to have other sides than the political and legal, from which sides alone it is now approached in college. . . . While, however, I have been, as well as am, in the fullest sympathies with your views . . . I can perfectly understand and respect the hesitation of the Corporation with its present means, to take so considerable a step in a wholly new direction."

In a paper on "The History of the Fine Arts,"[1] Norton wrote: "In the memorable address delivered in 1867 by John Stuart Mill, as rector of the University of St. Andrews, after a wide survey of the intellectual and moral education which the system of schools and universities is intended to promote — Mill went on to speak of a third division of human culture, 'not less needful,' he said, 'to the completeness of the human being,' 'the culture which comes through poetry and art, and may be described as the education of the feelings, and the cultivation of the beautiful.'

[1] See *Educational Review*, April, 1895.

And this, he declared, 'deserves to be regarded in a far more serious light than is the custom in these countries,' that is, in Great Britain. . . .

"To English hearers his words were as novel as they were weighty. Nowhere in English-speaking lands had culture in the arts been admitted as an essential portion of education. They had been regarded as of trivial concern; the study of them had been relegated to professional artists or to mere dilettanti, and the idea that a complete and satisfactory education could not be obtained without some knowledge of their character and history, and without such culture of the aesthetic faculties as the study of them might afford, appeared strange and unacceptable to many even of the most enlightened thinkers on the subject of the education of youth.

"It was about seven years after the delivery of Mill's address that the chair of the history of art which I have the honour to occupy was established at Harvard, and, so far as I know, it was the first of its kind in our country. By its establishment this great branch of the humanities was recognized as having an equal position in the scheme of college or university studies with the other branches, and as needful a function as any of them in the work of education. It was a noticeable step in educational progress."

Before passing to the record of all these years which exists in Norton's abundant correspondence, a word should be said about the individual quality of his work as a teacher. It is to be remembered that the subject of his teaching was open to a wide range of interpretations, and that he belonged to a generation which, in terms of intellectual purpose, had set its stamp upon American life before the achievements of applied science had done so much to obscure the values of a more spiritual culture. As in Norton's eyes the end of a liberal education was the training of the imagination and the consequent widening of the horizon, to that end he gave himself with definite intention in his university lectures. It mattered not if the subject were Egyptian art, Greek art, or that of the Renaissance; an intelligent reading of the Rosetta Stone of the arts could be interpreted in but one way: the way of culture and heightened enjoyment; of practical application of a noble ideal to life.

Believing, too, as he did, that the human being is vitally affected by environment, Norton sought to bring into the intimate possession of youth that understanding of the Fine Arts which should most directly create what is desirable. "Hitch your wagon to a star," he might have urged; but he would have added, "know well the road you mean to take." And of youth he begged, "think clearly." For mere enthusiasm lacking intellectual training and guiding reason, and therefore likely to end in unfruitful labour, he had a limited indulgence. Following, like his ancestor, John Norton, "that way which was purely independent," he appealed with uncompromising directness, and in terms lit by conviction, from mediocrity and irresponsibility to a higher aim and vision. But in this appeal there was no lack of sympathy and helpfulness for those who were not qualified to make an immediate response.

When his eightieth birthday was celebrated, Professor Palmer said of his teaching: "The methods of Mr. Norton were superbly out of date in our specialistic time." This was less true at the beginning of his teaching than at the end of it, when learning "made in Germany" had more firmly established itself as a University standard. In his later years Norton himself said that his utterances in class-room and elsewhere would not have produced the effect they did, had not the country been so unacquainted — broadly speaking —with the fine arts and their power to rouse the imagination and influence the individual life. It was the shower on a thirsty land that quickened the soil.

Inwrought with ethical suggestion, Norton's courses in the University inevitably took on, as the years went by, a character of their own.[1] His classes became very large. His own recognition of the callow or ingenuous undergraduate who elected "Fine Arts IV" as a "snap course" was complete. Once when the number of applicants was so great that the first lecture of the term had to be given in Sanders Theatre, the opening words of it are reported to have been: "This is a sad sight." But Norton, if he smiled at the "sad sight," did not despair of awakening the interest even of the idle, or of implanting in their unaccustomed breasts some other knowledge and ideals than those of the athletic field and the comfortable club.[2]

[1] See "Norton's College Lectures," Appendix B.

[2] In one of Norton's notebooks, he entered — undated and unnamed — under the heading "Idiotika: From Examination Books!" scraps of undergraduate learning which gave him special amusement — for example:

And it was in the lecture-room, as in his public addresses, that the inherited spirit of the preacher constantly expressed itself. Norton's eldest son once invented for these college courses the definition, "Lectures on Modern Morals as Illustrated by the Art of the Ancients," and told it to his father. Amused by the phrase he gave it, in words not precisely recalled, his humorous general assent. A statement of his own regarding the function to be fulfilled by instruction in such subjects as those with which he dealt may be found in his article in the "Educational Review" from which a quotation has already been made: —

"It is through the study and knowledge of the works of the fine arts, quite apart from the empirical practice of any of them, that the imagination, the supreme faculty of human nature, is mainly to be cultivated. . . . And nowhere are such study and knowledge more needed than in America, for nowhere in the civilized world are the practical concerns of life more engrossing; nowhere are the conditions of life more prosaic; nowhere is the poetic spirit less evident, and the love of beauty less diffused. The concern for beauty, as the highest end of work, and as the noblest expression of life, hardly exists among us, and forms no part of our character as a nation. The fact is lamentable, for it is in the expression of its ideals by means of the arts which render those ideals in the forms of beauty, that

"The chief title to fame of Boccaccio was Don Cameron." "The origin of Florence is wrapped in mith and mistery." "Giotto was one of the greatest *genii*." "The Roman Church put a great restraint on the passions of men in the Middle Ages; for Hell and damnation were a great cheque to them."

Facsimile page from a College Lecture Notebook of Norton's

V. Assyrian Art.

'Η Νίνος μὲν, ὦ πορθμεῦ, ἀπόλωλεν ἤδη
καὶ οὐδὲ ἴχνος ἔτι λοιπὸν αὐτῆς, οὐδ' ἂν εἴποις
ὅπου ποτὲ ἦν· ἡ Βαβυλὼν δέ σοι ἐκείνη ἐστὶν ἡ
εὔπυργος, ἡ τὸν μέγαν περίβολον, οὐ μετὰ πολὺ
καὶ αὐτὴ ζητηθησομένη ὥσπερ ἡ Νίνος·

Λουκ. Χάρων. 23.

Need of imagination to reconstruct the
lives of races now extinct. The function
of the historic imagination in its relation
to character, & the present time.

Babylonian Empire   circa B.C. 2230 – 1270
  Destruction of Nineveh B.C. 625
  Conquest of Babylon   536.

Buildings of clay & wood; consequence;
use of this material.
Palace architecture, gorgeous barbaric splendor,
  enormous extent, prodigality of labour.
No standard of excellence; no idea [...]
ple.
Decorative & pictorial sculpture.

the position of a people in the advance of civilization is ultimately determined."

Though Norton here refers to the "concern for beauty," it was beauty informed by a spirit of sanity, and expressing itself, through perceptions of structure and proportion, which was always in his mind; and in saying this, it may also be said that for him the Parthenon summed up almost a code of æsthetics.

Against his declaration of need and purpose in the study of the Fine Arts it is well to place some recognitions of the results of his instruction. These are to be found both in the printed and in the unprinted word.[1] Mr. William Roscoe Thayer has written of Norton's work at Harvard: "The secret of his influence as a university teacher lay in his power to humanize knowledge. In his elucidation the mere special fact became irradiated by its connection with general laws. Thus the pertinence, the applicability to yourself of whatever art or history or nature presents to you, he unfolded very simply, but with unforgettable impressiveness. What he touched, lived: there was no dead knowledge; even erudition took on an unwonted glow. . . . For many years he has been at Cambridge the Oracle of the Humanities; and from Cambridge his influence has been shed afar."[2]

Two private letters, written in 1912, give a personal

[1] Since these words were written a poem to Norton's memory by one of his earliest pupils — Mr. G. E. Woodberry's Harvard Phi Beta Kappa poem of 1913 — has given expression to Norton's influence in terms of happy appreciation and understanding.

[2] *Harvard Graduates' Magazine*, December, 1908.

expression to the relation of master and pupil. Each is from a man whose name and work have an international significance. These letters are typical of a mass of such tributes to Norton the teacher, and are exceptional only in the vigour with which they express what others have said in different terms.

"Norton," says the first of these letter-writers, "had an extraordinary influence over me when I was at Harvard in 1887, more than he knew and more, I am sure, than he would have approved. But looking back upon it after the lapse of years, I doubt if any man ever did me more lasting good. At first his influence provoked in me a vain attempt at imitation, at which, as I look back upon it, I can only smile. I remember his once saying that 'a plain handwriting was a part of good manners,' and I at once set myself to copy his own beautiful hand! That perhaps was the least foolish thing I did in that way. Later on my own nature began to react on what I had heard from him, and I think these reactions, all determined in part by him, were among the healthiest movements of my mind. It is in that way that the best men influence us all in the long run."

The second letter-writer describes the teacher of more than thirty years ago as "*the* great influence in my life. All that I have been and am was and is affected by his teaching and his character. He was the only *real* 'master' I ever had. And if indeed there is a place for the spirits of the good, and if as the wise pretend (all this is of course Tacitus), great souls are not extinguished with the body, may he rest in peace!

He gave me a desire to think clearly and speak accurately, and an admiration of elegant scholarship; he implanted in me the seeds of a loathing of affectation and vulgarity; and he conveyed to me a minute part of his own exquisite scrupulousness of taste which, while it has caused me to suffer many things acutely, has on the other hand been the source of my greatest joys."

It is in a sense touching to record that the writer of this letter had, on leaving Harvard in 1881, written the following words to Norton himself: "And will you allow me to take this last opportunity of expressing my appreciation of all that I owe to you? You have lifted my life to an entirely different plane and you will have my heartfelt gratitude as long as I live. Should I be fortunate enough to accomplish anything good in this world it will be owing chiefly to your instruction and friendship."

To the position of influence truly indicated by expressions such as these Norton came by a gradual process, of which the beginnings are seen to have lain, at least partially, in his personal need for definite occupation. The first stages of his work at Harvard, the interests that engrossed him during the early days of the professorship, are reflected in his letters of the period.

To J. R. Lowell

CAMBRIDGE, May 30, 1873.

We reached home safely last Monday evening, — after a fair, though not pleasant, voyage, — and we found all the friends dearest to us well and happy. The local changes during the last five years are much more marked than the personal changes. Everything seems strangely familiar, and yet to my heart strangely different. America never seemed to me so far from Europe as it does to-day; — and my past life is cut off from my present life by a sea wider and deeper than the Atlantic. . . .

Shady Hill and all Cambridge are at their best with the beauty of apple-blossoms and lilacs, and the fresh green of the foliage of the trees. The spring has been cold and tardy, so that the oaks have hardly leaved as yet, and few of the trees have their full leafage. Cambridge is greatly changed and improved by the building that has gone on during these years; but alas! it is no longer your and my old Cambridge. When I recall it as it used to be, I feel as if I had lived in prehistoric times. . . .

Emerson was a capital sailor, and made the voyage pleasant to me. We celebrated his seventieth birthday on Sunday the 25th. He lamented the date as the close of youth! "Alas, that youth's sweet-scented manuscript should close." But he has a spirit of perennial youthfulness. He is the youngest man I know. One notes a few signs of age in his head, but none in his heart and temper. He was as active as a boy on shipboard; and he talked more than all the rest of the company put together. At times he made me internally impatient with his inveterate and fatalistic optimism; he admits no facts that bear against his philosophy, — a philosophy that has its rise in the pure atmosphere of the America before 1830. . . .

To John Ruskin

ASHFIELD, July 17, 1873.

This little village and its people are as good as I used to report them to you. After six years' absence from them I am not disappointed on coming back. Here is a simple, cheerful, humane, intelligent community, far enough from perfection, but made up of people who for the most part lead sweet, wholesome, helpful lives.

The township is about ten miles square, it is all hill and dale, well-wooded hills of hard, granitic forms, the sinking waves of the mountain range that gives its name to Vermont. The village itself lies on a little high plateau perhaps 1200 feet above the sea, with hills rising close enough around it to give it shelter and protection, but not so close as to overshadow it. In the village there are forty houses, most of them with barns, three country stores, one schoolhouse, one tavern, and four churches; — all built of wood. There are two or three hundred people here, and in the whole township not more than 1100 men, women and children; — plenty of room for them in the ten miles square. The population has diminished slowly in the last thirty or forty years. The soil is too thin, the hillsides too rocky, the winters too long, for the love of birthplace and home to contend with unvarying success against the temptations of Western prairies and of a gentle climate. Each year some family deserts the solitary, outlying farm, and migrates to easier life. The country pays its tribute, too, to the cities. The well-grown, hopeful boys go off, eager to make money, and attracted by the activity, the promise, the wider variety, the glare of Boston and New York. Even the girls are tempted to seek their fortunes elsewhere. They grow restless at home. Life on the farms, with hardly a neighbour's house in sight, is too lonely, too hard, too monotonous for the bright girl who has been at school, and is fit to teach school herself, who reads Longfellow and Bulwer, and the beauties of Ruskin, and the weekly newspaper. And so, here and there, one sees old black farm-houses, tenantless and decaying, doors gone, windows gone, roof falling in, the pathways overgrown with grass and weeds, and only the grandmother's garden flowers and herbs, — honey-suckle, sweet marjoram, lilacs and lilies, — still holding out against neglect, and lifting the sweet banners of tender memories. The half cultivated land quickly falls back into wildness. Nature instantly reclaims it. We have not been settled long enough in New England to tame the earth, to subject it, much less to bring it into sympathy with man. It has not taken the imprint of his likeness.

The surface of Italy has been moulded by the hands of men, like clay on the potter's wheel. England has been shaped by the English of two or three thousand years into a curious image of themselves. But here the soil has not been worked long enough to show many marks of old labour, and nature at once reasserts her full rights over the fields that man deserts after but a partial conquest of them. It may be this resistance of the Earth to man, this brief period of culture as compared with the immemorial tramplings and diggings and hoeings and ploughings of the Old World that in part accounts for the ugliness and bleakness in our common landscape of which you are wont to complain. But even you would see some prettiness, some beauty in Ashfield, in the midst of what is rough and ill-composed. Nature certainly did not show half so much poetic imagination in the construction of America as she did in Europe. She finished you off with exquisite elegance, and she left us very much in the rough. At least all the Western side of Europe was obviously a labour of love, — toward Russia nature began to get impatient and moulded in the flat with a very coarse thumb.

I was interrupted here by our good village doctor driving up in his open wagon to ask me to accompany him on a long drive to see a little sick child in a neighbouring town. I like the doctor. He is a man who has seen something of life, having served through our war as a regimental surgeon. He is perhaps thirty-five years old; with a good heart, and a clear intelligence, and ready sympathies. He knows enough of human nature and of medicine to know that the administering of drugs is but the smallest part of his art. The afternoon was one of the loveliest of the summer; our way took us along pleasant roads through a pretty country, the doctor's horse is a fine creature, and the doctor entertained me with accounts of the families whose houses we, from time to time, passed by. The houses, with scarcely an exception, were neat and comfortable, with an air of pleasantness about them;

and I was the more interested in his talk because it curiously fell in with, and confirmed what I had just been writing to you. He knows this people as well as they can be known, and he has nothing but good to say of them.

He said that whenever a stranger came to town he liked to take him with him on his rounds, sure that he would stop at no house where the stranger would fail to receive an impression of the worth and excellence of its occupants. This was true of all Ashfield; it could not be said of some of the neighbouring towns; there was a great difference in the spirit of different, though bordering, communities. "Our people are all kindly and thrifty folks."

It is pleasant to live where nobody is suffering want, where everyone has self respect, where there are no great differences of condition [1] . . . . If Ashfield does not disappoint me, I admit that the general prospect of America does not encourage me. . . .

I am glad, very glad, you are at work on the new Elements of Drawing. I am like one of the bells in the old nursery rhyme, always dinning the same tune in your ear. Stick close to art, —

ars longa, vita brevis,
fors incerta, mundus levis.

Good-by, with faithful love

Ever Yours,

C. E. N.

---

[1] The population of Ashfield at this time was almost without exception "native born."

To Miss Constance Hilliard

SHADY HILL, CAMBRIDGE, MASSACHUSETTS.
October 15, 1873.

. . . A little more than a month ago I came back here
with Sally as my only companion, to this old home
where all the chief events of my life have been trans-
acted and all its most precious memories concentre.
Here I was glad to be alone for a time to face the past
and the present by myself. After a week the rest of
the family joined me, — and since then we have been
leading busy days.

There is much to be done in the house and on the
place after five years' absence. The place has grown
even more beautiful during our stay abroad, and you
would not find many prettier narrow views in New
England than that from our piazza down the fields
on either side of the avenue, belted as they are with
old pine trees and oaks. We seem to be far in the
country, for not another house is in sight, and the
woods apparently extend far away; but we are on the
edge of a busy town and surrounded by all that is suburban and ugly. . . .

How you would light up this study of mine could
you come into it to-night. It is a room so pleasant as
to be worthy of receiving you, — two rooms opening
into each other by wide folding doors, both lined with
books from floor to ceiling, leaving spaces for the windows, and one wall for my pictures. There are cabi-
nets for photographs and engravings, and for old vases;

and big tables covered with books and portfolios and litter of all sort, — and your portrait[1] stands on a ledge of one of the bookcases, and there are drawings and sketches wherever one can find place, — and I keep as hard at work as I can. . . .

To Thomas Carlyle

Sunday, November 16, 1873.
SHADY HILL, CAMBRIDGE, MASSACHUSETTS.

. . . There is nothing in my life to take the place of our walks. My walks are now for the most part solitary, — and all life is likely to be solitary in America to one who cannot share in that confident spirit of cheerful optimistic fatalism of which Emerson is the voice and the prophet. Longfellow was complaining the other day of the decline in the interest in literature and in the taste for it. Nor was he mistaken, — this generation is given over to the making and spending of money, and is losing the capacity of thought. It wants to be amused, and the magazines amuse it. I spend my time with books, — writing a little, reading a great deal, but finding very few new books that I much care for.

I have not read Mill's "Autobiography." One who knows anything of the "Vita Nuova" and of the "Divine Comedy" may be pardoned if he smile compassionately at poor Mill's experience of love. There is room for improvement, doubtless, in the regulation of our passions, but to regulate them out of existence is to go too far.

[1] By Ruskin.

Not many men could have been so comically sincere and so tragically ignorant, as to be able to write the sentence about the cutting short of the life of the worthy and suffering Taylor.

I have read lately another little volume of translations by FitzGerald from an Oriental poet, — "Salámán and Absál, an allegory, from the Persian of Jámí." . . . I care less for it than for the sceptical quatrains of Omar Khayyám, but it has beautiful parts, and throughout a true Oriental flavour, a mixture of sensual and spiritual, like the odour of musk. It is, however, —

> "No tale of I and Thou,
> Though I and Thou be its interpreters."

. . . .

My little Sally is true to her old love. She will never forget him. . . .

Leslie Stephen, writing in November, 1873, to Norton, says, in an unpublished letter, "I had a walk the other day with our old friends, Carlyle and Froude. Carlyle attacked me, not unkindly, for certain remarks about hell which I made in a recent article upon Jonathan Edwards. The old prophet loves hell and assured me on the authority of Dante that it was made of Infinite Love. . . . This is the kind of thing which riles me: but I can never contradict old Thomas, nor indeed speak to him as if I had the honour of belonging in the same rank of created beings. I have an infernal turn for inappropriate modesty."

To J. R. Lowell

SHADY HILL, November 24, 1873.

You will not wonder that since coming back to Cambridge I have been little in the mood for writing, — but my heart has turned very often to you. I miss you constantly, and Cambridge is not home to me without you.

For a long time I did not go near Elmwood, — but the other evening I walked up there, and lingered along by the fence.[1] Everything was wonderfully unchanged in aspect, but I was changed, and you were absent, and the friendly lights beckoned from the windows, but not to me. How many happy associations have I with the gate, the path, the door, and all that lies within! There are very few places on earth dearer to me. I thought that Elmwood looked as you would like to have it look; that, had you seen it, as I saw it, you would have been fonder of it than ever, and glad that you were to come back to it before long. Do come! We need you.

My last letter to you was written, if I rightly remember, about the time when my Mother began to show some signs of recovery from her illness in the summer. From that time she went on steadily gaining, till now she seems, I think, not less well and not less strong than she did when you last saw her. Our lives run in very quiet courses, but this is not on her account. All the rest of us are well. Jane and Grace have recov-

---

[1] Thomas Bailey Aldrich was occupying the place during Lowell's absence in Europe.

ered from the effects of last summer's fatigues and anx-
ieties, and are not worn out by their devoted care of the
children. Eliot is going to a dame's school where he
does well, and is very happy. We have a sweet and
excellent Governess for Sally and Lily and Rupert.
The two younger children are learning too much by
themselves to be put to regular lessons.

I employ myself in study, in writing a little, in reading a good deal; but the spring of voluntary work is
broken, and I should be glad of some steady employment to which I should be compelled by regular engagement. I am busy just now on a paper on the
Santa Maria dei Fiore, to accompany my account of
the Duomo of Siena. In writing it I live over many
happy Italian days. I wish I knew that you were in
Florence, or about to be there, for then I should ask
you to do me a kindness. What a pity we were not
again in Italy together! I find America much farther
away from Italy than it used to be. . . .

The other day in walking through what used to be
the Green Lane, and then became Linnæan Street,
without losing all of its pretty character, I found
the street full of city carts and labourers engaged
in grading it, and laying out straight sidewalks on
either side with fine granite curbstones. I cannot
forgive the cutting down of the elms, — the great one
in the square, the beautiful one at your corner. The
College Yard is no longer ours, and the Delta, — well,
perhaps you may like the big building that covers it
better than I do.

My own place, Shady Hill, is outwardly unchanged,

and my children are growing familiar with the trees
and the fields that I used to belong to; but how long
this will be so is doubtful, — but certainly not very
long. We shall be taxed out of it; and I have alas!
already been to consult the City Engineer in regard
to the laying out of the streets by which the place is
to be cut up. Next year, I fear, the work will have to
begin; let us hope not till after you have seen the old
place as it is once more.

Longfellow is delightfully unchanged. He seems no
older; and the sweet wine of his life runs clearer and
clearer as the years go on. . . . Wright comes almost
every Sunday to us. His powers increase rather than
fail. He has just written for the Academy a Memoir of
Mill, which is an admirable piece of clear analysis and
vigorous, precise statement, in a style of unusual excellence.[1] He is always pleasant and sweet when he comes
to us; full of tender kindly ways to the children. . . .

But I live almost altogether alone, and depend very
little on even the friendliest society. It will not be so
when you return. The circle of sympathies naturally
widens as one gains wisdom; but with their extent the
sympathies lose something of their depth. And here,
in this flourishing land of ours, you and I and the few
men like us who care for the ideal side of life, are left
from year to year in a smaller and smaller minority.
Even Longfellow, optimistic as he is, complains of the
decline in taste for literary culture, and of interest in
literary pursuits. We stop at the high-school level.

[1] This Memoir was printed, without a signature, in the Proceedings of
the American Academy of Arts and Science for 1873–74, and later was
included in Wright's *Philosophical Discourses*.

Charles Eliot expresses himself very strongly in regard to these matters. He finds great difficulty in getting Professors and even examiners for the different departments of the University. You will not be pleased with America when you come back, however fond of her you may be, or however many excuses are obvious for her faults. She is not a pleasing child; and not so hopeful, does not give so good promise as when she was younger.

The wind is buffeting my north-eastern windows, and the moon has in vain tried to break through the clouds. There is a little snow in the air, and by to-morrow morning I dare say the ground will be covered thick with it. Thanksgiving Day comes next Thursday, and this is fit weather for it.

I wish I knew that you were to-night in some place familiar to me. I seek for you in vain in the wide uncertain spaces. If you go to Siena, do not forget to go out to the Villa Spannocchi, and send me a leaf from one of its olives.

How much love this letter takes to you both! and yet you always have it.

Ever Your loving

C. E. N.

To J. R. Lowell

SHADY HILL, December 4, 1873.

My letter to you had not been gone an hour last Friday when yours arrived from Venice. It was most welcome, not only for the good news it brought us of you, but as breaking the too long silence between us,

and as coming from the city that is dearer to me than
any other in Italy. Your words about Venice meet my
thought. . . . I am especially glad that you should have
seen Tintoretto, for to *see* his pictures is the same as to
recognize him as the most imaginative and interesting
of painters. He is more a poet than any of the rest. It
seems to me no exaggeration to put him side by side
with the two or three greatest imaginative creators.
The more I studied him, the more wonderful, the more
original, the more comprehensive his genius seemed to
me. His best portraits go far beyond Titian's in insight
and truth of characterization. But there is no end if
one begins to write of Tintoretto and Venice. I have
been reading much about them, and have in mind to
write a Study of Venice in the sixteenth century. . . .

Charles Eliot has asked me if I could tell him anything about your wishes concerning the Professorship.
I told him that I supposed you intended your resignation to be final, but that I could not positively say. . . .
He desires, in case you wish to resign, that I should
take your place next year; and if I am to do this I
should want to set about the special preparation for it
at once. I have a double feeling as regards your resignation, as I have often told you. I should regret it very
much on account of the College; . . . I should rejoice at
it on your account, as leaving you free for your own
pursuits, and as lifting from you a wearisome load. . . .

I have been spending the day with Emerson at
Concord. He is very well, and as young in heart as
ever. . . . He has been reading to me from his English
journals of 1833 and 1848, — and I found the passages

he read of the greatest interest, — impressions, anec-
dotes and sayings of Carlyle, of Tennyson, of Wordsworth, of Dickens and many another of the best men
whom he saw. He asked especially of you; he would
be glad to have you at home and at the College again.
"We cannot spare such a star from our firmament."

No, we cannot spare you much longer. In eight
months I hope you will be here. It is a gain to begin to
count your absence by months.

We are all well. My Mother is delightfully fresh and
cheerful, and to appearance vigorous. She sends much
love to you both, as does each one of us great and
small.

To Edward Lee-Childe [1]

SHADY HILL, CAMBRIDGE, MASS.
December 20, 1873.

. . . America received us very kindly, but with a certain questioning look; as if a little conscious that there
was that in her which might not be all that her children,
so long absent from her, could have desired to find. But
there was nothing strange or unexpected in her aspect.
It is still the land of material prosperity, and of the
light-mindedness that results from uninterrupted success. We sow many a wind, but have escaped the
harvest of whirlwind. It is coming by and by. No
serious man who knows anything of human nature and
of history, can cherish the optimistic fatalism that is
still characteristic of the American temper, and that

[1] The son of General R. E. Lee's sister, Mrs. Lee-Childe, at whose house
in Paris, Norton in 1850 had found himself so cordially welcomed, and met
so many persons of note.

finds expression in the general confidence that some-how, however men may act and behave, everything will come out right in the end. There was never a people more reckless than ours to-day, and I often wonder whether we or the French are giving the strongest evidence of national folly. The evidence we give is less conspicuous, but hardly less convincing.

A number of cultivated and excellent Englishmen have been here this Autumn, and they all are dazzled by the spectacle of our amazing prosperity. They are like Gladstone, whom I heard one day, just before I left London, talk like a spread-eagle Western man about this country. He looked at it from the side of the budget. But to an American who must look at it from other sides and in other lights, there is much that is dark in the prospect. . . .

To Thomas Carlyle

SHADY HILL, December 22, 1873.

MY DEAR MR. CARLYLE, — . . . Four or five weeks ago I had a note from Emerson in the course of which he said, — "Another impulse of my three-score-and-ten-ship was to say that I shall like to know that I may confide to you the entire file of Carlyle's letters to me from 1835 to 1872, nearly a hundred, I believe; that you may hereafter make what disposition or de-struction of them you shall find fit; — to which I might add, I believe, some manuscript notes of him taken in 1848."

This is the essential part of his note. I answered, — that I was deeply touched by the confidence he put in me, and that though at first suggestion I shrank from accepting such a charge, yet on reflection I was willing to do so, for I knew no one to whom it could be more sacred, or who through affection and respect for you and for him, would be more desirous to fulfil the charge in a manner, whatever the needful fulfilment might prove to be, such as he and you would approve.

A fortnight ago I spent a day with him at Concord. He is best at home, and it seemed to me that I had never seen all the sweet qualities of his nature in happier activity than on that day. He was well in health, in good heart, and save for an occasional slip of memory, in full vigour of mind. The freshness of his perennial youth was restored; and his serene confidence in the order of the universe, his joy in life, his hopefulness, put to shame my weaker faith in the actual and instant supremacy of good. He reflects himself in the world; — and if men were but all Emersons one might share his confidence! As I left him he put into my hands a large parcel of your letters. They are now in a case at my side.

It is not unlikely that they may yet go back to him, to find some other destination. Why should he not outlive me? . . .

I do not like to have this trust in my hands, and in my heart, without your knowledge of it, and your concurrence in it. Emerson may not write you of what he has done, — and yet, I feel that you should know it, and that your leave should be asked. I shall feel the easier about it. . . .

In a work of this nature, as we have said, there are gaps that can be only indicated by a few words stretching to horizons just beyond those contained in the available letter. We have no letters that will illustrate Norton's relation to his brother-in-law, W. S. Bullard, — the head of the firm in whose employ he had gone as supercargo to India, — yet during the period immediately following Norton's return from Europe in 1873, and before his appointment to a Professorship at Harvard, William Bullard's counsel, encouragement, and strong interest were a valuable factor in shaping Norton's course in the direction it took.

From the time of Mr. Bullard's marriage to Norton's eldest sister, until his death in 1897, the relation between the two men was a close one. William Bullard well represented the vanished class of Boston shipping merchants, whose sagacity, integrity and public spirit gave them an important place in the life of the little city; but to those who knew him intimately there was a note of sentiment and intellectual power in his character, which distinguished him from the class he otherwise represented. Punctilious — according to the standards of to-day — in his courtesies and refinements, withdrawn by taste and a certain gravity of purpose from purely social intercourse, he had come after a youth of limited opportunity and hard work to the position he held; for left fatherless when still a boy, he had been obliged to enter a business office to help support his widowed mother. These early experiences left their stamp on the grown man, and those near him recognized "the helper and friend of mankind" in his attitude toward life. So it was that the bonds which drew him and Norton together were more than those of family affection.

To others Norton was writing of the matters which he and Mr. Bullard were constantly discussing at this time.

To John Ruskin

SHADY HILL, CAMBRIDGE, January 10, 1874.

. . . I want to be made Professor in the University here that I may have hard work forced on me, and may be brought into close relations with youths whom I can try to inspire with love of things that make life beautiful, and generous. I have some ardours left, — and no whit of faith in the good as good, and to be aimed at whether attainable or not, has vanished from my soul. While one is treading the wine-press alone and in the night, he may yet take comfort in knowing that there is happy labour and daylight for others. . . .

We have had a pleasant Christmas and New Year. The children were very happy in their little gifts and gaieties. . . . Child and his wife and their four pretty little children were here, and three or four other friends, one of whom is a great magician and juggler.[1] He entertained us all; and Child and his three little girls performed the ballad of Young Beichan, with wonderful costume and dramatic effect, and we had a magic lantern, and a sugar-plum bag, and one of the little Italian "presepios" with all the plaster figures of the pretty story of Bethlehem, — and when the eve-

[1] Chauncey Wright.

ning was at its end I read to them the marvellous tale,
so beautiful, and then we all, standing round the piano,
with Sally accompanying on her violin, sang the old,
sacred ballad, —

> "While shepherds watch'd their flocks by night,
> All seated on the ground."

I wish you had been with us. Good-night. All good
be with you.

Ever Yours,

C. E. N.

To J. R. Lowell

SHADY HILL, January 15, 1874.

Your letter from Florence, written on Christmas
Day, came to me three days ago. . . . As to the Professorship, so far as I am concerned your intentions and
your actions have been in every way those of the most
considerate and generous friend. . . . I should, indeed,
be glad of definite, regular compulsory occupation, and
this a Professorship would give me. . . . But it is not
certain that I shall remain without such occupation as
a Professorship might afford. The Corporation have
it under advisement to create a Professorship of the
History and Literature of the Fine Arts, and if this is
done, the place may be, probably will be, offered to me.
This much is certain, that if I chose, I may accept a position as "Annual Lecturer" in this new Department,
with the study made an elective for the Juniors and
Seniors. I have some strong objections to this latter
scheme, but I may give them up for the sake of the
benefit of regular hard work. . . .

So yóu will come back to take up your old work, and to have me, very likely, as colleague in the Faculty, — at any rate, to have me, as for almost a quarter of a century now, your fellow-student, and faithful and grateful friend. . . .

To J. R. Lowell

SHADY HILL, January 19, 1874.

. . . There is another matter concerning which I wish I had written earlier. I have not heard of old Seymour Kirkup's death, and take it for granted he is lingering on in squalor and spiritualism. You know he sold his library some three years ago, but he still, so far as I know, retains his mask of Dante. It is the best and most authentic of the copies from the original mask, and I wish we could get hold of it. I have, as you know, a cast from it, as well as one from the Torrigiani cast, now in the Uffizi. Its superiority to the Torrigiani cast, and to the bronze cast at Naples, is manifest. If you have a chance, pray go to see the old fellow. He would not be at all shocked at an immediate proposition to him to part with his mask, and I would give any reasonable sum for it. It would be a treasure worth having in America.

If you should have left Florence before this reaches you, perhaps you will see Marsh, and he might interest himself to get it for us. If you should see old Kirkup, and you can make him hear what you say, pray give him my remembrances. . . .

There is nothing new about the Professorship, but you would be pleased could you hear the strong expressions of satisfaction in the prospect of your resuming your place in the College. I trust that after all, on the whole the balance in your own mind may incline to your taking up the work again, as the best settlement of the knotty question of a tolerable *modus vivendi*. You will find the College a much better place to work in than it has been in past times.

Leslie Stephen's dedication [1] touched me. . . . It would once have pleased me without a pang. Your words about it are better than itself. I agree with what you say of the book, — but a man is forced to make the best of his position. If he be in earnest he must want other men to agree with him, and must try to convert them. The book will not have the recognition it deserves, for it goes against the grain of too many people, and there is a vast deal of the Marchioness's "make believe very hard" left in all circles in England. . . .

To J. R. Lowell

SHADY HILL, February 6, 1874.

I fancy you in Rome, — with roses and violets and anemones, and warm haze over the Sabine mountains. Here we are in deep snow; the winter delayed its most vigorous assault till now, and now, with the thermometer near zero and a foot of snow on the ground, it looks as if he would not raise his siege before April. Accidente! I wonder we are not all spoiled by our climate. I have just had to send back to Ruskin an old Florentine piece on panel, — two heads that Filippino Lippi

[1] See vol. i., p. 475.

might have painted, or even the great Filippo himself, because the wood seasoned by four hundred years in Europe, and strengthened by cross bars beside, would not, could not stand the strain of our dry air, but lost its old firmness and began to split with a deep crack from end to end. I feel a most sincere sympathy with it. I, too, warp and crack in this dry, clear atmosphere. . . .

Eliot — I mean President Eliot — has gone to England for two or three months. Before he went I promised him that I would take a class next year to give it instruction in the History of the Arts of Construction and Design, and their relations to Literature. I hesitated at first because the Corporation were unwilling to establish a Professorship, and I did not care to engage in the work for a year or two, as an instructor with an annual appointment. But on receiving assurance from Eliot that the Corporation would undertake in a short time to turn the post into a regular professorship, I determined to take the place. . . .

We are all well. There is no news with us since Jane wrote to you. I should tell you of what I am thinking about public affairs, but that I trust you see the "Nation." — Longfellow has been shut up with a cold, . . . I saw him day before yesterday. . . . Howells came in to dine with him; plump and with ease shining out from his eyes. He has passed his poetic stage, and bids fair to be a popular American author. As for art in American letters, — recent numbers of the "Atlantic Monthly" forbid one to think of it. There are no artists left but Emerson and Longfellow and you! . . .

To John Ruskin

SHADY HILL, February 10, 1874.

... I have undertaken to give instruction in the
University here, in the next year, in the History of the
Arts of Construction and Design, and their relation to
Literature. The work required of me will be laborious
for the want of proper text-books in English. It will
include both recitations (three a week) and lectures.
I am not sorry to be forced to work, — the inner motive has lost its ring and must be replaced by external
pressure.

My plan is to give my class at first a brief sketch of
the place of the arts in the history of culture, of their
early developments, and then to take them to the
Acropolis at Athens and make them study it in detail,
till they shall have some notion, however faint, of its
unique glories, and shall illustrate their Aeschylus and
their Demosthenes and all their other Greek books
with some images of the abodes and figures of the
gods and men by whom the Acropolis was inhabited.
I have it much at heart to make them understand
that the same principles underlie all the forms of
human expression, — and that there can not be good
poetry, or good painting or sculpture, or architecture,
unless men have something to express which is the
result of long training of soul and sense in the ways of
high living and true thought. . . .

After we have done with Athens, I propose to go to
Venice; show the similarity and the difference in the
principles of the two Republics, and the result in

their spirit and work; — and so fill up the year. I am already trying to fill up some of the gulfs of my ignorance — but as fast as I fill one, another yawns so wide as to threaten to swallow more than industry can supply. . . . Ever your loving

C. E. N.

Norton was a constant observer of the birthdays of his family and friends. Nearly always, when the 22d of February came round, there was a birthday message to Lowell; and the coincidence of the date with that of Washington's birthday was not always ignored.

To J. R. Lowell

SHADY HILL, February 23, 1874.

MY DEAREST JAMES: — As we still keep Sunday as a fast and not a feast, we did not celebrate your birthday yesterday, except in our hearts, but to-day all the bells have been ringing, and the guns firing, and the flags streaming, in honour of the happy anniversary. . . .

I am beginning to work in preparation for my new department. Fortunately I am impressed with a sense of my ignorance, and I shrink from making an exposure of it; so that I am driven to work hard. The gulf to be filled is very deep, and too wide to be spanned by any suspension bridge.[1]

I thought Howells would be here to-night to read me

[1] Near the end of 1874 Norton wrote to Carlyle of himself as "occupied now, mainly, with a class of some forty young men in the college here, whom I am trying to make less ignorant than I am myself."

part of the new novel he has just finished. . . . It is a pleasure to see him now-a-days, he looks so much at ease, and his old sweet humour becomes ever more genial and comprehensive. He is in just such relations to the public that he makes the very editor needed for the "Atlantic"; — there is not much in the magazine that is likely to be read twice save by its writers, and this is what the great public likes. There must be a revival of letters in America, if literature as an art is not to become extinct. You should hear Godkin express himself in private on this topic. He speaks with more than his usual vigour. . . .

To J. R. Lowell

SHADY HILL, March 13, 1874.

Yesterday your "Elegy"[1] came safe. Such poetry, being meant to live, would insure the safety of any ship which bore it across the ocean. It is a noble poem, manly and forthright as you wished it to be; full of fine characterization, of genuine feeling, of literal truth sublimated by the heats of imagination. I like no part of it better than the passage about Clough. You do scant justice in comparison to Emerson.

Emerson was here this morning and I read the poem to him, to his great interest and delight; — he had to hurry away at the end, to go to a recitation (he was in Cambridge as one of an examining committee) and had only time to say, — "How large and fine a work!" and bid me give you all affectionate regards from him. He seemed in excellent health and heart, — far better than

---

[1] Lowell's "Agassiz." Agassiz died in December, 1873.

a year ago. He had been much moved by Sumner's death; but this death touches Longfellow more nearly than any one else. I saw him this afternoon. He was serene as usual, but he looked as if he had had a heavy blow.

Poor Sumner! What a sad life his seems to one who looks beneath the shows of things! He illustrates the difference between bigness and greatness. He will hardly look more heroic to future generations than he does to us, but his figure will fill a large place in our history. I have a very kindly feeling to his memory; I should like to have more respect for it.

We shall try to get Hoar[1] for his successor, but our Massachusetts politics are so "mixed" just now that I am afraid some much inferior man will get the place. Butler's recent course has at length really aroused the spirit of honest men, and the forces are drawing off on either side for a battle that shall decide the fate of the Republican party. If we win it, the party is safe; if Butler wins it, we will break up the party. The better portion of the party will follow the lead of Massachusetts. I have been in New York, staying for a few days with Godkin, and, after much talk with him and Olmsted, came home to have a three hours' talk yesterday with John Forbes. He has taken his gloves off, and you know what that means when the Scotch blood is up.

I wait for your next letter to know what you wish me to do with your poem. I have my own wishes about it, and I hope yours will not be very different. It is too

---

[1] Judge Ebenezer Rockwood Hoar, of Concord, was at this time a Representative in Congress.

beautiful and fine a poem for the "Atlantic." But I am no critic of your poetry, — save as a lover is the best critic of all. I see you in it all, and seeing and feeling you in the lines I know them to be good from first syllable to last, good in the high sense of the word with all its best associations. . . .

To J. R. Lowell
SHADY HILL, March 15, 1874.

I wish you could have seen Howells's face yesterday afternoon when (having received your letter from Rome in the morning) I took to him your poem, — there was more pleasure in it than I have seen in any grown face for a long time. "Oh!" said Mrs. H. when he told her what had come, "*oh!* how splendid! why, that will carry the 'Atlantic' for six months." There was something touching and pretty in the little woman's delight in the lift to her husband's work. It was as if he had accomplished something great himself; she knew at least that he had now got a good handful of pure wheat to offer in the place of his common sackful of the most unnutritious chaff. And then I read them some parts of the " Elegy," for I am sure such a poem needs the interpretation of the voice, and it was pretty again, and pleasant to me, to see their common sympathy of appreciation and delight.

The manuscript is in perfect order. No words omitted or illegible. I asked Howells to let me see the proof, and I will make sure that no great blunder occurs in the printing. One line I think must be changed, but I shall ask Longfellow's counsel. I cannot recall it

exactly, but it is the line in which you speak of Agassiz's quiet and kindly disregard of Tyro while "He
puffs his smoke with inattentive ears." That's not
the line, yours is far better, but the "puffing with the
ears" is what jars on mine. No doubt some easy correction of the verbal ambiguity will suggest itself.[1]

You are to have not less than $300 for the poem; and
if you do not desire me not to do so, I will put the
amount in a bill of exchange and remit it to Barings
on your account. Do not allow your debt to them to
make any dent on your mind. Did n't they keep
monies of yours for years? Spend, dearest boy, and
accumulate debt at 4 per cent. You never will run in
debt so cheaply elsewhere. . . .

Poor Sumner lies buried in Mount Auburn. I took
Eliot and Rupert [2] to see the funeral procession this
afternoon. They were disappointed in the show, for
there was no music (as there should have been) and
there were no soldiers (as there might have been); only
a detachment of mounted police, then a carriage or
two, then the hearse with outriders, then a long line of
carriages.

Sumner's gift to the Library is most welcome, and
is gracefully and feelingly made. I feel very kindly to
the poor fellow, for I knew him best when I was a boy,
and he was very kind to me. I should have liked to
pay him all tender respect as to an old friend, but I
could not join in honouring him as statesman. At this

[1] The passage as finally printed stands: —
    "The long-trained veteran scarcely wincing hears
    The infallible strategy of volunteers."
[2] Norton's eldest and second boy.

moment it looks as if the attempt would be made to
exalt him into an ideal character; he is very near
apotheosis. And there is poor Mrs. Sumner! . . .

To John Ruskin
SHADY HILL, CAMBRIDGE, March 18, 1874.

. . . I am reading hard at Greek history and anti-
quities, and rejoice if I get anything better than a fact
out of the books. I have been studying Penrose on the
Parthenon, a book full of curious investigations, but
with not a hint to help one in the enquiry as to the
moral and physical elements of the Athenian nature, —
and why the Athenians alone should have invented
such subtile laws of harmony in building, and required
their adoption. . . . The prevalence of this sense of
balance, rhythm, proportion, symmetry, — resulting
in a sense of form very different from any that the
modern world possesses, was as characteristic of the
Athenians, as the sense of colour was of the Venetians.
But why, and what did it mean? . . .

To Miss Constance Hilliard
SHADY HILL, April 28, 1874.

. . . You say that when we meet next you will be
much graver from having learned more of the sorrow
and *sin* of the world. I hate that word sin, and I trust
you may never use it as people often do for most trivial
faults, and may never consent, in spite of the Liturgy,
to call yourself or be called "a miserable sinner." If
you try to believe or make believe you are so, you are
perverting your own integrity of heart and under-

standing. And don't burden yourself about the sin of
the world. To keep sweet and sympathetic, and kind
and cheerful, and constant, is far better than to grow
grave and bitter over evils that your brightness might
do something to expel. I do not mean that it should
be

> "Roses, roses all the way"

for you, but I do mean that it is not worth while for you
to go out of the way to prick yourself on the thorns. . . .

To Thomas Carlyle

SHADY HILL, CAMBRIDGE, MASSACHUSETTS
May 7, 1874.

If I have not written to you it has been partly
because life has been hard with me of late, and my
mood has been one of silence; partly because when I
think of writing to you your own image rises before
me as if saying, — "My good fellow, do not you
yet know that 'beyond all speech that is good for
anything there lies a silence that is better'?" and before I can reconcile the inconsistency of this image,
or special illusion, with my better knowledge of your
real self, the opportunity for writing has gone. In all
these months when I have not written, I have not
failed to hold you in constant memory. You have
often been my honoured companion in my solitary
walks, and I have gained much from the memory of
our last year's talk. I have had no one to talk with this
year. . . . Lowell, upon whose friendship and companionship I greatly depend, has been in Europe for nearly

two years past. I will send you an elegy he has just written on Agassiz. It is manly and vigorous verse, worthy of

"Deep-chested Chapman or firm-footed Ben,"

and, beside its merit in this respect, it is an excellent and truthful portrait of the man whom he celebrates and laments. There can be no better "character" drawn of Agassiz. You will like the lines, too, in which Clough is worthily commemorated.

You see that your old — what shall I call him, for "friend" will certainly not do? — Sumner is dead. We have had a great wake over him, and the echoes of it have scarcely yet died away. We are to erect many monuments to him and statues of him, — and are well on the way to make a mythical hero of him, — one of the emanations of the dawn, or types of the sun. In dying he did a good thing by leaving all his books and manuscripts and a fund of $50,000 (about) to the Library of the University here. I prize them chiefly for the sake of a volume, an album I believe, that has Milton's autograph in it, — his signature appended to the verses, —

"Or, if Virtue feeble were
Heav'n itself would stoop to her."

It will be some months before we shall be able to smile concerning Sumner, and probably many good people will till their death regard one who could speak of him with qualified admiration as giving evidence of "a bad heart." You say you find it hard to keep a supply of good books. May I send you ten or twelve

thick, royal octavo volumes of Sumner's Orations and
other performances? Motley has been asked to write
his Life. Poor Motley! He will decline because of ill
health. Somebody told General Grant that Sumner
had no faith in the Bible; — "Well," said the General,
"he did n't write it."

Just after your letter came to me, a pleasant note
arrived from Emerson, proposing to spend next Tuesday night with us. He is to read a lecture on Tuesday
evening before the Divinity School. What can he have
to say to-day to the students in an Unitarian Divinity
School? To Roman Catholics or good Calvinists there
is much that might be said to advantage; but to Unitarian Divinity students I conceive there is only one
thing possible to say, and that is, — "You can't stay
here. You must either go back or go forward." Emerson said his word to them in his beautiful discourse
thirty-six years ago. I shall give him that night the
copy of the portrait of Knox that you have sent to
him. It is a very credible likeness, and a face that may
well stand for that of the Reformer. I am very glad to
have it. The past becomes real to one in proportion as
one can see the men who filled it. I value a good
portrait even of an unknown man beyond almost
all other works of painting or sculpture, for the
painters or sculptors who had imagination of force
enough to give vitality to their works are as few as the
poets, — to be counted on the fingers. The third copy
of the portrait that you have sent me I shall take the
liberty of presenting in your name to the Massachusetts Historical Society, which has the honour of
counting you among its Honorary Members. . . .

And you must accept still warmer and more grateful thanks from me, for your kind words respecting Emerson's disposal of your letters to him. . . .

I am busy in preparing myself for work that I have undertaken to do at the University here. I found myself in need of work which I should be compelled by a definite engagement to accomplish, and was consequently not unwilling to accept a proposal to take a class of elder students to instruct in the history of the Fine Arts and their relations to Literature. It is not my intention to enter on the disputed territory of Esthetics, but I shall endeavour to give to the students some definite notions of the fine arts as modes in which men in past times have expressed their thoughts, faiths, sentiments and desires, to show the political, moral, and social conditions which have determined the forms which the arts have taken in different periods, — and to quicken, so far as may be, in the youth of a land barren of visible memorials of former times, the sense of connection with the past and of gratitude for the efforts and labours of other races and former generations. The field is so wide and so rich that there is no end to the work requisite for cultivating properly even a small part of it. . . .

I send you the best wishes I know how to wish, and end, with all respect,

Your truly affectionate
C. E. Norton.

May 9th. A year ago to-day I left you on Forster's steps. It is by such dates that one reckons life.

THOMAS CARLYLE

HIS BROTHER JOHN AND NIECE MARY, IN 1868

To John Ruskin

Friday, July 10, 1874.

To-day I have your second letter from your cell in the monastery,[1] — what a place to live in! Do you read the "Fioretti di S. Francisco"? It used to be one of my favourite books. And do you know the poems of Fra Jacopone? I should like to read them by your window, looking down on the valley below, and watching the life go on there in the same simple ways in which it went when Francis, looking at the little stream where you saw the peasant with his flock, wrote —

"Laudato sia mio Signore per sor aqua:
    La quale è molto utile, et humile, et pretiosa, et casta."

S. Bonaventura's "Life of S. Francis," too, is a book that one would like to read in the cell where it was written. I have an old copy of it that once belonged to the Library of S. Pietro in Montorio, — and if you have not the book, I will send it to you for the sake of its associations. I think you would have got more good from the seventh chapter of the Rule of S. Francis De modo serviendi et laborandi — had you happened to read it that morning — than you could have got from the ninth of Jeremiah.

You have too much of the old Scotch Covenanting blood in you to make Jeremiah healthy reading for you; he is too much in your own vein.

Do you think I urge you to draw and to give yourself

[1] Ruskin's letter dated Monastery of Assisi, 21st June, 1874. See *Ruskin-Norton Letters*, vol. ii, 79.

to work that no man can do so well as you, in a light spirit? Not so: it is because I am sure your influence will be made deeper, more permanent, and more helpful by patient work of this kind, than by your impassioned and impatient appeals to men who will scoff at your words. You have sown seed; let the summer show where it has fallen, some at least will be found on good ground.

Alas! poor Giotto. I cannot let him go. I believe in him still, in spite of your words. But I rejoice that you have discovered Cimabue for us. It is the choicest pleasure to redeem a worthy name from neglect; and to do so for a man like Cimabue is a fortune that hardly falls once in a century. I hope you will send me a little sketch of the Mater Dolorosa, — it would be a treasure to me. But Giotto, — because Cimabue is great, he is not little. Let us have two great instead of one. Have we not known that brave men lived before Agamemnon?

If you do not finish your work this summer at Assisi, shall you go back next year? In that case I might join you there, and then we would go over and see the Parthenon together, and you should have a chance to quarrel with my obstinate persistency in thinking that for a time you should give up the Monthly Letter, and keep yourself out of the newspapers. . . .

I wish I were with you, that we might talk together. I will write soon again. I wish I could serve you in all best things. May good be with you!

Your loving   C. E. N.

To Edward Lee-Childe

SHADY HILL, August 18, 1874.

Your letter from Plombières relieved me from much solicitude. I am truly glad to know that Mrs. Childe's health has not broken down under her heavy sorrow, and I trust that the quiet of the summer at your country home may be pleasant and serviceable to you both.

I wish you were able to take a more cheerful view of life. But we live in a time when it is hard for a thoughtful man to be gay, and which lightheartedness by no means befits. One may be peaceful, however, even if not happy, and accept the inevitable with serenity. The Devil is the only person who seems to have a good time in the world now-a-days, and the Catholics trouble *him* with holy water.

You are leading a rational life, and in securing the best culture for yourself you are doing good service to society. There is a great need of men who may keep up the standard of cultivation, without aiming at the cheap personal distinction for which most men strive. I know no worse calamity that can overtake a man than to have a thirst for publicity, and yet it is the common vice of able men in this epoch of the newspaper reporter.

I fear that in France, as in Germany, there is a decline in the interest in the highest branches of intelligence. The best thought whether in philosophy, politics, or physical science, (and the only poetry that has vitality in it) comes from England. . . .

To John Ruskin

SHADY HILL, August 30, 1874.

Your two notes from Lucca came to me yesterday and the day before. . . . Five years ago I was there with Susan; four years ago with you. . . . What you say of Giotto and Cimabue is of the greatest interest, and I am quite ready to believe in the deeper spiritual or mystic thought of the earlier painter. There was a distinct change in spirit in Italy in the thirteenth century, a decline in simplicity and purity and depth of feeling, and an increase of worldliness. In the "Vita Nuova," the book of his youth, Dante displays the quality of the earlier period; youths, especially young poets, are apt to have a touch of archaism, — but the "Divina Commedia" is plainly the work of a later, more material epoch. The reconciliation of the purity of youth with the power of maturity has never been achieved in life or art. I take it the Athenians of the days of Phidias came nearest to it; and how short is the interval before Euripides and the artists of realism and sentiment take the field in the place of those of imagination.

Italian architecture from 1150 to 1250 is certainly much nobler in design than that of the next century. It implies higher qualities of soul, but it lacks that quality of "mastery" which later buildings display. It is more solemn, serious, religious, but it corresponds little to the varieties of human moods and experience. . . .

I am solitary here, — working away against the

days. I spend half the time at Ashfield, but before long my Mother, and sisters and children will rejoin me here. . . .

From Thomas Carlyle

[London.] April 1, 1875.

. . . My bits of reading have been miscellaneous and insignificant. I could still be happy over a good book; but, alas, good books are like angel's visits. I will say nothing more about *them* to you just now. On the whole, though sensibly growing weaker year by year and almost month by month, I am still in what ought to be good health for a man in his eightieth year. Nor does the continual gaze into the dark Beyond, which is daily coming nearer and daily becomes more earnest and intense, give new pain; but rather becomes less painful, piously desirable and full at once of a kind of blessed sorrow and a love that nothing earthly can abolish. It is strange, it is high and great. *Allah Akbar; Allah kereem!* — I will add no more to-day only my blessing to your little Sally, who may be sure she is justified by the laws of reciprocity in loving me as well as she can. I send my blessings were they good for anything, to you and yours. I remain ever, dear Norton,   Yours,

T. CARLYLE.

To Miss Constance Hilliard

SHADY HILL, April 5, 1875.

. . . The winter has been a long and severe one with us, — but we have got through it well, till just now when my little Margaret has fallen ill with the scarlet fever. . . . I wish you could see them [the children]; they have all grown and developed in a healthy way, but they seem to me not to have lost the old characteristics that were familiar to you, and I believe that in ten minutes you and they would feel no novelty or strangeness, — but that it would seem as if you had parted from them not much more than a month ago! Sally's fiddle makes really pretty music now, and the little girl takes pleasure in it, and works with spirit at her practising. She and Lily are beginning to be great readers. They are now deep in "Tales from Shakespeare," and in "Tom Brown." Miss Edgeworth's "Frank" and "Harry and Lucy" have been great favourites with them of late, and I am glad of it, for I do not like the style of most recent story books for children. Even the book that everybody praises and that children enjoy, — "Alice in Wonderland" — does not please me. There is too little of simplicity in it, too much of the pantomime and the "grand transformation scene," too much nonsense and too little humour, too much factitiousness and too little nature. If you read any really good book for children, — I don't mean a "goody" book, but a healthy, simple, natural one, without sensationalism or sentimentality, and without ill-conceived and ill-drawn pictures (I have been disgusted lately by some of Walter Crane's picture-books, which are as bad in spirit as in execution . . .) — if you come on some sweet, tender, simple, natural, well-bred story, pray let me know of it. I don't want anything from the professional writers of stories, the John

Halifax Mulock Craiks, or the Charles Water Kingsley
Babies, or the Mayne Force Reids. May they never be
read! But you know what I want, — and you will tell
me. . . .

To Thomas Carlyle

SHADY HILL, CAMBRIDGE, MASS.
May 6, 1875.

. . . I trust that the Spring is not so laggard with you
as with us. The snow is scarcely gone, yet this morning
Sally brought in to me a few chilled violets, and a
handful of twigs of the golden catkins of the willow and
the red flowers of the maple. But we have no primroses and no larks. Nature has treated us New Englanders as step-children. . . .

The 19th of April was a great day for Concord. The
little town celebrated the hundredth anniversary of the
shot heard round the world. President Grant was
there, to remind men what an opportunity he had flung
away, and they had a big tent, and an enormous crowd,
and an oration, and a dinner, and speeches, and a ball.
The virtues of the fathers were duly commemorated,
and the sons were exhorted to emulate their sires. But
the day was one of the coldest of the spring, and the
performance seemed to me (at a distance) to share the
nature of the day. They were performances; we had no
right to expect anything else, for genuine unconscious
emotion is as rare here as it has been rare in all times
and places. One good feature of the day deserves mention; not a word was said either at Lexington or Concord that would have sounded hard to honest English

ears, or that tended to keep alive any old ill-feeling. Such feeling is, I believe, long since dead, and its ghost well laid. Emerson took part in the commemoration in his town, and it was pleasant to see with what common, national accord he was recognized as the chief figure and most characteristic product of the new American order of things. His invincible optimism is still the creed of the vast majority of us, and he will not live to lose one jot of his faith. He rebukes me for my doubts. I have seen him once since the anniversary, and he was in the happiest humour, full of cheerfulness and kindness. But he strikes me always now as *emeritus*, — happy alike in the past and in the present, but not likely to do any more work for his generation.

> A sweet attractive kind of grace,
> A full assurance given by looks,
> Continual comfort in a face,
> The lineaments of gospel books, —

will be blessings that he will bestow on his friends to the end.

That Allingham in his capacity of editor should have induced you to come into print again not only justifies his claim to the post, but wins him much gratitude. I have not read your papers, but I shall joyfully receive the volume in which they are collected, — sure of that rare "good book" which would content you for an hour or two, were it only by another author! I wish I had any good book to send to you. But there are no new books here of that sort. My reading has of late been pretty steadily of mediæval history, in the pursuit of knowledge of the thoughts and feelings and modes of

life of the generations who built the cathedrals and
castles, and who went on crusades. I lecture (Heaven
save the mark!) to a class of ingenuous youths, three
times a week, and am kept busily employed. It is a
touching kind of work; but there is, perhaps, as much
chance of good result from it as from most other modes
of work. One may at least have the hope of helping
some few of these young students to form such habits
of study, and to establish such principles of thought as
shall not be without service in later life. . . .

To John Simon

SHADY HILL, May 15, 1875.

. . . You remember Wright, whom you met at our
rooms in Paris. He is always here two or three times a
week. . . . He is not so much a companion as an agent
for mental activity; with uncommon natural powers
disciplined by even more uncommon training; the
clearest and the soundest thinker of my acquaintance,
with an admirable scientific but not poetic imagination; a man to talk with on all serious and difficult
subjects, but not exactly the person to talk with if one
be weary or in the mood to keep on the surfaces of
things. . . .

I have been busy all winter with my three lectures a
week to the students, bearing on the history of the fine
arts; attempting to set forth plainly the moral and
intellectual conditions of which they have been the
expression, and the political and social conditions
which determined their forces and the modes of their
expression. This has kept me hard at work. I agreed

to accept a Professorship, if it were offered me, and the nomination was made some weeks ago. But in the board (the Board of Overseers, as it is called) who have the power to confirm or reject nominations, objection was made on the score of my opinions in matters of religion. A pretty serious discussion arose, — and the result was that, after the meetings in which the matter was discussed, I was made Professor with but one doubtfully dissentient voice. I will send you some of the examination papers, that you may see exactly what I am doing, or, at least, attempting to do. I have been amused at the opposition to my appointment. We are far less outspoken and genuinely liberal than your best men in London. The reason of this is not difficult to see. In a society like ours, resting upon abstract theories of rights and carrying out in practice an extremely democratic system, any institution that has struck roots requires other treatment than in a society where the mass of conventions and traditions is weighty, and where there is an aristocracy whose culture, prejudices, prepossessions and interests serve not merely as a makeweight against tendencies to change, but afford a fixed standard in the midst of the fluctuations of personal convictions or popular emotions. The church is with us (though not established, and broken up into many sects) an extra-governmental organization of the highest importance to the order of society, and the maintenance of a strict code of morality. A wise man hesitates to undermine it by direct effort; and a man suspected, as I am, of holding opinions which if widely spread would weaken the influence of the doctrines on

which our commonwealth has hitherto rested, is justly
regarded with a certain degree of distrust if not of dislike. There is nothing to complain of in this. It is
difficult to see what would become of a democracy if
such views as you and I hold were rapidly to become
prevalent. There ought to be a slow process of acclimati-
zation. It was feared that I, occupying a chair from
which the professor might discuss any topic within the
range of the *omne scibile*, might become a preacher and
propagandist of a disintegrating scepticism. The
doubters did not know how conservative, how respectful for the old, how confident in the unforced progress
of the truth, I am. My work will be steady next
year, and on a small salary. . . .

To Edward Lee-Childe

ASHFIELD, August 4, 1875.

. . . I did not send you Lowell's Concord Ode at the
time of its publication, but I kept it back that I might
send with it a poem he read at Cambridge on July 3,
on the hundredth anniversary of Washington's taking
command of the army. This has just been published
and the two will go forward to you next week. You will
be touched and pleased, I am sure, with the noble
tribute to Virginia with which the later poem con-
cludes. The sentiment which inspires it has met with
the heartiest response from the North: indeed, I should
rather say, the poet but expresses the universal feeling
of his people.

The Centennial celebration of the Battle of Bunker's
Hill was the occasion of genuine peace-making. South

Carolina, Virginia, Maryland were all represented by men who had served through the war on the Confederate side, and they were welcomed, and they answered the welcome with deep and serious good-feeling, and with sincere intention of renewed good-will. The effect throughout the country was instant and great. I believe it was the beginning of a new period of Union. The mere politicians have been surprised at the depth and earnestness of the feeling manifested, and the result as regards national politics is likely to be most beneficial. There can be no "Force Bill" legislation after this. This Centennial year has come at a good time. I do not, indeed, look forward with much satisfaction to the monster exhibition at Philadelphia. A democratic community like ours is not good at organizing such a show. It needs an energetic autocrat at its head. If the affair turn out nothing worse than an overgrown bazaar, confused and confusing, and affording to the lively tradesman an opportunity of advertising his wares on a large scale, we shall have no right to grumble.

Here it is September 4, — my dear Childe, — and my letter has been lying for a month in my portfolio. I have been very busy with my lectures, — "Church Building in the Middle Ages," — a noble subject which I treat exclusively from the social, historical side. . . .

To J. R. Lowell

ASHFIELD, September 20, 1875.

. . . On one of the last beautiful days of last week I took a solitary drive to Northampton that I might be

present at Chauncey Wright's funeral. The day was
soft and gray, the landscape very beautiful, and very
much in harmony with my own mood. Wright is a
great loss to me. The sweetness of his nature showed
itself in the familiarity of home life, and his wisdom was
as marked in practical matters, as in his scientific
judgments. The children were all fond of him, and he
was always delightful in his ways with them. I had
counted much on the unconscious influence upon them
of his simplicity of character and clear intelligence; and
he was one of the few persons who, I had hoped, might
by and by give to the children some vivid personal
impressions of their Mother, for he had been very
much attached to her. But for himself death came
not unwelcome, and in the way he had desired, and
which I had long anticipated for him.

I spent the night at Northampton, — which has lost
much of its old, tranquil charm, and has put on the
showy looks and pert airs of a chromo-civilized country
town. There is nothing pretty, refined, or other than
inelegant in all its newness. It is plain that the civic
ideal of the dwellers in towns is very low, and that the
old sense of common interests and relations is falling
fast out of recognition. . . .

To Charles Darwin

ASHFIELD, MASSACHUSETTS
September 22, 1875.

MY DEAR MR. DARWIN, — I am sorry to have to
send you intelligence which I know will cause you
regret. Ten days ago our friend Chauncey Wright died

suddenly, apparently without suffering, from conges-
tion of the brain.

He was found in the morning seated at his desk in
an easy attitude, unconscious, but still breathing. He
died in a few minutes. He had apparently not been in
bed during the night, but had been writing. He was
busy with an article on your last book, which lay open
beside him. A week before I had brought down to him
from Ashfield a box full of specimens of Drosera which
my little girl Sally, knowing his interest in the plant,
had secured for him. The last letter any of us had from
him was a pleasant note to Sally telling her what he
had been observing of the habits of the Sundew.

He had stayed with us here for more than a week in
August, and had seemed uncommonly well. The last
time I saw him was about ten days before his death at
Cambridge, when he came to read me the proof of his
article in the "Nation" on "German Darwinism," and
to tell me of some changes which he proposed to make
in this essay which he had read to me in manuscript
some time before. I was particularly struck with his
animation and his cheerfulness, and with his readiness
to be interested in other subjects than that which for
the time was chiefly occupying his thought.

I believe that he had contemplated the probabil-
ity of such a death as it was his good fortune to die by.
He had no shrinking from death, and no desire to die.
He was far too much of a philosopher to form wishes
about life or death. And, so far as he is concerned, there
is no reason to regret his death. The prospect of his
life was not unclouded. But to his friends his death is

an irreparable, lifelong loss. The vigour of his intelligence was not more remarkable than the sweetness
of his heart, and the simplicity of his whole nature.
The clearness and power of his mind were plain in his
work, but only those who knew him most intimately
could know how wise and trustworthy his judgment was,
not only in matters of philosophy but also in those of
practical life, or how generously his wisdom was put at
the service of all who sought help from him.

His death, following so soon on that of Wyman,[1] is a
great blow, not merely to Cambridge, but to the interests of sound thought and scientific inquiry throughout
the country. But he was not widely known, and there
are but few persons who will know what a great loss we
have suffered. . . .

P.S. I ought, perhaps, to add that besides Wright's
interest as a scientific man in your work, he had a
strong moral and personal interest in it. Your work
was the illustration and exhibition of the spirit which
he sought in scientific enquiry. I think that in his late
years, he had no greater gratification than the recognition you gave to his work, and the occasional receipt of
a letter or note from you. He was radically modest,
but he was pleased with your expression of interest in
or approval of what he wrote. His visit to you was the
most prized experience of his stay in Europe, and from
that time his feeling toward you was one in which a
certain shy affection gave a still deeper character to
the complete respect he had long cherished.

[1] Professor Jeffries Wyman died September 4, 1874.

To Thomas Carlyle

SHADY HILL, CAMBRIDGE, MASS.
January 29, 1876.

I have just come from a meeting of the Saturday Club, (we meet on the last Saturday of every month,) . . .

We talked to-night for the most part about trivial things; but we had some talk about FitzGerald and his "old Mahomedan blackguard," and a little about the deep concerns of life. Emerson seemed well, cheerful, hopeful, youthful as ever. I felt myself the older — at least the less confidently hopeful — of the two.

Other men at the Club were your old acquaintance Henry James, with his Swedenborgian enthusiasms and eccentricities; Dr. Holmes, with his vivacious wit, throwing off sparks like an electrical machine; Judge Hoar, with his caustic humour, and shrewd good sense; Charles Adams with his shy and solid sincerity, that served him so well in England; Eliot, the President of the College, and the best executive head in New England; Gray, our six-and-half-footer Chief-Justice,[1] with a big head, well-stocked, and the face of a boy; — and half a dozen other men whom it is worth while to meet once a month.

I came out of town with Lowell, who is just now busy with a notice of Forster's Life of Swift for the "Nation." No man is better fitted to write a good notice of the book. . . .

[1] Horace Gray, then Chief Justice of the Supreme Court of Massachusetts, afterwards justice of the U. S. Supreme Court.

EDWARD FITZGERALD, 1883

To Thomas Carlyle

SHADY HILL, CAMBRIDGE, February 3, 1876.

The sad news of Forster's death came to me last night with an unexpected shock. I feel how great a loss he is to you, and it grieves me to think how much you will miss him. . . .

His last letter to me, three months ago, was, as usual, full of kindness and of thoughtfulness for others, but its tone was grave and depressed. Still it did not lead me to believe him more ill than usual, — and his book, that came with it, showed that his powers of work were unimpaired, and was a pledge that he was yet looking forward to busy years.

How tenderly he will be remembered for his friendliness, and his friendships! The quick sympathies that made him so good a friend made him, also, a good biographer. He seems as much the friend of Goldsmith as of Landor, as much the contemporary of one as of the other. The Club might make room for him at their table, and Goldsmith add a new portrait to "Retaliation." . . .

To Thomas Carlyle

SHADY HILL, CAMBRIDGE, March 24, 1876.

I am very much obliged to you for the Newcastle paper with the notice of Forster. Much of it, indeed, is poor provincial prattle, but there were two or three facts that I was glad to know. There is something of pathos in the thought how wrathful Forster himself

would be at reading it. He would not like to have so
minute a biography of himself as he has given the
pattern of. What a pity, at least it seems so to me, that
he should not have given his books and papers to the
British Museum. Precious things of the sort he had
belong there of right. They are out of place, and out
of the way, anywhere else, and especially in such a big
bazaar, and higgledy-piggledy omnium gatherum as the
Museum at South Kensington.

Yesterday Emerson came with his daughter from
Concord to lunch and spend two or three hours with
us. Lowell was here too, and we had much pleasant
talk. . . . We had all been reading the Life of Mr.
Ticknor,[1] and Emerson had been particularly entertained by it. It *is* entertaining, and I have been hesi-
tating whether to send it to you or not, but have determined not to do so for two big octavo volumes may
be troublesome, and you would, very likely, not care
to keep them on your shelves. But they are worth getting from the London Library. They are unique in the
picture they give of good society in Europe (mainly
the quality) and in America. No other American has
had such an entrée into the close circles of the old
world. Mr. Ticknor deserved all his success; he was
"a scholar and a gentleman" and had an attractive,
if not very deep, nature. His very defects—the worst
of which were the lack of imagination and of humour—served him in conventional society. He could
take it all as much in earnest as if he had been born

---

[1] The *Life, Letters and Journals of George Ticknor* was published in
1876.

with a title and an entail. If you read any part of
the book don't omit the account of his Spanish experiences in 1816 or '17; or the narrative, with which the
second volume begins, of his intercourse with Metter-
nich. And in reading I wish you might carry along
the impression which the book does not sufficiently
convey, of the essential simplicity and pleasantness
of the man. His wife was a sister of my mother, and
in my childhood they often stayed with us, and we were
familiarly at their house, and my earliest recollections
of him are of the gayest romps. It was always a
pleasant day for us children when "Uncle Ticknor"
was coming. . . .

To Edward Lee-Childe

ASHFIELD, September 24, 1876.

I am very desirous of hearing of Mrs. Childe and of
you, — and yet it is only to your pure benevolence I
could trust for a letter. I have been seemingly neglect-
ful of correspondence, but for a year past I have been
compelled to give up all but necessary writing. Work
of this sort, even the pleasantest, was apt to bring on a
persistent headache. I am now, however, getting rid
of this trouble, and I go back next week, the vacation
being ended, to my work at Cambridge with good hope
of being able to carry it on without interruption from
this cause.

But even if I had written frequently during the
past months I should have had little personal news to
tell you. Life has gone very quietly with us all. My
Mother has been, for the most part, well, and her life

has been made easier and more cheerful than for a year or two past, by the recovery of sight after a successful operation for the removal of a cataract. She is so fond of reading that to be able to occupy herself once more with books is a great pleasure to her. She, like everybody else, has been reading "Daniel Deronda." The English-speaking world should be grateful to Mrs. Lewes for supplying it for eight months with a topic of conversation as current and as interesting as the weather. It is a pity that one closes the book with a smile which the author did not intend to excite. To be led up to the Judengasse in the train of an enthusiast with a mission to restore the lost tribes of old clo'es men, is a surprising dénouement of a work of genius, — a situation at least as amusing as any in Thackeray's "Codlingsby." In George Eliot, if in any woman, one might have hoped for a sense of humour that would have saved us from this; and for a sense of proportion that would give to her work the excellence of artistic form, to the lack of which recent English works of imagination are compelling us to accustom ourselves. But no words of praise can be too warm for the insight displayed in the book into the complex feelings of modern character, for its delicacy and depth of delineation of sentiment.

There is no note of literature audible in America at this moment; hardly is there any symptom of intellectual activity. The great Centennial Exhibition may be counted a success, especially as it cannot be repeated. But the whole country is now excited by the political campaign, and in a condition of irrational emotion.

The best of the prospect is that a reorganization of parties seems not unlikely as an indirect result of the present contest between the Republicans and the Democrats. The better men of all sections are dissatisfied with both parties for good reasons, and there is a strong Reform sentiment which is gradually gaining head. But any radical change is not to be looked for. We shall stumble along; there are few optimists left.

European affairs interest me greatly. I see the "Times" regularly, and keep up some acquaintance with the aspect of events. . . .

To J. B. Harrison

CAMBRIDGE, January 3, 1877.

. . . I am more of a Republican than you, so far at least as I believe that more of the good principle and good sense of the people is to be found among its members than in those of the Democratic party. There is a radical and vast difference between my theories and principles of government and my conceptions of the American Commonwealth, and those of Mr. Tilden or of any man who had opinions and sentiments like his during the war. The war marks the division between us, and (though I now wish that Mr. Tilden may be our next President) I should have no satisfaction in promoting the election to the Presidency of anyone whose political principles in most important respects I profoundly dislike and distrust.

I think we must have a break-up of the old parties, whoever becomes President. . . .

To G. W. Curtis

CAMBRIDGE, May 20, 1877.

The intelligence which your note [1] has just brought me gives me great satisfaction. It is not a surprise. I have, indeed, thought it probable that the offer would be made to you, and I have formed definite hopes as to your decision. As those hopes are distinctly against my personal interest, I have some confidence that they are the result of right judgment.

I am strongly of opinion that you should accept the English mission, — for the sake of the country, of the administration, and for your own sake. As regards foreign affairs there is nothing more important than the increase of mutual good-will and respect between this country and England. The present time is especially favourable for their cultivation. There is no irritating question between the two countries. But to secure what is needed this country must be represented in England by a man truly representative of American principles and sentiments, trusted and known at home, and with the qualities required to secure personal confidence, esteem, and liking abroad. There is no one who unites these requirements in equal measure with yourself, besides adding to them the most desirable social qualifications. . . .

So much for the sake of the country. Quite as much is to be said of your going for the sake of the administration. But you, probably, see as clearly as I the gain

[1] On May 19, Curtis wrote to Norton: "Mr. Evarts offered my choice of the chief missions, evidently expecting that I would choose the English." See Cary's *Curtis*, p. 253.

that it would be to Hayes, and the strength it would give him, to have you accept the place.

What I fear you will not see as I do is, that it is desirable for your own sake that you should do so. I do not under-estimate the value of your services in your present position to the country and to the party. I see that your loss would be greatly felt in New York politics; that Conkling would be thankful to have you out of the way, — that from Blaine downward (if there be any lower depth than his) every selfish politician in the land would be glad of your absence. But the position in which you have served so long and so effectively, is not, and never has been, in every respect, satisfactory, and it offers no prospect of becoming so. There is no future to it. The years are going on, and such work as you have done for the paper cannot be continued indefinitely. It has told already upon you, and before long you will feel the necessity of rest, and of slackening the pace and amount of work. Some regard, — not too much, — but some regard is due from every man to his own dignity, and the time is near if it has not already come for you to accept a position which shall serve as a public recognition of your character and deserts. If you were absolute master and controller of the "Weekly" the case might be different, but you are, and are known to be, in employ of men inferior to yourself, and whose course you cannot always approve. Doubtless your services to them are so indispensable as to secure you a very considerable independence, — but still before the public you are associated with them as potentially under their command. They could, if they chose, dismiss you; that they would not do so does not affect the fact of their power to do so. You have now the opportunity to leave them for a position more suited to your real eminence, more publicly honourable, and not of less service to the country. And I think you should not let the opportunity pass. . . .

I wish I could see you to talk the whole matter over with you; for I could enforce with many arguments what I have to put briefly here.

If you, after consideration, resolve to decline,[1] even if you do not bring me to acknowledge the wisdom, I shall be perfectly sure of the uprightness of your decision. In this case I incline to think that you might write such a letter in declining the post as would make the Administration glad to have the offer made openly and with form. You might, I think, with propriety say as much to Evarts, and might also urge that, as you decline, it is but due to yourself that the offer should be known. But I trust there will be no need of this. — How I, — how we all, — should miss you! . . .

Following close upon Curtis's decision to decline the English mission came Lowell's acceptance of the Spanish. The ensuing letter was written soon after his departure for Madrid. Of this event F. J. Child wrote to Norton: "I saw Lowell yesterday and said good-bye. He more than half repents accepting his appointment. . . . Poor Jacobus was made quite wretched by Alexander, the Cunard man's getting up an escort for him to the outer light. The revenue cutter 'Galatea' and the

[1] Curtis declined the offer before the end of May.

steam tender 'Hamlin' (ought an ambassador to have anything to do with such political craft?) will convey the friends of the Hon. James Russell Lowell from Long Wharf to the stream, where they will take the 'Parthia.'"

To J. R. Lowell

ASHFIELD, July 24, 1877.

MY DEAR JAMES, — I hope that to-night you may be sleeping on dry land, and with that sense of being at home which is to me always a great pleasure on reaching England. I followed you with my heart after the crowd had left the ship, and wished you the last God-speed. The days of the voyage have not, I trust, been disagreeable. These days have passed with us in the most quiet and uneventful way, — while a great part of the country has been in a wretched, alarming and most instructive uproar. These riots [1] are full of political significance; — they show that some of the popular theories have no solid foundation, and that we are face to face with difficult social questions which our institutions were not framed to meet and to answer. Society, however, will protect itself, and will work out the solution of the new problem even at the cost of consistency of political theory, and even with changes in political institutions. It is plain, moreover, that the militia system, the "citizen soldier" theory, has failed in Maryland and Pennsylvania, and must be essentially remodelled to become an efficient force for the protection of life and property and the maintenance of order.

[1] In Pennsylvania, following the "Molly Maguire" troubles.

Last Thursday and Friday George Curtis was in Washington for the purpose of talking with the President, chiefly in regard to the reform of the Civil Service. I had read him what you had written of your impressions of the President, and he returned on Saturday night with very strong similar impressions. He had a great deal of the most open and frank talk with Mr. Hayes, and was convinced of his candour, and openness of mind, of the solidity of his judgment, of his good common sense, of his understanding of the scope of his own action, of his freedom from personal or partisan motives, and of his courage. . . . He found the President very much in earnest in the matter of the Civil Service, quite aware that the enforcement of his recent Order would throw the party into confusion, but entirely resolved to enforce it. The President said that he expected the Republican party would be defeated in every election this autumn, but that he believed in ultimate support from the people if they saw that the Reform was genuine, and productive of good results. . . .

Curtis dined one day with Mr. Evarts, and, the conversation turning on you, Mr. Evarts spoke with real warmth of his satisfaction in your going to Spain, and with a heartiness and fulness of expression which convinced George that you were absolutely mistaken in supposing that any one else could possibly have been more acceptable to Mr. Evarts.

George himself, who has a good party prescience, thinks there is dissatisfaction enough with the President's policy to turn many of the elections, and very seriously to embarrass the carrying out of the policy.

One thing I had forgotten, the President spoke with some feeling of the misrepresentation to which he is exposed, — part of it unintentional, part of it wilful, and referred, as an instance, to the statement circulated through the country that he had intended to exempt the members of the National Committee from the operation of his order in regard to office-holders in politics. Nothing, he said with emphasis, could have been further from his intention than any such exemption.

But enough of public affairs.

Last Saturday was Rupert's tenth birthday, and a very happy one. He had presents that pleased him, and, in addition to the presents I promised him, as part of the birthday festival, an excursion with the other children to Shelburne Falls, next Thursday, to see a Mammoth Traveling Menagerie and Great National Circus, which is to exhibit there on that day. So that this whole week has something of the pleasure of a protracted birthday.

The quiet of Ashfield is pleasant and serviceable to my Mother and Grace. They are both as well, and in as steady and cheerful spirits as I could hope to see them. They are natural, not overstrained, and they can take pleasure in the happy young life which still makes the house bright, — but which has its pathos to those who have experience of sorrow.

Good-bye, for to-night. I think of Elmwood as I say Good-night, for so I localize and hold fast yourself.

My Mother and Grace send special love to you both,
— so do I. With faithful love

Ever yours

C. E. N.

The sorrow to which Norton refers at the end of this
letter was that which had come, late in May, to his
family in the death — after a brief illness — of his
older sister Jane. Lowell, writing a few days earlier
to Thomas Hughes, had described her as "one of my
oldest and dearest friends," and his many published
letters to her show how natural had been the growth
of such intimate and sympathetic friendship with a
nature so capable as hers, in its unusual range and
generosities, of answering to his. In her death, her
family and friends — a wide circle — felt the irreparable quality that lies at the heart of such a loss.

The next letter is one of the first in a large portion
of Norton's correspondence from this time forth — the
letters to younger friends, usually known first as
pupils, and always followed with an active interest
through their careers in the larger world.

To G. E. Woodberry

CAMBRIDGE, October 11, 1877.

DEAR MR. WOODBERRY, — To-night is the first
free evening I have had since your letter reached me
six days ago, — and it is now near ten o'clock before I
have been able to begin writing. Here everything is as
usual, while with you the surroundings are changed so
utterly, and so much for the worse. Were you to come

in this evening it would seem that you had been here before on just such an evening; the books on the table are different from those of last year (not all of them indeed), but that is the only change. One book in oaken covers lies on the corner of the table, and this big volume I should like to show you. It is a manuscript of the "Divina Commedia," written in 1457 by a Luccan scribe.

The air outside is still and damp; the stars are a little dim behind the autumnal haze; within, the fire is cheerful, the room is warm and full of companionable objects.

The contrast with your bare solitude is complete. I should like to make it sharp to your feeling. I think the conditions of your life as you describe them simply odious; but did you not ever really come to the conviction that till a man had had the practical experience which could test his genuine Stoicism, — not his mere dilettante profession of the faith of Marcus Aurelius, — that he' could not be sure of his own manliness, and much less expect others to have confidence in it?

You are probably right in thinking that I would not pass three days in Lincoln.[1] I am getting on in years and have no days to waste. I do not want to go West. But the day after I spoke my Commencement part I entered a counting-room on a wharf in Boston, and for a couple of years used to freeze in winter and to roast in summer overseeing the warehousing of thousands of bags of Rio coffee, or thousands of bales of Calcutta

---

[1] Mr. Woodberry was at this time Professor of English at the University of Nebraska.

hides; I had to run errands, to do work that even a Freshman would not expect to do. It was against the grain, but it had to be done, and I stuck it out, and am not sorry now that I did so. I learned something of the world, and more of myself. There is no fear of your becoming barbarous. You will come back more fastidious (I trust) than ever. I do not expect to see you with war-paint and feathers.

It is worse than you expected. Well, so you may find all the rest of life. I do not believe you will, and I think that even when this note comes to you Lincoln will already be less intolerable than when you wrote.

What a chance it affords to study Primitive Institutions! I wish I had as clear a conception as you are getting of the first doughy stage of a modern civic community. It is all elucidation of history.

I shall not forget that you want to come East. I am not unsympathetic with you, and I am,

Very sincerely your friend,
C. E. NORTON.

To John Ruskin

CAMBRIDGE, November 2, 1877.

. . . I hold to my old desires for you. I can't think it good for you or for mankind that you are carrying on nine books at once, and a monthly serial as well. No man can pull nine bows at once so as to hit a bull's eye with every arrow, — and as your aim is no common bull's eye, but the eye of the Minotaur himself on the one hand, and the dull eye of St. Theodore's slimy dragon on another, and the white belly of the Python on the third, — good Heavens! it is plain that your hand, strong as it is, cannot bring these monsters all down at once. I wish you would practise at one, or two, at a time; and get leisure to give us the laws of Fiesole, such as they had come to the ears of her,

> "L'altra, (who) traendo alla ròcca la chioma,
> Favoleggiava con la sua famiglia
> Dei Trojani, di Fiesole e di Roma.'

. . . We have had a southerly gale to-day. The wind is down now, but it has left the trees stript. Here comes winter, — unwelcome, when the art of living is reduced to a wretched and degrading contest. As for me I am like the boy in "Evenings at Home" — no, he is in Berquin's "Fables" — I am steadfast in my preference for summer. . . .

To G. E. Woodberry

CAMBRIDGE, Sunday, December 23, 1877.

My long silence is no evidence of forgetfulness. I have had so much work to do that I have found no leisure for letter-writing. But the Christmas recess brings free days, and I am glad of the chance they give me to thank you for your letters. I need not tell you that I am truly sorry that you continue to find life at Lincoln so barren of good things. I wish it were otherwise, — but I still hold to the belief that this hard experience will not be without its worth to you, and that there is little danger of its resulting in substantial injury to the qualities and capacities in yourself which are best in promise, and for the cultivation of which Lincoln seems so unfavourable. The "Lines in Au-

tumn" that you sent me seem to me better than anything of poetry you had before written. It might be
objected to them that they are full of deeper meaning
to the poet than even the most sympathetic reader
would appreciate without special knowledge of his circumstances. One of my objections to verse-writing is
that so much verse is written by those who mean but
little by their words, and who have no real feeling, but
only an external substitute for it through acquaintance with its modes of expression, that verse inspired
by true feeling is less likely to receive due attention. . . .
But before I leave the subject of your verse, let me say
I would gladly hear, if you care to tell, what is your
"inner assurance of still longing for the laurel." I am
not so far past youth, and I hope I may never be, as
not to care for the hopes and the visions of those who
are still young, and not to rejoice when, in advancing
years, they fulfil the prophetic ideals of their youth.

Your Commencement part came to me only a week
or two ago. I like it even better now, than when you
first read it to me; and it will be pleasant to me to keep
it as a record and reminder of a past year in the little
Holden lecture-room. The past is so hard to keep! I
care most (in these later days of life) for the present as
that out of which the past is distilled. A square acre
even of the gardens of Shiraz yields but a drop or two
of the priceless pure attar of roses.

I take it for granted that you get Cambridge news
from younger friends. I know very little of it. The
most interesting College matter is another step that
is taking toward the University of the future, in the

organization of a thorough, though at present, modest
system of post-graduate instruction. A Committee is
working out the details of the scheme, — and in a
month or two I hope we may issue such a scheme as
shall attract students who desire to lay deeper foundations of learning than is practicable in the undergraduate course, and may serve as a means by which the
standard of professorial learning and labour shall be
steadily raised. . . .

To Edward Lee-Childe

SHADY HILL, February 22, 1878.

Your letter is truly welcome, for it relieves me of
solicitude about you. I have had it in mind for a long
time to write to you to ask for news of your returning
health, but in a life like mine, in which reading and
writing fill up of necessity a great part of the time, the
pen is apt to grow tired, and correspondence is put off
till that season of leisure and of freshness which never
comes, but which so often seems close at hand. Letters
in the true sense are the offspring of leisure. The busy
man, even if poet and scholar, can only write a business
letter. One must live like Doudan, at ease, free from
the worry of office, the exhaustion of a lecture-room,
and from all wearing social claims and domestic duties,
if the fine art of letter-writing is to be cultivated and
improved. Art is always a jealous mistress; this valetu-
dinarianism was one of the sacrifices she required of
Doudan, — and which he did not make. Indeed troubles never should get into letters; and yet in the letters
of friends how large a place they are apt to fill! . . .

The year began as cheerfully as we could now hope, but it had scarcely begun when my Mother was attacked with alarming illness. . . .

Mrs. Cleveland is much with us, to my Mother's great happiness; and my sister Louisa spends great part of every day with her.

My children are all well and happy and the household life is cheerful with their happiness and gaiety. I had a party of them this evening in my study, that I might read to them at their own request some stories out of the Bible, and show them the engravings from Rafael's designs and Holbein's Bible cuts. They have been greatly interested in these for some time past; and I am struck at seeing how much more they are impressed by Holbein than by Rafael, though the prints from the Stanze are so much bigger and more showy. The strength, directness, liveliness and truth of Holbein's conceptions are enhanced by the feeble grace and mannered indirectness of most of Rafael's designs. Two or three of Rafael's deserve to be excepted, especially one that we were looking at to-night, "The Finding of Moses," where the group of women on the river bank is beautiful with the beauty of Italy, — a kind of beauty unseen by Holbein or any other German.

Longfellow was here the other day, more truly delightful than ever in the sweet mellowing of his old age. The world will be greatly poorer in the best things — things "that are lovely" — when he is taken from it. I wonder that I do not see him oftener, — but visits like letters are fruits of leisure. Indeed I am too tired almost every day when my work is done to care to talk. . . .

To J. R. Lowell

SHADY HILL, May 19, 1878.

Your letter of a month ago was very welcome. I have wished that we were writing more often to each other, but a common feeling has made our letters infrequent. I miss you all the time, more than ever, — and am far more solitary in Cambridge (though I incidentally see people enough) than I ever was before. You speak of feeling old, — I too have been conscious of growing old this year. Losses set one forward in life; they shift the balance from the future to the past. Children, too, push one on. Eliot is almost as tall as I, and will soon be taller. He is getting on toward College, and will take his first examinations next year. Sally will soon be in long dresses, — and Richard will be going to school. I don't regret all this. I have had a full share of happiness and of sorrow for a long life, and many men who live to eighty have had far less experience of life and the world than I.

The days go on with us very quietly. My Mother's condition does not essentially change. She is physically to all appearance as strong as she was before her attack in January. Her mind is clear, but its vigour does not return. . . . Her state is full of pathos, and it brings a hard and constant strain to poor Grace, who bears her trial with admirable courage and self-forgetful cheerfulness. The children keep the house bright and happy. You must not have gloomy thoughts of us. There is a great deal of sunshine left. . . .

Child and I walked home together last evening from

Faculty meeting. He was good as ever. He has been doing a vast deal of work this last six months of a sort that I begrudge, as it takes him from work that he alone can do, and which he has already put off doing too long. . . . When you write to him I wish you would spur him up about his "Ballads." I want him to begin to print. He ought not to delay.

Godkin is coming back to his house in June,[1] and Olmsted and his wife are proposing to spend a good part of the summer with him. This is an excellent arrangement, for Godkin's social nature requires company, and he could not have better company than Olmsted. There is nothing in public affairs to make Godkin, or any other thoughtful man, cheerful. Our politics have never been in a worse state. The administration is a failure. Hayes lacks capacity to take advantage of circumstance and position. Evarts has neither dignity nor weight of counsel. Sherman blows cold and hot, and has aided in demoralizing the public sentiment in regard to the resumption of specie payment, and the general good faith of the nation. Schurz means and does well, but makes many enemies. The rest of the Cabinet is too feeble to count. This reopening of the Presidential question by the Democrats is not likely to have any worse consequence than to promote a disquiet state of feeling and postpone that revival of confidence which is essential to prosperity. Business is not likely to revive during the summer, and people feel poor and uncertain of the future. There is scarcely any house-building, and mechanics of all sorts

[1] Godkin was at this time living in Cambridge, near Shady Hill.

are out of employ. The natural consequence of these
conditions is an outcrop of all the socialism and com-
munism, and all other growths of idleness and ignorance in the country. The "National" party, whose
principles are the destructive fallacies of ignorance, is
having ominous success in the elections at the West.
There is already a strong anti-resumption and un-
limited-issue-of-Greenbacks party in New England.
The prospect is not bright. It will not be surprising if
we have a repetition of last summer's strikes and labour
riots. President Eliot is doing what he can to promote
the rifle club and drilling among the students. He
thinks the time may very likely soon come when they
will need to know the use of arms, — not to defend the
college, but for service in some one or other of the
cities.

The College itself is doing well. Two great buildings
are to go up this summer; the new Gymnasium between the Holmes house and the Scientific School; and
Sever Hall, for lecture and recitation-rooms, which will
probably be set just back of Lane's house, between, but
a little back of, the Library and the Chapel. This is to
be a very large hall, 180 by 80 feet, and I have given
up all hope of any College building being other than
ugly. . . .

To J. R. Lowell
ASHFIELD, August 4, 1878.

. . . Yesterday, after dinner, I went across the fields
to George Curtis's to ask him to join me on a walk. He
was sitting on the piazza with Anna, and with Mrs.

Leonowens who had come over from Amherst to spend
Saturday and Sunday with them. Mrs. L. is teaching
Sanscrit in Dr. Sauveur's summer school of languages.
Conversational Sanscrit is a novelty, but Mrs. Leon-
owens has vitality enough to revivify the deadest of
tongues. . . .

The two ladies went off to drive. George read me,
while I smoked, a number of his late letters, — one,
and the best one, from the President. It takes a long
time to educate Hayes, but he is educable, and when
he leaves the White House he will be a good President.
He lacks the energy of an aggressive leader, and his
position is essentially aggressive. But this letter to
George Curtis indicated that he was beginning to feel
that there was little chance of success for his policy
unless he convinced his opponents that he was resolved
to take all upright and legitimate means to secure it.
I trust there will be fewer inconsistencies and fewer
faults in the Administration as Hayes learns that there
is no hope of harmony in the party, and that concilia-
tion by temporary desertion of one's principles is
always a weak and always a disastrous policy. His
Cabinet is greatly against the President. Sherman and
Evarts are enough to ruin the attempt to establish a
civil service reform, and they succeed in giving to the
attempt, on the President's part, in popular estimation
the air of a mere politician's game. . . .

My days are generally very quiet. I have been for
the most part indolent, for I was very tired when we
came here, and I have not yet got wholly rested. But
I am doing a good deal of reading on the Renaissance;

— I have read more of Machiavelli than ever before, and I have been rereading Vespasiano, and a good deal in Muratori, and the Archivio Storico. It keeps me in Italy. . . .

To J. R. Lowell

ASHFIELD, September 17, 1878.

. . . George Curtis and I have been taking a long walk this afternoon. The sunlight had an autumnal pallor, but the air was soft; the goldenrod fringed the roadside with its splendid plumes; here and there we saw and left many gentians; the blue jays were bickering on the edges of the woods; the streams were full with last week's abundant rains. For sweet, easy, daily pleasantness George has no rival. It is perpetual summer with him. There is no change in him, except each year makes his good still better. Time improves the best things. He is as busy and as serviceable in politics as ever, — and our long daily talks are more occupied with the shifting aspects of affairs in New York, or Maine, or Massachusetts, with the errors or good deeds of the Administration, with the prospects of the autumn political campaign, than with all other topics put together. He has a capital, practical estimate of forces, and his judgment has been disciplined by long experience. He is one of the most prominent figures in New York politics just at this moment, but he looks on at his own part in the mêlée, and gives and takes heavy blows, with as much unconcern as if he were a third person to himself. We were laughing to-day at the heat of the battle around him, while he remains a cool

spectator from the hills. His position has been one of
real difficulty and delicacy, and is likely to be so, so
long as Conkling succeeds in holding a majority of the
Republican party in New York. . . .

Horace Gray has been here for two or three days
between two terms of Court, and his presence made
talk upon politics only the more active. And Woodberry — the young fellow to whom you were so kind
— was here at the same time, and as Godkin has just
taken him on to the "Nation," and he is beginning to
write a part of its political articles, he was something
more than a merely observant listener.

Godkin is pleased with Woodberry's beginnings.
His work seems to me more than promising; it has
absolute, accomplished excellence. . . .

I have been reading much on, — or rather *in* the
Renaissance this summer, mostly the R. in Italy.
Lately I have been cantering through Ariosto. I never
read the whole of the Orlando before, but now I have
read on and on for the sake of the pictures of Italy
which shape themselves to my vision on the screen of
Ariosto's magic lantern. The phantasmagoric wonders
reveal real figures in scenes of real life. His easy,
graceful, natural fluency is delightful. It must be
vastly more difficult to sustain verse at such an even
level of elegance, than to help it out with buffoonery
like Pulci, or with verbal playfulness like Casti, whose
consummate cleverness might indeed be equal to any
task in versifying.

I hope you are not studying too hard. I am always
afraid of the next month for you, after one of your

protracted debauches of hard reading. Your late letters have made me happy with their good accounts of yourself, and I want this happiness to last. I am glad that they are beginning to find you out over there. . . . And I am glad, too, that you have begun to feel the charm of Spain and to discover the Madrid of Cervantes. . . .

To J. R. Lowell

SHADY HILL, February 22, 1879.

I have celebrated your birthday in my heart, glad and grateful for all that my life owes and has so long owed to your love. Few men can look back on so many years of mutual affection as you and I can do, absolutely unshadowed by even the most passing cloud of difference. Fewer still have been so blessed in a friend as I in you.

It is long since we heard from you; but I take your silence to mean only good. I hope with all my heart that you are well and contented. I wish that on the first of every month you would send a postal-card to me with the two words *Buenos días.* I will do as much. And, indeed, on my part there is little need of more, for the days pass so quietly with me, and one week is so like another, and each so like those that you have known, that there is little to tell you of personal experience. In essentials there is no change here since my last letter.

It is late in the evening. I had meant to begin my letter earlier, but just before tea Godkin came in, having been dining at the Saturday Club, whither I did not go to-day because I had some work that I wanted to accomplish. I had not seen Godkin since he went to New York at the beginning of November. He is well, and seemed in good spirits. He has come on to spend a few days with the Gurneys. I fear he is tried by the condition of the "Nation"; the subscription list declines, and the paper still depends on him so exclusively that he can get no release from constant work. He can find no one to relieve him, and the prospect of continuous labour is unlighted by any hope of a competent assistant. . . . The trouble is that he is so eminent in the field of political writing himself, that there is no second to him. He stands alone, without even a squire at his side. It is a great pity that he is thus unaided. It is, indeed, part due to character, and I see nothing for it but that he must continue to work, till he grows too weary to work longer, and turns the paper over to some wholly new hands which will hardly be able to carry it on at its present level of ability.

Woodberry is now established in Cambridge for a few months, writing regularly for the "Nation," and studying Italian with a view to the study of Venetian history. Godkin had not gone this evening when he came in to read me an article on the effect of our institions on literature, suggested by the reading of old Mr. Dana's prose and poetry. It was a thoughtful and interesting essay which I hope will appear in the "Nation" of next week.

When I referred to your birthday, Woodberry spoke with warmth of your kindness to him. He is growing fast in power; the experience of life is serviceable to

him; and if he keeps his health, and has sufficient
energy, much that is good may be fairly expected from
him. He has no successors in College with literary
gifts that approach his in quality. I see him once a
week regularly, for he is one of a class of young graduates and of Seniors, — eight in all, — with whom on
Tuesday evenings I read Dante. It is interesting work,
for they are a picked set, and all full of fresh interest
and zeal in the study. By the end of the year we shall
have read the whole "Divine Comedy," and there will
be eight more lovers of Dante in the land. In the ideal
University I should like to be Professor of Dante.
When you come home you and I must go to work on
the edition of the "Divine Comedy" which we have so
long planned. I was pleased the other day to receive
from the good old Witte a new volume of his collected
essays on Dante. . . .

The year 1879 marks a date significant in Norton's
association with Ashfield. His letters from this summer
refuge have already shown the reader how highly he
had come to value, for himself and for his family, the
restful charm of the place, and the simple terms upon
which life could be lived in it. To Curtis he wrote in
1877: "I am sorry you are becoming so interesting to
reporters; every time that 'Ashfield,' 'Summer Home
of . . .' etc., 'Pretty Village,' 'Wooded Hills,' etc., are
seen in a New York paper, a bit of our wall of defence
against the public is thrown down, and I see summer
visitors climbing in through the breach to break up the
precious seclusion and leisure of our summer days."

In the same year he drew for Lowell a village scene in which the friendliness of the little place stands forth: —

"I wish you had been here last Saturday evening. George Curtis had just arrived and had come over to greet us just after dark, when we heard the village band coming up the road, and received word that a serenade was to be given to me, and that afterward George was to be serenaded. George fled homeward that he might be there to receive his guests, and missed the pretty sight of the band with their lanterns under our heavy maples, — the light thrown out from the lamps in uncertain flashes up and down the road, and on the villagers who had gathered to hear the music, and on two or three wagons full of people from distant parts. The music was better than I had expected, though I had heard praises of the band, and the whole affair was pleasant and the scene was unusual and picturesque."

Again to Lowell he wrote in a later year: —

"Last night I was at a meeting of the Trustees of our Academy here — good men of the village, all of them, the excellent products of democracy; we discussed the questions of town schools, town debts, town accounts, all with good sense and right purpose.[1]

"To-night, 'by request,' I am to give a talk on Longfellow to the townspeople. To-morrow night George is to preside at a general meeting of the taxpayers for discussing some of the questions we had in debate last time."

These passages, drawn almost at random from a mul-

---

[1] Two years after Norton's death an Ashfield woman with whom he had worked on Village and School Committees, said in speaking of him to a stranger — "We always felt he was one of us."

titude of references to Ashfield and to Norton's personal
identification with the concerns of the town, illustrate
an element of deep interest in his life from this time
until its end.

That the Academy in Ashfield should especially have
enlisted the services of such a citizen as Norton was
natural. This Academy, once a flourishing school,
founded by Alvan Sanderson, of Ashfield, in 1817, had,
through the indifference of its trustees, become little
more than a name when Norton and Curtis first made
Ashfield their summer home.[1]

To restore the ruinous old building, to engage a good
teacher, to provide the children of Ashfield with much
needed schooling beyond the primary stages, became in
Norton's early summers in the town a great interest
with him. He talked, he stimulated, he worked; the
village became interested and worked too; and Curtis,
not less readily than his friend, gave himself to the
cause.

When in 1879, the "Academy Dinner" was started,
it was to provide funds (from the sale of tickets at one
dollar each) which should help eke out the small in-
come of the School. With Norton to preside at those
"dinners"; with Curtis, whose persuasive eloquence in

[1] Mary Lyon, who founded Mount Holyoke Female Seminary (now
College), the first institution for the collegiate instruction of women in
America, was an early pupil of the school, and from 1822 to 1828 an assistant
principal and "preceptress." The *Hampshire Gazette* for October 24, 1827,
contained the following advertisement: —

"SANDERSON ACADEMY. — The winter term of fourteen weeks in
this Academy, commencing on the 12th of December next, will be devoted
exclusively to the instruction of FEMALES, under the care of Miss Mary
Lyon. The course of instruction will be essentially the same as was pursued
the past winter, with the addition of Chirography."

the fearless exposure of corruption can never be forgotten by anyone who heard him speak; with Lowell,
Howells, Choate, Moorfield Storey, Booker Washington, and many others, guests in Ashfield and speakers
at that midsummer feast, it was not surprising that
the occasion became, as the years went on, well known.
It was regarded from outside as an event of national
interest, since the speakers addressed an audience that
listened from beyond the encircling hills of Ashfield.
Their words might be denounced as "Mugwump oratory"; they might themselves be regarded as "rene-
gade to party"; but this did not deter these lovers of
America, these leaders in such causes as those of Civil
Service Reform, Tariff Reform, Negro education,
Anti-Imperialism, from coming to Ashfield to speak on
subjects about which free speech was expected there.[1]

For twenty-five years these "Academy dinners," in
the Ashfield Town Hall, continued their course. In
1903 the last one took place: after that year Norton's
failing strength made it impossible for him longer to
"carry" the occasion, which since Curtis's death had
lost its most important speaker, and with that loss, a
charm and quality that could not be replaced. The
summer of Curtis's death (1892) the dinner was
omitted; the following year it was arranged as a memorial to him.

In the early autumn of 1879 Norton's mother died
at Shady Hill, after some months of sad illness. Death
brought in this case the comfort that suffering had

---

[1] For list of speakers at Ashfield Academy dinners see Appendix C.

ended, but it brought a vital change. One thinks of
Gray's words in a letter about the loss of his mother:
"It is thirteen years ago, and seems but yesterday; and
every day I live it sinks deeper into my heart." Mrs.
Norton's long life, so closely bound to her husband's
and to her children's — of the very fabric of theirs, it
might be said — had, through a quality of devotion
quickened by intelligence and moral purpose, the clear
outline of a noble simplicity.

> "Oh dignity of life that dignified
> All common life around, as some fair hill
> Ennobles all the landscape seen beside, —
> Grove, road, and meadow with its little rill!" [1]

What Norton's relation to his mother had been his
letters have shown; and if other token were needed, her
carefully preserved letters to him complete the tangible
record. Among these letters there is a touching little
packet of now faded scraps of writing, — requests in
her hand, in regard to errands to be done, messages
delivered and the like; little phrases of affection for him,
pinned at night to his jacket to meet the little boy's
eye when he started early for school before seeing her:
all these kept and labelled in a boyish hand.

Not long before his mother's death, Norton had
written to Ruskin: "My children must have a country,
and on the whole this is best for them. I am bound
here by duty to them and to my Mother. For my life
would doubtless be better in many ways in Europe;
but I should be after all of less service there than
here." About the same time, in a letter to John Simon,

[1] "To C[atherine] E[liot] N[orton]," *King Arthur in Avalon and Other Poems,* by Sara Hammond Palfrey.

Norton said: "Your letters make me feel sharply what I am losing in life — pleasures, opportunities, happiness, indeed, of a sort that nothing else can supply. I envy the man whose roots draw full nourishment from his native soil. I am half starved here, — and in the old world I should be half starved for this strange new one. A thousand years hence, perhaps, America will be old enough for men to live in it with comfort, and with complete satisfaction. 'To live for the future,' as we are told to do, is to live on the windiest and least nourishing of diets."

To the same kind friend he wrote of that event which now brought one period of his life to a definite close.

To John Simon

CAMBRIDGE, September 25, 1879.

I do not want you to hear by mere common report of my Mother's death. She died tranquilly at midnight, last night. . . . Euthanasy would have been a blessing at any time for a year and more past; and, of late, to abridge her life would have been a duty in any society more civilized than ours. The relief has come at last, with its strangely mingled emotions, — thankfulness, pathetic tenderness, memories of past gladness, and a sense of an indefinitely immense change in life, not merely in its daily interests, cares and associations, and in the severing of closest ties, but (much more impressive) in the balance between past and future. With her so much goes over from me into the past, the henceforth forgotten, irrevocable and unknown! So long as she lived somebody was in the world who knew and

cared for me as nobody else ever can, — who shared
with me memories exclusively our own. I feel as if it
were great part of the historic me that had gone into
extinction, on its way to dust, and the stopping of a
bunghole. I don't know that I regret it much. Such
mutation sobers, but not saddens the heart.

CHAPTER X

THE FIELD OF INFLUENCE

(1880–1889)

No years of Norton's life were more productive than those that followed immediately upon his taking up the duties of his Professorship at Harvard. His indefatigable industry spent itself not only during term-time in college duties — for many years he gave six or more regular lectures a week — but at all times in carrying on other labours in wider fields. Several of these self-imposed and large undertakings had their beginnings at almost the same time with the institution of the Ashfield dinners. In all of them Norton's faculty for enlisting the interest and active enthusiasm of younger men — an influence partaking the spirit of Goethe's dictum: *Lehre thut viel, aber Aufmunterung thut alles,* — was a large element in the final success of the various objects in view.

The first of these enterprises was one with which Norton's name has had scanty public association. Yet his correspondence for some years from 1879 onward shows that he bore an important part in the movement which resulted in the state reservation of Niagara Falls. One of the chief agents in the enterprise was Frederick Law Olmsted,[1] and with him Norton was in

[1] Norton's letters to Olmsted have perished, but Olmsted's to Norton are full of interesting evidence in regard to their joint labours in this undertaking, held at heart by both.

close and constant touch. An early step in the work was the securing of influential signatures, American and foreign, for a memorial in favour of the reservation. Norton's friends at home and abroad were the very men whose names were needed, and he spared no pains to obtain them. As the Loyal Publication Society during the Civil War had brought the newspapers to bear upon public opinion, Norton now set a similar influence at work on behalf of the salvation of Niagara. In the summer of 1881 Mr. (now Sir) Henry Norman,[1] then just leaving Harvard, and in the following summer the Rev. J. B. Harrison [2] — each instigated by Norton — wrote effectual letters from Niagara to many newspapers. Ascribing to him a large measure of the impetus given toward the salvation of the Falls of Niagara, — "that is, the voting of enough money by the State of New York to buy enough land round them to prevent their actual destruction forever, and to buy up the Gas Works and Oneida Community's factory on the cliff," — Sir

[1] Member of Parliament, traveller and author of *The People and Politics of the Far East, All the Russias,* etc.

[2] Norton wrote at this time to Harrison: —

"I should be glad to have you write something to indicate to the mass of unreflecting, uneducated Americans what the value of noble scenery may be in its influence upon life and character; to show to them how it should be regarded, and to point out to them the need of self-education in order properly to appreciate the beauty of Nature, and to recognize the lessons for life which are to be drawn from it. The mass of the visitors to Niagara go there to look at it as a curious phenomenon, one that excites their wonder, and stimulates their national pride, as being the finest and most famous waterfall in the world. Very few of them recognize in it one of those works of Nature which is fitted to elevate and refine the character, and to quicken the true sense of the relations of man with that Nature of which he is a part, to the beauty of which he should be sensitive, and of whose noble works he should feel himself to be the guardian."

Henry Norman has recently written to a member of Norton's family:

"When I was leaving Harvard and coming home for good, he said to me, 'Norman, do you wish to do a piece of good work before you leave America, that needs doing, and that several people have tried to do and failed, and that you, if anybody, can do?' I replied that I would attempt anything that he wished me to do. So he told me the job was to spend a couple of months at Niagara, to write letters and articles for any paper that could be got to publish them, and so to arouse public opinion to the shame of the imminent destruction of this unique American possession of natural beauty that the State Legislature would be led to vote enough to save it. I spent two months at Niagara, all my expenses being paid, at your father's request, by Mr. Howard Potter the banker; and I wrote a large number of articles which appeared in newspapers all over the United States.[1] The following year I happened to be at Albany and went to call on a Senator, who took me on to the floor of the Senate. I said to him, 'What is the business before you at this moment?' He replied, 'we are about to vote the Niagara Falls Appropriation Bill.' I went to the telegraph office and sent a message to your father, congratulating him."

If more recent industrial progress now urgently renders still further protection of Niagara Falls desirable, it is appalling to reflect upon the destruction that, but for the activities of Norton and his friends about thirty years ago, might have continued unchecked.

[1] These, and J. B. Harrison's letters, were republished in pamphlet form.

An enterprise with which Norton's name is, however, inseparably connected was the founding of the Archæological Institute of America. In 1879 he prepared, and, in coöperation with others, issued a circular proposing to establish a society for the purpose of furthering and directing archæological investigation and research. The high conception of the value he believed to lie in such work was expressed in an address of later years: "Reckoned by the period of man's unrecorded existence, written history dates only from yesterday, and its earliest and longest parts are full of gaps and still fuller of errors. But as geology has within a hundred years indefinitely extended our conceptions of the age of the earth on which we live, so archæology, dealing with what Livy calls the *incorrupta rerum gestarum monumenta*, has indefinitely lengthened our view of human life, and thrown back the date of human activity into a past hardly dreamed of by our ancestors. 'The night of time far surpasseth the day,' said Sir Thomas Browne, and it is the task of archæology to light up some parts of this long night with its torch, which burns ever with a clearer flame with each advancing step into the darkness."[1] Still later Norton wrote: "The chief motive which has led me to undertake this task was the hope that, by the establishment of such a Society, the interests of classical scholarship in America might be advanced, and especially that it might lead to the foundation of a school of classical studies

---

[1] From an address, "The Work of the Archæological Institute of America," delivered at New Haven, December, 1899.

in Athens where young scholars might carry on the
study of Greek thought and life to the best advantage, and where those who were purposing to become
teachers of Greek might gain such acquaintance with
the land and such knowledge of its ancient monuments as should give a finality to their teaching unat-
tainable without this experience. It had become evident that, if Greek literature and art were to have
their proper place in the education of American youth,
fresh effort must be made and new means taken to promote their study." [1]

How were these desires fulfilled? The answer is
found in a few words from an address by Professor W.
F. Harris before the Archæological Institute soon
after Norton's death:

"To the gratification of all scholars and lovers of
learning throughout the country, the idea of the Institute met with cordial coöperation on the part of our
leading colleges and universities. The School at
Athens was almost immediately founded. The Institute became one of the important means for the ad-
vancement of sound learning in America. Under Professor Norton's catholic direction the work took a wide
range; investigations were conducted at Assos in the
Troad and in the southwest of our own country; the
interests of architecture were fostered; the higher intellectual pursuits in the community were aided by a
study of the close relationship of the art and thought
of the ancient world to our own. And more than all
else, he started a stream of American scholars to

[1] *Journal of the Archæological Institute of America*, vol. vii (1903).

classic lands.[1] These men have been inspired by an increased realization of the vitality and splendour of the
life and literature of the people who dwelt around
the Mediterranean. And this inspiration they have
brought back to innumerable pupils in this land, so
that the seed of Norton's sowing has gone on, ever increasing."

A more concrete expression of the feeling that Norton was himself the Institute is found in an anecdote
related by Professor Harris: "'Archæological Institute of America?' queried one who did good work in
the service: —

"'No!'

"'Archæological Institute of New England?'

"'No!'

"'Archæological Institute of Boston?'

"'No! Archæological Institute of Shady Hill!'"'

The files of Norton's wide correspondence bear
eloquent testimony to his unbroken and far-reaching
interest in the society. Through all the years, during which Norton said of the Society, — "It had
scanty funds, it had often to live by faith," — it was
indeed at Shady Hill from 1879 up to the end of his
life that a vital portion of the work of the Institute was
done.

Societies neither have a beginning nor continue to
exist without the devotion of one or more unselfish persons. A third enterprise of this period which owed its
origin to Norton was the Cambridge Dante Society. His

[1] To these services of the Institute must be added its establishment of
the School of Classical Studies at Rome, and the publication of the *American
Journal of Archæology.*

letters and his publication so early as 1859, of "The New Life of Dante, an Essay with Translations," have shown how strong and enduring his interest in the study of Dante had been. Of his other contributions to that study, and of the founding of the Dante Society, no one is better qualified to speak than a friend and pupil to whom Norton in later years was indebted for many expressions of whole-hearted kindness, — Mr. William Roscoe Thayer, the distinguished student in the fields of Italian history and literature. From his paper, "Professor Charles Eliot Norton," in the Annual Report of the Dante Society (Cambridge, Massachusetts) for 1909, the following pages are drawn: —

"In the early sixties, Longfellow took up his translation of 'The Divine Comedy,' and Lowell, Norton, and a few others gathered on Wednesday evening every week in the study at the Craigie House, listened to the new section of translation, pondered it, and gave to Longfellow suggestions, some of which, as he acknowledged, he gladly adopted. Mr. Howells, in his delightful volume, 'Literary Friends and Acquaintance,' has described these meetings of the 'Dante Club,' to which he, then recently settled in Cambridge, was invited. 'Those who were most constantly present,' he says, 'were Lowell and Professor Norton, but from time to time others came in, and we seldom sat down at the nine o'clock supper that followed the reading of the canto in less number than ten or twelve. The criticism, especially from the accomplished Dantists I have named, was frank and frequent.'

"Even before this Mr. Norton himself undertook to translate 'The New Life,' the first specimens of which he printed in 1859. Thenceforward his quality as a Dantist was publicly recognized. . . .

"A few years ago I asked him for information in regard to the founding of the Dante Society, and he replied in a letter dated July 29, 1904, from which I quote: —

" ' It was, I think, in 1880 that some members of the class which I was conducting in "The Divine Comedy," hearing me speak of the possible service which a club for the promotion of Dante studies might render, came to me to say that they wished such a club might be founded, and would be glad to do what might be in their power to give it a good start. (I recall especially John Woodbury [now secretary of the Metropolitan Park Commission] and Professor Hart as interested in the matter.) I told them that I thought that the success of the effort would depend on whether Mr. Longfellow would consent to take the presidency of the proposed society, and that I would consult with him about it. Longfellow was cordial in his approval of the scheme. He saw in it, especially, the means by which the Dante library of Harvard might be strengthened and steadily increased, and also he believed that such a society as was proposed might justify its existence by undertaking the publication of the "Comment on The Divine Comedy" of Benvenuto da Imola, of which only fragments had hitherto been printed. This had been long an object of desire with him, and he and I had often talked of how to bring it about. The existence of a society, the members of which could be appealed to, to contribute to the cost of copying the manuscript of the "Comment" and to the further cost of printing it, seemed to open the way to the accomplishment of a work of the first importance to all students of "The Divine Comedy."

"'Longfellow readily consented to be president of the society. A few persons were asked to become members. A meeting of them was held at the Craigie House, and Longfellow was, as usual, the most genial and delightful of hosts. I think more than one meeting was held there; by-laws were adopted, officers were elected, circulars were prepared, the aims of the society were thoroughly discussed, it was determined to send to Florence for a copy of the Benvenuto manuscript of the "Comment," and, if I remember rightly, Longfellow undertook to defray the cost of the copy.'

"So was founded the Dante Society, which for nearly thirty years has persevered in the mission then laid down for it. It has called out several important studies in Dante, achieved two invaluable concordances, stimulated by its annual prize the zeal of university students for research and criticism, and contributed to the assembling in the Harvard Library of a Dante collection accessible to scholars throughout the East and second in range only to that given by Professor Willard Fiske to Cornell University. In his account of the founding, Mr. Norton, with characteristic modesty, attributes to Mr. Longfellow's coöperation the element indispensable to success; but, in fact, as the original members will be the first to testify, it was Mr.

Norton himself whose active sympathy created the
society and caused it to flourish as long as he lived.
Mr. Longfellow served it as its first president, — a
beautiful and willing figure-head, lacking neither in
helpful counsel nor in practical support. On his death,
in 1882, James Russell Lowell was chosen to succeed
him; but Lowell was then in England, nor did he ever,
after coming home in 1885, take root again in Cambridge. But his name shed a far lustre, and his favour
and advice sustained the prestige of the society. When
he died, in 1891, Mr. Norton became president.

"Thenceforward, every May, on the evening of the
third Tuesday of the month, he held the annual meeting at Shady Hill, and nobody who attended one of
those meetings will ever forget the way in which he
presided, so informally, yet with that unfailing dignity
of which he alone seemed to have the secret. In a few
penetrating sentences he would review each of the half
dozen Dante books of the year; point out new work
that the society might undertake; praise, in words
which held no flattery, the labours of Professor Sheldon
and his colleagues on the concordance; and summarize
the quality of the essays handed in to compete for the
Dante Prize.

"Until a year or two ago, — indeed, until last year,
— though he seemed at each season a little frailer in
body, we noticed no slackening of intellectual vigour;
but last year, while his mind was as clear as ever, he
asked Professor Grandgent to give an account of the
new publications which he had himself been unable
through illness to keep abreast of. To the end, however,

the 'gracious amity and unequaled intuitions,' which Mr. Howells recalls of him at the meetings at Longfellow's forty years before, shone in his manner and in his criticism. Almost his last words, before the meeting of the society in 1908 broke up, were to urge that Dante be read *naturally*, for his evident meaning, and especially for his significance to us to-day, and neither as a maker of linguistic and philogical puzzles, nor as a conscious exploiter of recondite theories.

"In 1891 Professor Norton published his prose translation of 'The Divine Comedy,' — a work which at once took its place as the best. It is hardly likely to be superseded, for metrical translators of Dante sacrifice too much of his meaning in order to give us a metrical residue which in nowise corresponds to his *terza rima*. It is significant that the best metrical version in English, Longfellow's, in hendecasyllabic blank verse, comes nearest to prose. Readers to whom the originals of the few world masterpieces are inaccessible will more and more resort to the best prose renderings. Among these Norton's ' Divine Comedy' unquestionably belongs. To understand the care with which he worked, one should compare the first edition of his translation with the last. In the intervening ten years he literally went over every word afresh, weighed every phrase, listened to every new suggestion, and made even commas serve instead of exegesis. His critical faculty was so delicate and so exacting that he was satisfied with nothing short of perfection in his own writing. 'It is the final thumb-nail touches,' he used to say to me, 'that count.'

"Besides his translation of 'The Divine Comedy' he brought out a revision of 'The New Life,' and he contributed to Warner's Library a monograph, unfortunately too brief, on Dante's career and genius. The latter fragment was compiled in part from lectures delivered by him on the Turnbull Foundation at Baltimore. He could never be persuaded to amplify them into a volume which should transmit to posterity the interpretation and criticism of the foremost English-speaking Dantist of his time.

"I call Mr. Norton the foremost Dantist advisedly, for I had the rare privilege of being a pupil both of him and of Lowell, whom Norton himself called his master. But Lowell was never the minute and indefatigable searcher of texts that Norton was; and Lowell never felt Dante as Norton felt him. Lowell's essay will long deserve to be read, not only because it is one of the best literary essays produced in America, but also in its wit, in its flashes of insight, in its occasional waywardness, and in its Romanticist exuberance, it is characteristic of his brilliant talents. But to read Dante with Mr. Norton was almost an act of worship. There was in his voice something wonderfully stirring and wholly incommunicable. . . . He explained fully from every side, — verbal, textual, literary, spiritual; and even when he did not pause to suggest the parallel between Dante's examples and our modern instances, he left no doubt of their pertinence to ourselves. Yet with all this there was no hint of preaching, no attempt, so common among German expounders, to twist Dante's text to fit a theory.

"Looking back upon those hours of high instruction, I find it hard to say whether the final impression Mr. Norton's illumination of ' The Divine Comedy' made upon me concerned the spiritual signficance or the supreme beauty of the poem. That one should blend into the other was, after all, what he intended, for he never divorced the spiritual from the beautiful. . . . In his interpretation of Dante he had one immense advantage which neither Lowell nor any other English-speaking Dantist has possessed: he had a specialist's knowledge of mediæval art. So the thirteenth century lived for him not merely in its poetry, theology, and chronicles, but in its paintings and statues, in its churches and town halls, in its palaces and dwellings. These arts, needless to say, had then an extraordinary representative value which they do not possess at all to-day; and only he who knows them intimately can compass the whole circle of the experience and the ideals of that world of which 'The Divine Comedy' is the supreme expression in language.

" Mr. Norton had this erudition, but, as was his wont, he never gave it out as mere erudition; he always vitalized it by his sympathy, and so endued it with immediate human interest. He scorned loose thinking; he despised inaccuracy or misstatement. His critical keenness made him instinctively take care to be sure of his facts, but he unconsciously presented his facts with charm, as Nature hides pollen or seeds in her flowers."

The final words of Mr. Thayer's paper are: "As long as any of us who knew Charles Eliot Norton survive,

we shall feel that his benign influence accompanies us
and bids us Godspeed." In this year 1913, a fourth
volume of concordances to Dante has been published
under the auspices of the Society, with a dedication
which gives expression to a continuance of the spirit
that Mr. Thayer so happily described:—

> CAROLO ELIOT NORTON
> Aurea qui quondam vitæ praecepta modestae
> DANTIS amans docuit, Graius homo ipse animo,
> Nunc ad iustitiam multos informat ut olim,
> Fulgens ceu mundi sidera perpetua.

The activities of the busy years in which Norton's
interests were so broadly extended are faithfully reflected in his letters of the period, though but as in the
convex mirror. When the first of them was written,
Lowell had just been appointed Minister to England.

To J. R. Lowell

SHADY HILL, January 22, 1880.

The letters of the last two weeks from you and John
Field have lightened our hearts, and made the beginning of the year happy for us. . . . By this time I wish
that Fanny [1] may have got her invalid chair from London, and be able to move from room to room, and
enjoy the fresh air at the windows.

I hope she is pleased with your appointment to
London. I take it for granted that the Administration
consulted you before making it, and appointing your
successor at Madrid. It pleases me that the place
should be offered to you, whether you accept it or not.

[1] Mrs. Lowell was recovering slowly from a desperate illness.

Mabel writes to me, "I do so hope that Papa will feel he can afford to take the English mission. I can think of nothing better, for they just wish to get away from Madrid as soon as may be." I do not think the question of "afford" ought to enter among those to be discussed in coming to a decision. It is an immense mistake, it seems to me, to think it necessary to live at a great expense and in a grand style as Ambassador. You can live with dignity and propriety in London on the Minister's salary, and be just as much liked as if you spent double, and more respected. I think Motley never gained by his lavishness, but on the contrary exposed himself to criticism that was not unfounded. I am sure John Field will confirm me about this matter of expense in London, and of the way in which our Minister ought to live.

There seems to be but one feeling throughout the country as to the fitness of your appointment, and a general expression of gratification in it. I inclose a note from Brimmer which has just come to me and will show you how people feel.

Howells and Curtis and I did our best to bring this about last June, — but the weather grew hot, and Congress and the Cabinet left Washington, — and then Fanny was taken ill.

I hope with all my heart that you will not suffer now from any reaction from the tense life of the last six months. Take care of yourself, my dear old fellow, for Fanny's sake now.

Your faithful friend,
C. E. N.

To Henry C. Lea

CAMBRIDGE, March 20, 1880.

DEAR SIR, — I am much pleased that the scheme for a conference of Independent Republicans before the Chicago Convention meets with your approval. I have great confidence that if a proper organization is effected, the defeat of Grant or Blaine, if either of them should receive the nomination at Chicago, would be assured. And it seems to me a far less evil that there should be a Democratic Administration for four years, than that there should be a corrupt Republican Administration.

Vigorous and courageous action on the part of the Independents will be supported by the same class of men as those who were the original founders of the Republican party.

I am entirely of your opinion that the Conference should not be called for some weeks to come, and that the form of a call should be so worded as to make sure that the conference shall not assume the character of a nominating convention. . . .

To J. R. Lowell

ASHFIELD, June 27, 1880.

. . . I do not remember if I told you I was printing a volume of Studies of Church Building in the Middle Ages, — made up of studies of St. Mark's, and the Duomo of Siena, and that of Florence. It was finished a month or two ago, but the Harpers keep it back for publication in the autumn. It makes at least a very handsome volume. If I have the leisure during the coming year I mean to follow it up with further studies of the same sort of Cluny, St. Denis, and Chartres, for which I have most of the material ready.

The only new book of much interest is Howells's new story [1] which I hope he has sent you. As a mere story it is very slight, but in the delineation of character he has before done nothing so good as Dr. Boynton. It is a genuinely imaginative creation, and shows a range of thought, and a power of speculation hardly indicated by his previous work. As an artist his stroke is strong and felicitous throughout. The picture of the Shaker community is charming. Howells is very well, and seems happy. He is coming to make us a little visit in August.

I have had a good deal to do during the last year with our new Archæological Society. It has begun well as you will see from the first Report, of which the Secretary of the Institute will send you two or three copies for such use as you may like to make of them. We are just now busy in raising money for the work of this year, and, though we shall not get all we want, we shall get enough for us to undertake explorations at Assos with hope of interesting results. The main grounds for the choice of Assos as the site of investigation are set forth in the last paper in the volume that contains the Annual Report.

Curtis has not got to Ashfield yet. My vacation does not really begin till he comes to share it. He was greatly needed and missed at the Chicago Convention.

[1] *The Undiscovered Country.*

Had he been there we should hardly have had to endure
the wretched anti-climax of Arthur's nomination. The
"Nation" will give you my politics. . . .

In the autumn of 1880 the book mentioned in the
foregoing letter, "Historical Studies of Church Building in the Middle Ages: Venice, Siena, Florence," was
published. Norton's letters from Italy in 1869 and
1870 have shown him at work on the original investigations that form the substance of this book, and more
than any other work of his, it represents his study of
the subjects to which his teaching at Harvard was
specially devoted. Its purpose — as expressed in the
book itself — was to show the relation of a great art to
the times in which it flourished, and to impress "the
truth which has determined the character of all
supreme artistic production — that in the highest
forms of human expression morality and beauty are
inseparable." The volume marked an important point
in Norton's career in establishing with the general
public the place as an historian and critic of art which
his work as a teacher was winning for him at Cambridge.

To Thomas Carlyle

ASHFIELD, MASSACHUSETTS, July 26, 1880.

MY DEAR MR. CARLYLE, — . . . I sent you not long
ago a volume of Archæological papers which I hoped
might entertain you for an hour or two. I don't
care much for our American Archæology (though as
president of the society I must say this under my

breath), but it is worth while to try to get what exact information we can about the semi-barbarians concerning whom so many wild fancies have been current ever since the days of the Spanish conquest, fancies which the amiable Prescott confirmed by his pleasant romantic narrative. But I do care much for the Greeks, and believe that the more the influence of their sane thought and modes of life can be brought to bear on our modern youth the better will it be with the coming generation. I hope we may get an American School at Athens where, before long, our young students may go to drink deeper from the classic fountains than they can at home. My interest in this new Archæological Institute of ours springs from the confidence that it may do something to promote Greek studies among us. This next year we are going to work at Assos, and the exploration is to be in charge of a fine young fellow named Clarke,[1] whose "Notes on Greek Shores" you may have looked at in the aforementioned volume. The two tracts in history in which man has reached the highest level are that occupied by the Greeks, and that held by the Italians from 1200 to 1500.

I have not seen Emerson since the winter, but I heard lately that he was physically well. His memory is quite shattered, and at times his mind moves as in dreams. I was told of his speaking the other day of the pleasure he had once had in a visit from you at Concord. The spiritual impression was too strong to be mastered by the feeble memory of fact. He has his

[1] Joseph Thacher Clarke.

good days, however, and I see it announced that he is
to read a lecture this next month at a "Summer School
of Philosophy" at Concord of which your old acquaintance, the potato-and-apple Evangelist, Alcott, is the
High-Priest. The teaching is marvellous; and the
intuitionists have it all their own way, and the con-
tradictoriness of the intuitions of the different sages is
the supreme test and evidence of their truth. Is not
truth polygonal? Are not the ego and the non-ego
resolvable in the last analysis into a single affirmation?
You know the kind from of old. All the doctors of this
Faculty are not to be found in the New World. The
only novel development is, that we have female sages;
modern Pythias, or at least pytholepts of an Hegelian
Apollo, and reported by the daily press. Whereat we
profane, standing far off, marvel.

In this little village among the hills from which I am
writing we "suck on country pleasures childishly" as
Donne says; — the fields, the woods, the rocks, the
garden, horses, cows, dogs, kittens (one was just now
playing with the fallen leaves by the long window at
which I am sitting). Chickens, wild birds, flowers,
berries afford us amusement and occupation. We
have lessons, and practising on violin and piano, and
Scott's novels and the Arabian Nights, and a swing and
a hammock, and other ways of passing the time. . . .

Wherever I am, I am always, with grateful respect
and affection,

Faithfully yours,

C. E. Norton.

Norton's narrow margin of surplus physical strength reveals itself from time to time throughout his life. On October 14, 1880, he writes to the Rev. J. B. Harrison: "During the last part of the summer my head gave me so much trouble, from a tendency to blood in it, that at the end of the vacation I made up my mind that I would give up my college work for the present. But I have been persuaded to carry on a part of it, and the doctor has consented to my doing so on condition that I give up all other occupation that involves intellectual fatigue — and among the matters forbidden are serious conversation, and letter-writing."

Though "forbidden," letter-writing, at least, suffered no marked intermission.

To G. E. Woodberry

CAMBRIDGE, January 31, 1881.

. . . I began on Saturday evening by receiving the men of the Greek play [1] for a rehearsal in my study. It was a most interesting exhibition, and a new experience in College life. Professor White is the head of the undertaking, and the actors and the chorus have taken up the work with the same spirit with which our men have devoted themselves to the work of the crew or the nine. Their zeal and their industry are rewarded by a surprising success. Riddle has the part of Œdipus, Opdycke of last year that of Jocasta, Howe of '81 is Creon, Guild of '81 Teiresias, Manning of '81 is the priest. They already have the larger portion or the whole of their parts to perfection. They rehearsed about

[1] *The Œdipus Tyrannus* of Sophocles.

half the play the other night. Riddle's voice and his
pronunciation and delivery of the Greek are admirable,
and the other men are all excellent. The tragic quality
of the drama is forced home upon the spectator with an
effect one would not have anticipated. The music for
the choruses is striking, too modern in quality to accord perfectly with the character of the play. But we
cannot give the play as the Greeks represented it: we
must be content with what will be a very striking
modernized reproduction. It is a great gain for culture
that this interest in a classic work should be so strong.
Our expedition to Assos will help also. It has started
with the best promise. . . .

To J. R. Lowell

SHADY HILL, February 11, 1881.

Eliot [1] left us an hour ago for New York, whence he
sails to-morrow in the "Rhein" for Southampton. He
will be in London for a day or two, before proceeding to
join Mr. Clarke at Munich, on the way to Assos,[2] and
I have told him to see you and to carry you my love by
word of mouth. . . .

I do not know that you have heard of the expedition
in which Eliot is to take part. He will tell you of it.
Clarke, who has charge of it, is an admirable fellow, and
the whole party is made up of men of such character
and acquisitions that I am glad to have Eliot brought
into close association with them. The expedition is
creditable to America, and I look forward with great

[1] Norton's eldest son.
[2] The scene of the first excavations of the Archæological Institute under
the charge of Mr. J. T. Clarke.

confidence to excellent results from its work, — provided only that the vexatious delays which the Turkish Government is interposing before granting the
necessary firman for the work, do not prevent its success. The firman was asked for in October by the Department of State. It was promised by the Turkish
Government, and Mr. Longstreet [1] wrote that the
Minister of Public Instruction had told him that he
should have it on a certain fixed day. But in spite of
Mr. Heap's (our Consul General at Constantinople) [2]
and Mr. Longstreet's persistent urgency the issue of
the firman is delayed, till now I cannot but feel some
solicitude lest it should finally be refused, notwithstan-
ding reiterated promises to the contrary. If you are
on friendly terms with your Turkish colleague at the
Court of St. James, I wish you would make a personal
representation to him concerning the matter, and get
him to write to his home government about it. It is, I
believe, the first request of the sort that our State
Department has ever made. The Expedition has no
private ends. And terms, similar to those which the
Turkish Government has imposed in similar cases, — as
for the German explorations at Samothrace and Per-
gamon, — will be acceptable. . . .

To-night I go to Longfellow's to attend the first
meeting of the Dante Club, of which he has consented
to be President. Your acceding to become a member
of the Club gave great satisfaction to the young men
who have been active in getting it up. They will ask

---

[1] James Longstreet, U. S. Minister to Turkey.
[2] Gwynn Harris Heap.

you, I believe, to be the Vice-President. I do not know that much good will come of the Society, beyond the cherishing of the love and honour of the poet in the lives of a few of the better class of students of a generation younger than our own. This is enough.

Nothing is definitely known concerning Garfield's cabinet. It seems likely that it will not be made up in a way to satisfy the better elements of the Republican. Garfield has much of the modern American politician in him. He wants to "harmonize," to conciliate the irreconcilables, and to keep the party united. There can be no surer way of breaking it up.

Of course you will remain abroad as long as you like. And how long will that be? I do not want you to come home as long as you like to remain abroad, but it will be a glad day for me when I hear that you are coming. . . .

The next letter, to Mrs. Alexander Carlyle — Carlyle's niece, Mary Aitken, shortly before this time married to her cousin — is one of the first in a long and detailed correspondence bearing upon Norton's work in the editing of Carlyle's Letters and Reminiscences. The results of this work, undertaken at Mrs. Carlyle's request, are found in the seven volumes of four publications: "The Correspondence of Thomas Carlyle and Ralph Waldo Emerson" (1883); "Early Letters of Thomas Carlyle" (1886); "Correspondence between Goethe and Carlyle" (1887); and "Reminiscences of Thomas Carlyle" (1887). Even without the later volumes of Lowell's and Ruskin's letters and Curtis's

Orations, this important body of work would have given Norton a conspicuous place as an editor.

At this late day, nearly twenty years after the death of Froude, it is unnecessary to revive in detail the violent differences of opinion with regard to his handling of the biographical material entrusted to him by Carlyle. With a full measure of restraint, Norton in his life-time made his own carefully considered estimate of it clear—in an article in the "New Princeton Review" (July, 1886), and in the volumes he edited; pointing out the countless errors—whether of careless transcription or of printing, it mattered not — and the frequently resulting alteration of meaning intended by Carlyle.

Merely for the sake of final record and for reaffirming Norton's beliefs regarding Carlyle's essential character, a few passages from letters to Mrs. Alexander Carlyle, containing frank contemporaneous expressions to Carlyle's nearest representative, may rightly appear in these volumes.

To Mrs. A. Carlyle

CAMBRIDGE, MASSACHUSETTS, April 15, 1881.

It was very kind in you to write me, and your letter has touched me deeply. The incidents of your uncle's last days of which you tell me, held sacred in your memory, will be held sacred in mine. To have known and loved him, and to have received such expressions of his regard as he gave me, are among the most substantial and permanent blessings of my life. . . .

I have read the "Reminiscences" with deepest interest. I have the same feeling as you in respect to Mr. Froude's publication of them. More than once I spoke to your uncle, with even more freedom, perhaps, than was altogether becoming, of my mistrust of Mr. Froude. He used to assure me that if I knew him better I should think better of him. Reading as I did between the lines of the Reminiscences, with such illustrations of their meaning as my knowledge of your Uncle afforded, there were few sentences that I regretted to read, — could they have been read only by me and a few others who could rightly interpret them. It was only as they would give false impressions to the curious public, and be misinterpreted by it, that I regretted certain passages. I feel for the pain which the publication of what never should have been given to the public has brought and must continue to bring to you.

But the clamour against the book and the misinterpretation of it will in great part be short-lived. The great and noble qualities of your uncle's character are too manifest in the book for it not to become to many persons one of the most precious of their possessions. It is one of the most human of books; as sincere and serious a record of life as exists anywhere; a book to strengthen and to elevate whoever can read it aright. The very parts of it with which most fault is found are either evidences of an uncompromising sincerity, or of an exaggeration of expressions that indicate the simplicity and tenderness of the heart from which they proceeded.

To my eyes there is not a word in the book that

distorts or dims the image of your uncle in my heart,
— an image formed with as strict a sincerity as one
would learn from his example. I hold him but the
dearer for it all. . . .

To G. E. Woodberry

CAMBRIDGE, May 22, 1881.

. . . I should be much interested in what you have
written of Clough. He was distinctly a forerunner.
His complaint concerning Carlyle marks his own position. He could not give up altogether the sentiment
of the old faith. He was too intellectually sincere to
hold to the old beliefs in spite of himself, as Lowell tries
to; but he never gave up the hope that they stood for
something that was real and existent. For him God
had not wholly disappeared, — "Whoe'er, whate'er
thou art." Clough expressed better than anyone else
the moment of transition from faith to scepticism, from
dogmatism to agnosticism. He was in the desert, and
fancied there might yet be a promised land. Had he
lived but five or ten years longer he would have found
out that the desert was the promised land itself; and
the discovery would not have shocked him or sent him
back to the flesh-pots of Egypt. Clough led the way to
independence for many souls. He had passed his own
leaders, and had left Carlyle and Emerson behind him;
he himself was to be passed by his companions, but
only because he fell dead along the road. He was the
most courageous of poets. He really trusted his own
soul. . . .

The play has been more than a success; — it has

been the most interesting event in College life and studies for years, and it will have great effect in quickening the interest in classical studies. The most powerful
impression it has made is that of the excellence of the
Greek drama, — especially in form. The unities have
asserted and justified themselves. The old play, produced under conditions so different from those under
which it was originally brought upon the stage that its
whole external character was changed, has proved of
such intrinsic power as to have hardly less effect upon
a modern and foreign audience than upon its first hearers. The dramatic quality of the play was marvel-
lously brought out in the acting. The acting was all
as good as perfection in knowledge of the parts, and
general intelligence, could make it. But it was all too
sentimental and realistic; and full of incongruities to
one who measured it by Greek modes of expression.
The young fellows[1] have really done themselves high
credit, and Mr. Goodwin and Mr. White are greatly
satisfied and pleased. . . .

To G. E. Woodberry

ASHFIELD, July 31, 1881.

MY DEAR WOODBERRY, — What you say of the
Colorado landscape and the remoteness of Nature
from man is no doubt quite true. For the interest of
nature is not in herself, save from the scientific point
of view, but in her effect on man and in his relations

---

[1] A number of rehearsals for the play had taken place at Shady Hill, and
through the familiar intercourse they brought about, Norton's relation to
some of the actors, among them [Sir] Henry Norman and Mr. Owen Wister,
developed into the friendship of later years.

to and dealings with her. Mere natural beauty leaves us cold; even the picturesque grows wearisome; a new country, though it be more beautiful in aspect than Greece, is dreary except for its promise of human history. Nature to be really beautiful to us must be associated with the thoughts and feelings of men. An Italian sunset is better than a Californian for this reason: a daisy of more worth than a mayflower. The landscape to be dear to us must say, —

"Here in old time the hand of man hath been."

This is the reason why Turner's pictures are of such worth. The heart of his landscape is the deeds or sufferings of man. If he paints mere nature, as he seldom does, he is only technically better than our American landscapists. And this, as it seems to me, is the real power of Wordsworth. His conception of the ministry and sympathy of Nature is often carried too far, as if the mere winds and waters and rocks and flowers could help and answer; but at his best he is conscious that only as man finds associations with man in nature she becomes a really serviceable mistress, except to those who are jaded and diseased by having the world too much with them. Then, for such as these, a course of barbaric and solitary nature may be needed as a restorative. Nature has no mind, and it is by an open fallacy that men speak of her as exhibiting the thoughts of God. If she did! . . .

In the summer of 1881, the assassination of Garfield, the two hundredth anniversary of the Hingham meet-

ing-house with which Norton's earliest American ancestors were associated, and the sensation created by
Wendell Phillips's Phi Beta Kappa oration at Cambridge, gave occasion for a longer letter than usual to
the absent friend.

To J. R. Lowell

ASHFIELD, August 31, 1881.

Every day for the past two months my thoughts
have been with you even more regularly than usual,
for in every day's paper I have turned to Blaine's dis-
patch to you as the best summing up of the President's
condition, and have shared with you in the alterna-
tions of hopes and fear. This protracted anxiety, these
partial reliefs, and frequent disappointments have been
very wearing, and have made us restless and uneasy.
Many people, like the doctors at the bedside, have
grown visibly older. It has been a comfort to have
George Curtis close by, for there has been news to exchange, and hopes and fears to share; and, at such a
time, there is a sort of relief in the mere speculation
with such a friend concerning chances and consequences; and in the simple expression to each other of
a common feeling.

Yesterday there seemed reason for hope. No paper
has reached us yet to-day. We should have had a special telegram sent up from the office, six miles away,
if there were any decidedly ill news, so that I am beginning to hope that to-day's accounts will continue
encouraging.

If Garfield were to die now, the country is in a much

better condition to meet the blow than if it had fallen two months ago. There has been much servicable reflection and determination in these weeks. It is hardly possible that Arthur, who is not a dull man, should not have had some important lessons forced home to him. Conkling's fate would have been very different had Arthur become President on the 2d July. But, perhaps, nothing has been of more service than the example of patience, fortitude, simplicity and sweet domestic worth shown by both Mr. and Mrs. Garfield under a trial so severe, and made enormously more grievous by the terrible glare of publicity in which they have had to endure it. This exhibition of admirable character has produced a great effect. The impression made by it is very deep. It is a blessing for the country that such a standard should have been held up.

I have felt how hard it must be for you to have to wait so long for the daily details from which you might form your own judgment in the case. It cannot now be many days before we shall be assured of life or death. I do not venture as yet to have any confident hope of Garfield's recovery.[1] . . .

I have had one occupation this summer quite out of the common course. There was to be a commemoration of the two hundredth anniversary of the building of the old Meeting-House at Hingham. It was built when my ancestor was the minister of the parish, and the Committee for this year's celebration appealed to me to make the address. I did not want to do it, but

[1] President Garfield died Sept. 19, 1881.

five generations of my ancestors who had worshiped in that house were too strong with me: filial piety prevailed, and I undertook the task. The commemoration came off three weeks ago, and was altogether a successful occasion so far as giving satisfaction to the people and the parish was concerned, and in celebrating the venerable old building. These two centuries have been so very long in this country, if measured by change, that the old meeting-house seems older than many a building of far greater antiquity as measured by years in the old world. I was not sorry to read a good deal of the New England theology of the end of the seventeenth century, and to read over great part of the "Magnalia" and altogether to refresh and enlarge my knowledge of the early Colonial period. The second volume of Sewall's "Diary" is quite as good and entertaining and instructive as the first, and if you have not had it, you should have it sent to you. It would steep you in New England. It is quite invaluable for its sincerity; its very dryness is delightful as a reflex of the times, and every page is full of genuine human nature. One learns to feel both respect and affection for the old judge. He was as tender-hearted as he was stout-hearted, an upright, provincially-minded, clear-headed worthy. I often wished for you while I was reading and writing. New England is your province; and I wanted you to give your Imprimatur to my words.

I wished for you, too, for your own sake at Phi Beta. George Curtis was staying with me, having come to receive his LL.D. from Harvard, an honour that pleased

him greatly. Commencement Day and Phi Beta were
two of our loveliest summer days. Cambridge never
since she became a city looked so pleasant at the end
of June. There had been no canker-worms, or so few
as to make no inroad on the beauty of the trees. The
spring had been late and wet, and the June rains had
been frequent, so that the foliage was far more abundant and richer than usual. There was a great crowd to
hear Wendell Phillips, and he was well worth hearing. . . .

There he was, the most admirable natural orator of
our time, artist to the last point in the forms of oratory,
with all the power that perfect libertinism of speech
secures for the speaker. As Longfellow was leaving the
stage he said, "Yes, it was marvellous and delightful,
but preposterous from beginning to end." As Phillips
was speaking I could not but contrast him, and his
looks, and his speech, with Emerson and his Phi Beta
discourse.[1] Phillips's face reveals his temper. He has
lost nobility of expression. His features moving or at
rest have a bitter and malign look, — they are not the
lineaments of Gospel books. It was a great and memorable performance. It will be one of the historic Phi
Beta orations.

Charles Eliot made a forcible and eloquent five-
minute speech at the dinner, vigorously rejecting
Phillips's doctrine and exposing the essential fallacy of
his discourse. He was surcharged with moral indigna-
tion, and without the slightest intonation, much less a

[1] Emerson's second Phi Beta Kappa address was delivered in 1867,
thirty years after his first.

word, that could give offence to Phillips, gave expression with characteristic manliness to the offended sentiment of serious men. . . .

In writing of the oration to Mr. Woodberry, Norton said: "It was truly not a rhetorical but an oratorical performance; almost faultless and completely subordinated to its end. Had the substance of thought, of judgment, of character in the piece been equal to its delivery, it would have been worth coming from Colorado to hear."

Curtis, alluding in an address on Lowell to Phillips's oration, said in 1892: "He was never more himself, and he held an audience culled from many colleges and not predisposed to admire, in shuddering delight by the brilliancy of his unsparing censure of educated men as recreant to political progress."

To G. E. Woodberry

CAMBRIDGE, Christmas, 1881.

Your remembrances for the children, and your note for me have come this morning, and have given as much pleasure as you could wish. Last night we had a little party of cousins and friends, twenty in all, and after "twenty questions," and capping verses, and other games, and supper, we all sang the Christmas Hymn, —

"While shepherds watched their flocks by night," —

and then the folding doors of my study were thrown open and there was the inner room quite full of presents for young and old, and we had one of the pretty half hours. When it was all over the children all declared that they had had a better time than they had expected, and that their presents were "perfectly splendid." Dick expressed the feeling, as he went to bed, that was common to them all, "I don't want anything better."

I wish you had been with us.

It seems to me that you have one more lesson in philosophy to learn, in the real philosophy — that of life; not to be saddened by the imperfection of men and of nature. In the very cherishing of ideal aims, in the clear recognition of the rarity and preciousness of beauty and of joy, an equal recognition is implied of the solitude, the weariness, the prosaic course of daily life. Before we win the last victory, we must be content to be without hope, — and to be ready and cheerful for the day *Even though* the struggle nought availeth. This is probably what I meant by your "incomplete pessimism." If we cannot accept the worst that can come to us, without being overcome, we are still incomplete pessimists. It is you or I against the world, and to lead the life which you or I care for we must be stronger than the world. The long traditions of Heaven, paradise, and happiness have enfeebled the spirit of manliness in us. We who give up the quest of happiness and paradise, can be gladder than other men in the gladness of the earth, and have joys deeper than those that others count such, for even in grief it is a joy to have reason to be so sorry.

Is this too esoteric for Christmas? Well then, let us

join in the song of the angels, and let us obey the new commandment.

Ever Yours,

C. E. NORTON.

I wish you a happy New Year.

To J. R. Lowell

SHADY HILL, February 22, 1882.

MY DEAR JAMES, — Here is the same old love for you on your birthday, and the same old wishes that have in past times often been fulfilled as nearly as the best wishes ever can be fulfilled. Your birthday comes in in sunshine. It is a splendid midwinter day, the air crisp and clear, and the earth white with new-fallen snow, through which the first tracks are as yet hardly made. Spring is a long way off. Child makes believe that his crocuses have started; but he gets up a little private Spring of his own, keeps it shut tight in boxes under glass, and compels some violets and hyacinths from it. There is no harm in this, and it makes him happy; — but the violets, poor things! and the primroses, we who have gathered them on Italian banks and in English woods may pity these hot-bed darlings.

Child, dear old fellow! is well, and is actually beginning to print the great Ballad-book on which he has been at work so long. I have sometimes, of late years, been afraid that he would never do it, but would carry off with him all the learning of which no man ever had the like. Part of it, at least, will now be saved, and for this I am glad. . . .

I did not see Wilde when he was in Boston, for I

was then at Princeton where I had gone to give three or four lectures at the College. But Eliot did honour in my stead to your note of introduction. America has taken Wilde very well, not *au grand sérieux*, but with a good-natured smile dashed now and then with a grain of contempt, such as any hard-headed and pure-minded Yankee would naturally feel for such a Sir Piercy Shafton. *Préciosité*, like measles, never wholly disappears, but it seems to be more prevalent than usual, and to have become seriously epidemic, in some circles of English society. As yet we have only rare sporadic cases. . . .

To J. R. Lowell

SHADY HILL, March 28, 1882.

. . . You have been much in my thoughts during these last days. I have wished that you were here, and I have felt how much you would wish to be here. I have known how deeply Longfellow's death would touch you. It is an immeasurable change and loss for us who have known him so long and loved him so well. His friendship has been one of the steadiest and longest blessings of my life. It dates back almost half a century. I have gifts from him given to me when I was younger than my own Richard. I have a book in which he wrote my name forty-one years ago. And in all this time I have not a single recollection of him that is not sweet, pleasant, and dear. It is a delightful retrospect. Even the memory of his sorrow is beautiful. His life has been an essential part of the spiritual atmosphere of yours and mine.

Last Sunday week, the 19th, was a beautiful day, soft with the early breath of Spring. I went to see him in the afternoon, and heard, to my regret, that he was in bed with a cold, taken the day before, but that he was not seriously ill. An hour later I met Mrs. Ernest Longfellow, who told me that there was nothing alarming in his attack. I had felt anxious, for of late he has seemed to lack vigour, and he has suffered from inability to do any mental work and from shifting neuralgic pains. One of the last times I saw him, I said as I entered his study, "I hope this is a good day for you." "Ah, Charles," he answered, with a not uncheerful smile, "there are no good days now."

On Tuesday and on Wednesday I heard that he was better, but on Thursday I was alarmed at hearing that Dr. Minot had been sent for by Wyman for consultation, and on Thursday evening I saw Wyman and he told me there was no hope. He said that on Saturday Longfellow had been walking on his piazza in the afternoon, and came in feeling a chill. As the evening went on he became ill, he had a night of sickness, and "when I saw him on Sunday," said Wyman, "he was already very ill, and his strength very much gone." . . . On Wednesday he slept much, but was cheerful when awake, and said, "I don't understand all this anxiety." On Thursday it became plain that the end was not distant. He wandered a little from the effect of the opiates that were administered, but was for the most part tranquil and without pain. I saw Wyman again on Friday noon. Death might come at any moment, he said; and in the afternoon at a quarter past three the meeting-house bell began to toll. He had just died.

There is no reason to wish for his own sake that he had recovered. He did not desire longer life. A year ago I dined with him on his seventy-fourth birthday, and he said, "Really I cannot think I am so old, it seems that the numerals have been reversed, the four should precede the seven." But since then there has been a great change. He had greatly aged in the twelvemonth, but he lost nothing of his familiar sweetness, or of the brightness of his smile of greeting.

Thursday, March 30.

The funeral services on Sunday were in all respects what they should have been. The coffin was in the library, — the large back room, — and here were the friends, while the immediate family were in the study. George Curtis came from New York, and was with me. The most striking incident was Emerson's solitary approach to the coffin, and his long gaze at the face of the dead. Only the family and a few intimate friends went to the grave at Mt. Auburn. Emerson was there, — his memory gone, his mind wavering, but his face pure and noble as ever, though with strange looks of perplexity wandering over it from time to time. The afternoon was raw, grey, March-like. Emerson took my arm up the path to the grave, — and his arm shook as we stood together there. I could not but think of Longfellow's happier fate.

Yesterday I saw Alice and Annie. They were both well, sweet, simple, self-controlled as could be desired.

They would not wish that their father had lived longer.
There was nothing to wish different, and no reason to
desire longer life for him. Everything in the end had
been appropriate to the life. His greatest pleasure in
the last month had been in Edith's children. They
meant to live on in the old home, and to keep everything unchanged so far as was possible. They had
thought much of you, and of your sorrow with them.
It is almost twenty-one years since their mother died.
I stood on Sunday close by the spot where I had stood
at her funeral. . . .

To G. E. Woodberry

CAMBRIDGE, June 1, 1882.

. . . The last months have been full of change.
There was nothing to lament in the death of Longfellow or of Emerson, except for ourselves. Their loss
to us can never be made good. It makes me feel suddenly old, by shifting so much of what was best in life
from the present into the past, — by breaking the
continuity of associations which had stretched in a
pleasant line from childhood to to-day. Memory is
good, but the frequent renewal of living associations
is better. The spiritual landscape of actual life is greatly
altered, — there is a desert where once were greenest
fields.

I was greatly interested in your account of Oscar
Wilde, and I believe you saw and interpreted him
rightly. I have not yet seen him, and I wish I might
escape seeing him, but he is to be in Boston to-morrow
and I suppose we shall meet. . . . The man who loves

beauty merely for its outward seeming, and for the sake of selfish enjoyment, has little claim to regard. Beauty unveils herself not for him. She must be loved unselfishly before she yields even the hem of her garment to her lover's kiss . . . .

The first meeting of the Harvard Faculty Committee on the Regulation of Athletic Sports was held June 15, 1882. Norton was chairman of the committee, and for two years contributed much to its efficiency. The "Harvard Alumni Bulletin" (January 3, 1912) has said: "This first committee, under the skilful guidance of Professor Norton, at once took up with students, representing all the College athletic activities, various questions of discipline, training and management; and 'they found prevailing among the students most interested a sense of satisfaction that the Faculty had undertaken the systematic regulation of athletics.'" Among the specific recommendations of Professor Norton were: that no college club should play with professionals; the restriction of employment of trainers without the consent of the Committee; that no student should compete on a team without being examined by Dr. Sargent, director of the Gymnasium. These and other recommendations are notable both for what they suggest regarding the state of organized athletics when the faculty first dealt with them, and for their revelation of Norton's work in a field not commonly associated with his name.

Meanwhile his interest in the other affairs to which he was devoted continued without abatement.

To J. B. Harrison

July 23, 1882.

... I do not believe that we can bring the mass of Americans to recognize any responsibility for the preservation of Niagara, or to feel any of the higher motives for doing so. This work really, then, is not so much to save the Falls, as to save our own souls. Were we to see the Falls destroyed without making an effort to save them, — the sin would be ours.

The growth of wealth and of the selfish individualism which accompanies it (and corrupts many who are not rich) seems to weaken all properly social motives and efforts. Men in cities and towns feel much less relation with their neighbours than of old; there is less civic patriotism; less sense of a spiritual and moral community. This is due in part to other causes, but mainly to the selfishness of the individualism in a well-to-do democracy. . . .

To Mrs. A. Carlyle

ASHFIELD, MASSACHUSETTS, July 5, 1882.

... I felt much for you, and, I trust, with you, in reading Froude's two volumes of the Life. I have never read a book that gave me more pain, or that seemed to me more artfully malignant. I could not have believed, even of Froude, bad as I thought him, a capacity for such falseness, for such betrayal of a most sacred trust, for such cynical treachery to the memory of one who had put faith in him. I am at a loss to discover a sufficient motive for this deed.

No unbiased person can, I believe, read the Life without a conviction that the original text — the letters — does not support Mr. Froude's comment; that he has throughout glossed the letters in a false and evil spirit, that he has distorted their plain significance, and misinterpreted them with perverse ingenuity. The process is too open; he has revealed his own nature, and he has not succeeded in obscuring, for more than a brief moment, the real character of those to whom he has done wrong. His blows are vain, malicious mockery.

This misrepresentation of his is, indeed, not so much a sin against those whom he called friends, as a crime against human nature itself. To attempt to pervert the image and to degrade the character of a man like Mr. Carlyle, is to do an injury to mankind.

It is impossible to forgive him for the gross indelicacy of publishing the most private, sacred, and tender expressions of the love of two such lovers as those whose lovely letters he has ventured to print. But a more noble love-story is not to be read, — and these letters will be precious and sacred to many who will be the better for reading them, though they cannot but shrink from being the innocent accomplices in such a breach of faith. I wish that at some time you might print these letters by themselves, so that they should make their true impression, and be relieved from the ugly setting in which they are now preserved. Indeed, it seems to me that you may have to write the true story of your Uncle's life, or rather to give the true account of him.

You may perhaps remember that nine years ago Mr. Emerson confided to me your Uncle's letters to him, and that your Uncle approved his doing so. Since Mr. Emerson's death his letters to Mr. Carlyle have also been put into my hands. I propose to edit this most interesting correspondence, and though there will be little need of my saying much, I hope in the little I may have to say to be able to do something to redress the wrong that Froude has done. . . .

The record of Emerson's entrusting his Carlyle letters to Norton is fortunately preserved entire in a communication written soon after their return from England together. Emerson refers in the omitted passage to a letter which had been lost.

From R. W. Emerson.

CONCORD, November 11, 1873.

MY DEAR NORTON, . . . The purport of the letter was to pray you to record carefully all your experiences of Carlyle and his conversations, since I had been convinced in London, and on our voyage home, that you had heard better speech from him than probably any other of his acquaintance that I have met. He will be sure to be reported and injured by unskilful persons, and he deserves a masterly hand. Another impulse of my threescore-and-ten-ship was to say that I shall like to know that I may confide to you the entire file of Carlyle's letters to me from 1835 to 1872 — nearly a hundred, I believe — that you may hereafter make what disposition or destruction of them you

shall find fit;— to which I might add, I believe, some
manuscript notes of him taken in 1848.[1] It was you
who decided him to give his books to Harvard, and I
please myself with believing that you will take care
hereafter that his memory suffers no detriment on
this side the sea.

Yours affectionately,
R. W. EMERSON.

Confirming this commission of Emerson's, Carlyle
had written to Norton, 24 January, 1874:[2] "Understand then at once that I entirely agree with Emerson
in his disposal of these letters, and have or can have no
feeling on the subject, but that if he was going to do anything at all with the stuff he could not in the world have
found anybody better to take charge of it than yourself. Accept it therefore, I pray you; lock it by in some
drawer till I have vanished; and then do with it what
to your own just mind shall seem best. If my brother,
Dr. Carlyle in Dumfries, or Froude, who are appointed
executors, should ever want it, they will know that it is
in your keeping, and will get a just response upon it on
application. And that is all I have to say on this small
matter, — which I confess grows smaller and smaller
to me every day, and every year, for the last forty; the
wish rising stronger and stronger in me, were it possible, not to have any Biography at all in a kind of
world like this, but rather to lie purely silent in the
Land of Silence; intimating to all kinds of 'able

---

[1] See *ante* vol. i, p. 508.
[2] In answer to Norton's Letter of Dec. 22, 1873. See *ante* p. 26.

editors,' *blithering* stump orators, penny-a-liners, or guinea-a-worders,

> 'Sweet friends, for Jesus' sake forbear
> To dig the dust inclosèd here.'

This is all of essential I had to say. Needs only that I charge you with my friendliest, fraternal salutations, and thanks to Emerson, and hopeful gratulations on all your report upon him."

To John Simon

ASHFIELD, September 21, 1882.

... I have been occupied during the summer in arranging for publication the correspondence between Carlyle and Emerson, and it will go to press so soon as we can get from England some of the earlier letters of Emerson, which in some dishonest way have got into the hands of a man who wants to make money out of them. The correspondence seems to me of unrivalled interest. It is the sincerest expression of the genius and character of the writers. No relations could have been better than those which existed between them. The letters are the record of forty years of admirable friendship. They will dispel some of the false impressions concerning Carlyle which, thanks mainly to Froude, are so prevalent just now. "Froude is a villain," writes —— to me, and I do not think her far wrong. But Carlyle will always suffer from the lack of the sense of humour in mankind, and from the impossibility that the insincere should understand the frankness of genuine sincerity.

Sept. 22. It was too late last night when I finished

reading to the children for continuing my letter. We have been reading this summer "Guy Mannering" and "Rob Roy," and now, for a change, have taken "Little Dorrit," in which we are all greatly interested. Whenever I read these books I acknowledge a new debt of gratitude to their authors. They are admirable introducers to life, — and our world owes more to them than it will ever recognize. What a century this has been for literature! Put the literature of this century into one scale and that of all preceding time into the other, and the balance would not hang very uneven. This last year has brought a great change in life to me, by the death of Longfellow and of Emerson; not any marked change in the course of common days, but in the spiritual background of them all. There is a great blank without them. It is as if two of the noblest, most familiar, best loved objects had disappeared from the landscape, and half its beauty had gone. For me their death throws much of the best of life into the past. It is not the passage of years but such changes as these that bring old age. . . .

The reference in this letter to reading aloud may well be supplemented by a word in regard to a matter which in Norton's estimation had a distinct intellectual and social value — the capacity to read aloud well. Reading much to his children when they were little, hearing them later read to him, many an evening not otherwise occupied was spent in this fashion; and much of Thackeray, Dickens and Scott, books of the hour, memoirs, and poetry, were read together and

enjoyed through laughter and even tears. Is not the
hour still fresh in memory when Norton's youngest
boy, reading the account of Colonel Newcome's death,
said to his father, "perhaps you better read now," and
Norton's own voice when he took up the book, became
nearly as unsteady as the boy's?

Occasionally Norton made time, in later years, to
read aloud to a group of patients in a Catholic Hospital
for Incurables, which was established not far from
Shady Hill. The interest he took in this institution
was so great that the Sister Superior writing to him on
one occasion about some question in regard to the comfort of the patients in hot weather, refers playfully in
her note to "your big family here."

From the making of books and the teaching of
young men Norton was frequently turning to more
"practical" affairs. The constant personal element in
his work for the Archæological Institute is illustrated
in a brief letter — one of many — to a member of the
Assos expedition.

To F. H. Bacon

CAMBRIDGE, February 3, 1883.

I received four days ago your note of December 30.

I at once sent to the Treasurer to have a credit for
£80 sent to you, care of the Ionian Bank, Athens.
I thought it best to send you a little larger amount than
you asked for, in order that you might feel entirely at
ease about funds; and not be compelled to hurry home
through lack of money. If you find yourself in need of
more, send me word. . . .

I hope you are refreshing yourself after your long and exhausting work; and I trust that you were able to leave Assos with a satisfactory sense of having completed your work there so far as it was worth while for you to carry it.

Let me again express my own hearty satisfaction, and that of the Executive Committee, in what you have accomplished. . . .

When Norton left England in 1873 Leslie Stephen wrote to him: "You don't know what your friendship has been and will be to me. . . . It is really odd that of all the men I know, you and perhaps Morley (I can't think of a third) are the only ones with whom I can be sure of finding thorough sympathy in such conversations as we have had. . . . Now you are gone, I not only can't fill your place, but I can't get even a moderately good makeshift." [1] The published letters of Stephen show how active their correspondence was from this time forth. Unfortunately, Norton's letters to Stephen from 1873 to 1883 were not preserved; but those beginning with this year form an important part of Norton's record of himself.

To Leslie Stephen

CAMBRIDGE, March 1, 1883.

The best part of your last letter (barring the general good account of yourself and your household) was the sentence in which you told me that your wife's sentiments about Froude coincide pretty much with mine.

[1] Maitland's *Life and Letters of Leslie Stephen*, pp. 234-35.

I should feel safe in believing about anybody as she does; and I am glad no longer to have to suspect myself of lack of discrimination or of charity about a man of whom I have no better opinion than I have of Froude. I believe that some day he himself will compel you to give more than a half-hearted assent to your wife's opinion. Good women always recognize the true colours of Mephistopheles long before the Fausts find them out. It went against the grain with me that the closing words of Carlyle's letters to Emerson should be praise of this false friend and the expression of trust in him.

I hope you have received a copy of the "Correspondence" which I directed the publishers to send to you. I suspect that the book will be more interesting to readers over here than in England, for it throws a good deal of light upon certain literary and social aspects of New England in the last generation concerning which there is a rather lively curiosity, — not unnatural considering the figures who move across the scene. But apart from this local interest, the Correspondence will be widely and permanently interesting from its striking exhibition of the contrasted characters of the writers. Carlyle's letters will, I hope, do something to set right public opinion concerning him, which the questionable Froude has had such success in misleading and perverting. (I am tempted to follow your bad example, and to say "Damn him"! I save myself by quoting the words from you.)

What a task you have undertaken! You must have

immense confidence in your own patience.[1] I trust that you will have a staff so well organized that you will be spared a great part of the tediousness of the work over which you will preside. To edit a select Biographical Dictionary, if one could make one's own selection, would be pleasant enough; — but to have to attend to 900 A's of whom 850 had better be forgotten is surely worse than reading Guicciardini. I shall grudge you to the work, if it tyrannises over you, and compels you to give up the writing of books or essays of your own.

I am on the whole glad that Morley has got into Parliament. A man ought in the long run to be governed by his own genius, and Morley has long felt that his pointed that way. When you see him I wish you would give him a cordial message of regard and good will from me.

We are all well. I am, as usual, busy with much work, but lead a most quiet and domestic life. Child has just got out the first part of his "Ballads." You ought to see it. It is incomparably well done. Send me a line or two when you can.

Affectionately Yours,

C. E. NORTON.

To G. E. Woodberry

CAMBRIDGE, March 4, 1883.

Your note gave me much pleasure, and what you say in it of the Carlyle-Emerson Correspondence is of great

[1] On December 23, 1882, Stephen had written to Norton: "I have given up the *Cornhill*, and taken to a biographical dictionary [the *National Dictionary of Biography*], which will last me the rest of my life — if, that is, it succeeds in living at all." Maitland's *Stephen*, pp. 375–76.

interest to me. Your judgment of the characteristics
of the two men as exhibited in their letters coincides in
great measure with my own, *so far as it goes*, but I
should want to make additions to it that would essentially modify its effect so far as Emerson is concerned.
You judge him too exclusively, it seems to me, from a
personal point of view in which he is brought into relation of comparison with natures of a different order
from his own. He is not one of the Universal men in a
large sense; but a man of some universal sympathies
and relations curiously and instructively hampered by
local, provincial bonds, and narrowed by spiritual
traditions that were inherited by him as part of his
intrinsic nature. Not Plato himself escapes from the
cramping limitations of his own age. Emerson reminds
me of one of the Italian masters in the 13th century,
breaking loose from Byzantine bondage, and possessed with a new spirit not yet capable of securing for
itself full and free expression. If compared with other
men of his own time and country his genius is evident.
His imperfections — his coldness, his want of consecu-
tive and accomplished power of thought, his untrained
art — are all national more than individual defects.
His blindness to all but optimistic conclusions is an
American trait. But his finer spiritual insight, his purity
of tone, his elevation of motive, his simplicity and sincerity are essentially personal traits, and will continue,
I believe, to exert a strong influence for a long while yet
to come. I find him nearer to being a poet than any
other American. . . .

To John Ruskin

SHADY HILL, April 3, 1883.

. . . Your complaint that I had given no proper Epilogue to the Carlyle-Emerson book [1] touched me, and made me reconsider the motives which induced me to put nothing of my own into the volumes; but, on the whole, without altering my judgment. The letters seemed to me to form a complete and unique whole, needing no addition from any other hand. Who was I that I should patch on a piece of my work to a canvas like this?

> Ma io, perchè venirvi? o chi il concede?
> Io non Enea, io non Paolo sono;
> Me degno a ciò nè io nè altri crede.

The sentiment of the book was too intimate for a third person to intervene in it. Moreover, believing as I do that great and grievous wrong has been done to Carlyle since his death, and that the feeling toward him is still too excited to be set right, I thought that the best service to be rendered him was to let him show himself as he was in one of the most characteristic relations of life, and to allow the impression made by this display of his real nature to work its effect unaccompanied by any expression of a judgment that might be controverted, or charged with the partiality of affection.

The effect of the book in modifying the harsh and false opinion of the public, so far as I can judge of it,

[1] On March 10, 1883, Ruskin wrote Norton that he was "disappointed at having no word of epitaph from yourself on both the men," and "vexed for want of a proper epilogue of your own." See *Ruskin-Norton Letters*, vol. ii, 189–90.

seems to me to indicate that I was right. Even you, I
sometimes fancy, underrate the worth of the man, and
let the trivial and external traits of his unique individuality go for too much in your estimate of him. His
essential nature was solitary in its strength, its sincerity, its tenderness, its nobility. He was nearer Dante
than any other man. He belonged to the same order
of spirits. Like Dante his face was black with the
smoke of Hell, and the street-boys called him names
and threw mud at him. His stomach sometimes got
the better of his head, but that it did not master his
heart and break his will is a marvel.

Do you hear anything from Pisa? I wish we could go
there together once again and study out together the
problems of the old masonry. And, by the way, we
would go to Volterra, and if we did not find there the
walls to be like those of Fiesole, I would wholly with-
draw the innocent words which you found so wicked.
You taught me a great deal when we were in Italy in
happy days, for which I never cease to be grateful to
you, but how much more could you teach me now!

I am going to send you a book of which I am proud,
— my dear old friend Child's book of Ballads, the first
part of which is now ready, and is a masterpiece of
pleasant scholarship and character. It is not a book for
boys and girls, or for amusement, but a learned book,
and it may not suit your fancy. But you will like to
have it at Brantwood, to turn to when you want to find
out all that is known about some familiar ballad, and
to see how widely the story has been said or sung all
over Europe. It is a study of the favourite forms in which

the poetic imaginations of the common people shaped themselves, — the poetry of the cradle and the fireside.

Give my love to Joan, please. . . .

Good night, — with love as of old,

Ever yours,   C. E. N.

The summer of 1883 found Norton in England and Italy, sent there by doctor's orders, in the hope of overcoming the insomnia from which he had been suffering. Leaving home with his oldest son as his companion, he spent a few days with Ruskin on the way to the Continent; and again, on his return to England, Norton saw his old friend.

To his Children

BRANTWOOD, CONISTON, LANCASHIRE.
Thursday, June 28, 1883.

. . . We were not sorry to start for Brantwood yesterday morning. . . . The journey hither was . . . full of interest that touches the imagination, nay even the heart, deeply. . . . The contrast between the aspects of things that go by the same names in England and America is always a new surprise. . . . We passed through historic Preston, and still more historic Lancaster with its fine old castle crowning its hill, and then we passed along the broad sands of Morecambe Bay, a solitary stretch of sea-waste, with the mountains that stretch down toward it half hidden in the mist, — then we passed close to the ruins of Furness Abbey, stopping for two minutes where we had a full view of these beautiful and stately walls, striking in their ruin, still more striking in their suggestion of change as they look across to the intrusive railway station that has planted itself within the very precincts of the Abbey, close to the ancient church. The common Englishman has no reverence for the beautiful monu- ments of the past, — nowhere does the common man care much for such things.

We reached Coniston about four o'clock. Ruskin was on the platform of the station, — his heart un- changed, his welcome as loving as a welcome could be, and in an instant the ten years had gone, and we were talking as if we had met last week, so familiar did our voices seem to each other. It was raining a little, the day was dull and grey, but even without sunshine the drive along the border of the Lake from the vil- lage to Brantwood is of extraordinary beauty, — pure English beauty, in its kind not surpassed in the world, a beauty for living with and growing fonder and fonder of from day to day.

Joan,[1] with three charming children, met us at the door,— and we were soon settled in the drawing-room, and while Eliot went off with the children and was mak- ing them very happy, we elders, including Miss Shaw,[2] who is an interesting and pleasing woman, sat talking till afternoon tea was over, and then we moved . . . into Ruskin's study, and looked at illuminated manu- scripts, and Turner water-colours, and talked till

[1] Mrs. Arthur Severn, Ruskin's devoted cousin, who lived with him during the latter years of his life.

[2] Miss Flora Shaw, now Lady Lugard, author of *Castle Blair* and other charming stories; formerly head of Colonial department of the London *Times,* for which she has made special investigations in South Africa, Australia, Canada and the Klondike.

dinner-time; — and then more talk, and more talk till half-past ten and bed. . . .

Ruskin has aged a good deal in these late years. He looks as old as he is, — sixty-four. He stoops a good deal; but he seems physically well enough, and his mind is as active and perhaps as vigorous as ever. He has always been perverse and irrational, and he does not grow less so, but his heart has all its old sweetness, and Miss Shaw and I differ from him and laugh at his extravagancies of expression, and at his follies of sentiment, without ruffling the smoothness of his temper, or awakening a single flash of personal sensitiveness. He still remains one of the most interesting men in the world. . . .

I slept well last night, and am all the better for it to-day. . . .

To Miss Sara Norton

GENEVA, July 20, 1883.

. . . Dijon, where we spent Wednesday afternoon, and Thursday morning, is a very charming old city, with the most irregular roofs and chimneys of any city in France, I believe, and betraying in this picturesque fashion the individuality of its inhabitants. It preserves many of the monuments of the time when it was the chief seat of the Dukes of Burgundy, and there is enough of the remnant of the great days of its splendour to give one the impression of the old time. There are two or three interesting churches, and in the Museum are two magnificent tombs, greatly restored but still fine, of Philippe le Hardi and of Jean sans Peur. There is little left in the town that recalls Charles the Bold, but I noticed on a street corner the sign of "Rue de Quentin," and was reminded of our pleasant readings of three months ago. The Hôtel de la Cloche, where we stayed, is one of the pleasant, rambling, irregularly built, old-fashioned provincial inns, which I am afraid will have disappeared before you come to see Dijon, for a great new modern Americanized hotel with all the improvements is building, as much superior to the old as Aladdin's bright new lamp was to the dull and battered lamp by which he could find his way through the magician's caves. . . .

There is but little of interest at Geneva, except the lake, and the rivers, and the view of the mountains. The rushing of the Rhone through the heart of the city is superb; the river starts with splendid energy as if conscious of the great course before it, and of its own historic life; and the near and distant mountains combine in a foreground and background of heights that are hardly to be surpassed in grandeur of line and form, in variety of color and light and shade. And although in these days the clouds have been too heavy and too low, most of the time, yet they rise and fall and enwrap the mountains and disclose them in constantly changing motion and beauty. . . .

To Miss Elizabeth Gaskell Norton

PALLANZA, LAGO MAGGIORE
Friday, July 27, 1883.

MY DEAREST LILY, — I forget whether in my letter of last Sunday to Sally I said that we had given up going to Chamonix on account of the cold and cloudy weather. We were sorry to do so. However, on Monday we bade the Simons good-bye, and took the train which carried us along the shore of the Lake of Geneva, past Lausanne, past Vevey, past Chillon, up the valley of the Rhone, between walls of bleak mountains, to Brieg, the little town at the foot of the Simplon. The next day, in the coupé of the diligence, we went across the famous and magnificent pass. The clouds hung too low to let us see the upper snowy summits in all their glory, and when we reached the village of Simplon, near the top of the pass, the rain was falling steadily. In the rain we entered the superb gorge of Gondo, one of the grandest gorges of the Alps, with dark, high, precipices on either side, with scarce room between them for the dashing river and the road. It is in the pass that you cross the Italian frontier, and the change is instant and delightful; — the pleasant Italian people, the soft Italian speech, the gracious Italian manner, the pretty Italian villages, the colour, the landscape, the fertile and smiling hillsides and valley upon which you descend from the higher mountains, all have the quality of the South and possess a beauty or charm which is wanting in the lands from which we had come. Is it Tennyson who says "Love is of the South"? So it seems. We had gleams of sunshine as we entered Italy, but the rain was falling heavily when we reached Domo d'Ossola, the little city where we were to spend the night. It is a most Italian city, and in it one is far away from Switzerland. Wednesday was a day of complete sunshine. We took a little one horse vettura and drove up the beautiful Val d'Anzasca to Ponte Grande. The valley is one of the loveliest of those of the Italian Alps. Ponte Grande is a little mountain village whence the view of the snowy summits of Monte Rosa is superb. We spent the afternoon in wandering among the chestnut woods of Bannio, a charmingly picturesque, secluded little village still higher than Ponte Grande, and in drawing a full breath of high Italian air. The mingling of cultivated fields with the wildness of rocks and woods, the paved narrow ways leading up to the remoter heights, the handsome and smiling peasants with their greeting of "Buon giorno," or "Viva," the little village market-place, the church, the distant convent on the seemingly inaccessible height, the glimpses of snowy peaks, the rapid little brooks, the multitude of Alpine flowers, and a thousand other details of the scene, made me often wish that you were with us to enjoy them all and add to our enjoyment of them. At the inn at Ponte Grande were three Italians who entertained us greatly; a handsome Monsignore, perhaps sixty-five years old, with fine manners, and with a distinguished air in his priestly dress, and his sister and her daughter, the latter a true little Italian beauty, with soft eyes and a semi-demure, semi-smiling look. They had come from Mantua, Mantua the city of marshes, lying low on the banks of its sluggish river, — "the sleepy Mincio creeping to the Po," — they had come up here to the mountains and the rushing streams and the light air, and were obviously enjoying themselves. The Monsignore, divested of his clerical hat, came out on his balcony in a gay smoking-cap, while the elderly lady sat by knitting, and the little Mantuan beauty flitted in and out of the window with changes of talk and laugh.

We left Ponte Grande yesterday morning in good season, and drove here in five hours; — a great part of the way the scenery was exquisite, and this town is situated so that the views from it and around it of the lake and of the shores are really as beautiful as one imagines the views on these Italian lakes should be. . . . Our windows open upon the lake and directly before us are the famous Borromean islands, with their palaces and terraced gardens, and behind them the opposite mountainous shore, and to one side, closing the western horizon, the snowy summits of the Simplon. . . .

To Miss Sara Norton
BELLAGIO, LAKE OF COMO, August 11, 1883.

. . . We arrived at this lovely place, the most romantic in its pure essence of Italian beauty that we have seen, yesterday, and received, to our great satisfaction, a great parcel of pleasant letters. . . . They made a good day for us, and we read the last of them during the twilight in a boat upon the lake. Every day I wish you were with us, but I especially wish so to-day for your enjoyment of this delightful scenery would be very great, and we should like to be here together. The vast, conspicuous hotels, enormous democratic palaces, and the crowds of miscellaneous, hasty travellers, interfere in some degree with the sentiment appropriate to this and other beautiful places on these Lakes. But without much effort you can generally get out of

sight of the one, and of hearing of the other, and secure a scene of entire beauty undisturbed by inharmo-
nious suggestions.

Como is the lake of ideal villas, where it would seem
it might be easy to lead a poetic life; villas with their
stately or gay Italian beauty, with wide terraces, and
flights of steps leading to the water, with cool arcades
adorned with statues, with the soft dripping of fountains in their open courts, with hedges of oleanders and
thickets of roses, with alleys deep-shaded under dense
ilex trees, with gardens in perpetual bloom with plants
of tropic growth; — with the encircling mountains
from which the air comes fresh to temper the warmth
of the lake. The moon was shining bright on them last
night, and one could fancy that the nights were never
moonless. It is a pity that the impression cannot be
absolutely complete, but as in Venice so here. The
imagination has to exclude much of the intrusive life of
the prosaic days in which we live. The little smoky
steamers are puffing about with bustling speed too constantly, there are too many second-class travellers
with their second-class style, the vulgar democracy invades the sacred retreats of the Muses, and here at Bellagio the hotels and the shops for travellers give to the
edge of the lake the air of a cheap modern watering-
place, a place of trivialities and trinkets and dust and
fashion. . . .

We left Monte Generoso on Wednesday morning
(to-day is Saturday) and reached Milan at two o'clock.
We had a fine early-morning two hours' walk down the
mountain, to which I was sorry to turn my back, and

then went the rest of the way by rail. The day was a delicious summer day. . . .

In September, writing to John Simon from Brantwood, Norton says: "I find Ruskin in excellent condition, steadier, less excitable, more equable than when I saw him nine or ten weeks ago. I have had a very interesting, but a very touching day with him; touching because his solitude is so great, and because the past is a sad retrospect and the future a sad prospect for him."

To Edward Lee-Childe

SHADY HILL, September 29, 1883.

Your most kind note of the 12th September finds me here at home again after three too short months in Europe. . . . I found myself really more in need of entire rest than I had known to be necessary, and I fulfilled the injunctions I had received to avoid all the pleasures and fatigues of seeing old friends. The temptation was almost irresistible, but I hurried away from London and Paris and went rapidly to the Italian Lakes, where I stayed till it was time for me to hasten back to Liverpool to embark. . . .

No present age, no actual age, was ever good, I fancy, for idealists like you and me. In Europe I could not but feel with pain the ill wrought by the progress of democracy, — the destruction of old shrines, the disregard of beauty, the decline in personal distinction, the falling off in manners. Here, as we have less to lose, we have less to regret, and the spread of comfort,

the superb and unexampled spectacle of fifty millions of human beings living at peace and in plenty,
compensates in a certain measure for the absence
of high culture, of generous ideals and of imaginative
life. . . .

To J. R. Lowell

SHADY HILL, 10th February, 1884.

Your letter of a month ago was as good as a letter
could be. It is more than twenty-five years since you
told me that when assured of the affection of a friend
you could get on very well without his letters. I recognized the truth then, but less than I do now, that you
would not have felt so, had it been possible for you to
receive any letters as good as your own. You will
always lack one of the pleasantest experiences in life.
I am sorry for you; I wish I could make up to you
for your loss! . .

Woodberry's poem[1] has, I trust, reached you. We
have had no poem of such worth since you left off
writing. In its finish, its quietness, its sustained tone,
its pure English, its avoidance of the tricks of contemporary verse, its freedom from echoes save of long
extinct and noble voices, — it is strikingly unlike and
superior to most of the poetry of recent days. It lacks
inspiration in the highest sense, the God breathing
through the poet; but if it misses this it shows, perhaps,
capacity for such inspiration, in the making ready of
the soul and voice for the time when the God shall
arrive. The poet is at least higher up on the slopes of

[1] *The North Shore Watch.*

Parnassus than most of those who try the ascent. I find his poem better each time I read it, — an indication, perhaps, that it needs only familiarity and age to be ranked among those near the best.

In one of his letters I was reading the other night Horace Walpole says: "I do not ask you if Cambridge has produced anything, for it never does." Our Cambridge is no more productive than his was a hundred years ago. But it changes from day to day, and you and I grow strangers in our native town. Soon there will be nothing left except half a dozen old houses, and they with new people in them, of what we knew when we were boys. . . .

To G. E. Woodberry

CAMBRIDGE, February 25, 1884.

. . . You are a little hard on Horace Walpole, and yet I grant all you say and could add something to your depreciation of him. I should think a volume of extracts from him would be wearisome; — but take his Correspondence in full and you get not only the impress of the time and some vivid touches of life, but also the image of a man of no great size, yet who, in spite of a love of gossip, is seldom malicious, in spite of affectations has still a love of nature, who in an age of perverted taste liked better things than most of his contemporaries cared for, who lived purely and decently in the midst of corruption, who loved his friends faithfully, and had enough character to improve, in spite of flattery, up to his old age. And the vivacity and keen observation of this innocent man entertains you and me a hundred years after his death! Really we ought to see the beam in our own eyes. . . .

Again in the summer of 1884, Norton — this time accompanied by his eldest daughter — was in England, for the purpose of representing Harvard at the Tercentenary of Emmanuel College at Cambridge. His letters home give some impression of the crowded and interesting days spent there, but could hardly do justice (written as they were after full and fatiguing hours) to a memorable University celebration, — an occasion crowned by the warmth of expression to Harvard, through her envoy; and by Summer, which makes those incomparable College gardens and "quads" of the older Cambridge, with their flower-filled borders and thick greenery, so alluring to the American imagination.

When the functions in that little world of custom were over, Norton accompanied by his sister-in-law Miss Sedgwick (then in England), by his daughter and Burne-Jones's daughter Margaret, made a little tour among Cathedral towns; seeing Ely, Lincoln, York and other delightful places, and ending by a visit to Ruskin at Coniston: — golden hours for the younger members of the party, and perhaps not less so for Norton, who had not been in some of these places since his youth.

After a few other visits to friends and several weeks spent in London, Norton returned to America, leaving his daughter in England.

To Eliot Norton

ELY, 23 June, 1884.

I sent a letter to you this morning from London, and now this evening I take up the account of the doings at Cambridge.

At the dinner on Wednesday evening I sat between Dr. Ferrers the Vice-Chancellor of the University, a Puritan-looking man, stiff, hard, vigorous, a very fit figure for a chief place in this celebration of the Puritan foundation of Emmanuel, and Mr. Beresford Hope, one of the members for the University, a pleasant, social man, long in public life, a brother-in-law of Lord Salisbury, a high Tory and with an ease of manner that made it easy to talk with him through two or three hours. It was past eleven before the dinner was over, and then Uncle James[1] and I went to the rooms of one of the fellows of the College, where was a large gathering of University men, and where we stayed, much entertained, till past midnight.

The next morning there was an interesting service in the chapel of the College, with a fine anthem composed for the occasion by Sir George Macfarren, and an excellent sermon, as sermons go, by the Bishop of Winchester. This was over about one, and at half-past one we repaired to the Senate House where Dr. Boyd Carpenter, the Bishop designate of Ripon, and I were to receive our honorary degrees. Some two or three hundred people gathered in the hall, and the occasion was made pleasant to me by the presence of Sally and Aunt

---

[1] To Norton's children Lowell was "uncle by adoption."

Theo, of Uncle James and Miss Alice and Miss Annie Longfellow. There were other friends also, Miss Clough, Mr. and Mrs. Horace Darwin, Mr. Norman, and my new Cambridge friends and acquaintances. Dr. Carpenter and I were robed in our scarlet gowns, and stood near the middle of the hall, some twenty steps in front of the Vice-Chancellor, who sat in his robes of office, with an official bearing a silver mace on each side of him. Uncle James was near by in his doctorial robes, and behind us was a semi-circle of college dignitaries and youths. The ladies were seated on benches on each side between us [and] the Vice-Chancellor. Dr. Boyd Carpenter was presented first by the Public Orator, Mr. Sandys, in a Latin speech more than five minutes long. Then came my turn, and I was full of admiration at the extraordinary felicity of the Orator's speech. It was wonderfully graceful, ready, and well-turned flattery, which from being partially disguised in a classic tongue seemed more agreeable than if it had been uttered in a more familiar tongue. . . . It was altogether a picturesque scene, and well conducted public ceremony.

When it was all over and I had received the cordial expressions of many friends, the Registrary of the University, who had, previous to the ceremony, required me to sign my name in the volume containing the roll of the persons who had received an honorary degree from the University, carried me off to the hall where his books are kept, to show me the signature of John Harvard when he received his degree of A.B., 1631, and on becoming Master of Arts in 1635. Then once more to Emmanuel, to a sumptuous lunch, spread in a marquee, at which some 250 to 300 members of the College were entertained. I sat in a seat of honour next the Master, and on my right was a pleasant old gentleman, Archdeacon Watkins of York. There were many speeches, and I had to make one, which was not as carefully prepared as that of the night before, and therefore not as good, but it was very cordially received, — and, indeed, throughout the commemoration the heartiness of the expression toward Harvard, and toward me as its representative, was very great. I did not get away from the lunch till six o'clock;—at eight we had a dinner party at the Lodge, and as soon as dinner was over the Master held a reception in the Picture Gallery. . . .

I wish I had given you a more picturesque and animated account of it all, but I have had to write when I was tired. . . . Sally's letter will fill up the details of the story.

It is now June 25th. We are at Lincoln, having had two delightful days at Ely and Peterborough. I wonder a little that you were not more struck with Ely. It is a most impressive church, though I am quite ready to admit that it lacks the charm and the deeper interest of one of the great French Cathedrals of the best time.

As your birthday approaches, my heart is full of loving thoughts and hopes for you. . . .

Good night, dear boy,

Your loving

FATHER.

From Cambridge Norton had written to his son: —

"The presence of a representative from Harvard was worth more to the occasion than I had supposed it could be, for Emmanuel's services to Americans in her early days are the chief services she has rendered to the world, and Emmanuel men generally had not known how great they were, how honourable to their College, how illustrious they made her, till they were enlightened on all this by hearing the testimony given by an envoy from across the sea. . . . It was delightful to me to have Uncle James there. He gave to all the proceedings a touch of long association with the past which made them assume a very different character in my regard from what they otherwise would have had."

To Eliot Norton

BRANTWOOD, CONISTON, LANCASHIRE.
1 July, 1884.

MY DEAR BOY, — My heart is full of hopes and wishes for you to-day and I am sorry to be away from home on this special birthday of yours.[1] . . .

I was interrupted in my note, and during the last three days we have been travelling and sight-seeing so much that I have not found time for writing. It is now the fourth of July, we are at Warwick, which we reached from Lichfield night before last. Yesterday we had a delightful day at Stratford, weather perfect, scenery from there here as beautiful in tranquil rural beauty as any that England can show; —

[1] The twenty-first.

In thy green lap
Was Nature's darling laid.

The oaks and elms of Charlcote are superb, and the herds of deer, the rabbit warren, the pheasant boxes, the haymakers, and the stacking of the hay, the old church, the old house, the fields of grains just filling out their heads, a glory of red poppies, the hedges alive with birds, all these, and much beside made up a succession of English scenes of the prettiest sort, till we reached Stratford. Of Stratford, I believe, the girls feel too little has been said. They were not disappointed. Margaret is capable of deep sentiment, and her soul was stirred to its depths. Sally enjoyed the day not less, and with more vivacity of expression. They have been charming companions.

To-day we have spent the morning at the Castle, and now have come to the hotel, rather tired, for lunch. We are proposing to go to Kenilworth this afternoon, if the thunderstorm which is muttering in the distance does not come upon us. . . .

With constant love, and deepest desires for your good,

Ever, dear boy,

Your loving FATHER.

To Miss Sara Norton

THE ADELPHI, LIVERPOOL, 16 July, 1884.

I could be quite homesick for you to-day, but I steadily resist the temptation. We have had a happy time together this last six weeks! and we shall be glad enough when we see each other two months hence!

Yesterday's journey was fast. . . . What pleasant
recollections came up to me as we stopped at Rugby
and at Crewe! But they made me feel very solitary.
I wanted you and Margaret in place of the two girls
for whom I was getting biscuits and sandwiches. I
did not offer them a bun; buns were sacred. . . .

Good-bye, dear child.

Your very loving

FATHER.

To J. R. Lowell

SHADY HILL, 16 November, 1884.

. . . I cannot tell how Cleveland's election will affect
your position. Some people, of as good judgment and
means of knowing as others, think he will wish you to
remain in England. But I am inclined to believe that
he will accept your resignation, not at once, but after
some months. He has borne himself in a manly way
through the most trying, and by far the most disgust-
ing political campaign we have ever had. But the test
of his "staying" power is yet to come. Godkin is very
confident that he will do well, but Godkin has been a
very ardent, as well as very able partisan, and is convinced of what he desires to believe. The touch of
Ithuriel's spear was not more effective in disclosing the
true nature of his adversaries, than the issues of this
campaign have been. Most of our friends have stood
well. Judge Hoar is the only one who has failed; and
his failure has been redeemed by the vigorous protest
of his sons. The young men have been mostly on the
right side. But though Blaine is defeated, the narrow

margin of victory is disappointing, even discouraging. It displays the low average of moral sense in the people, which the defence of Blaine's course and the methods of his active supporters have done much to lower still farther.

I could wish that in your admirable discourse on Democracy — which is as wise as it is brilliant — you had dealt with this danger of the lowering of the moral standard in a democracy like ours to the level of those whose moral sense is in their trowsers and not their breast pocket. You give me pause when you say the people are "learning more and more how to be worthy" of their power. Perhaps so; but this is more questionable than it seemed ten or twenty years ago. It is not because I am ten or twenty years older that I say so, but because unfavourable influences, only nascent then, have, in recent years, been working with full force to affect the character and aims of the great body of the people. I have as strong a conviction as you that "democracy" will work; but it may work ignobly, ignorantly, brutally; here, at least, it does not look as if the better elements of social life, of human nature, were growing and flourishing in proportion to the baser. You will find the quality of the democratic climate changed not for the better during your absence.

Your letter was very interesting. I lay part of it to heart; but I am getting old. To-day is my fifty-seventh birthday. I do not feel so near threescore. . . .

Matthew Arnold and Mrs. A. spent some days with us, two or three weeks ago. He was most pleasant, and simpler than he appears in London. Mrs. Arnold quite won the hearts of my girls. Materially speaking his lectures are a success. He will go back with some money. His delivery is not good, but is striking from its thorough Anglican seriousness and awkwardness. It does not hurt the substance of his lectures, or their effect on the audience. Indeed the common hearer seems to be impressed by the fact that it is the matter not the manner of his speech that is of primary consequence.

The lecture on Emerson is a piece of large, liberal, genuine criticism; but, being criticism, has aroused the provincial ire of the pure disciples. On the whole Howells was right when he said that as he was listening to it he was constantly thinking, "Ah! that is just what I should have liked to say!" I have read the piece very carefully (for Arnold left it with me to have it printed for him) and I quarrel with no part of it. He has never written anything more picturesque than the opening pages, — never a sincerer criticism or one from so high a point of view. . . .

To Edward Lee-Childe

SHADY HILL, CAMBRIDGE, MASS.
29 November, 1884.

Your letter was very welcome and very pleasant except for its little tone, — undertone, of depression. You do not carry your pessimism far enough. We absolute pessimists accept this as the best of all possible worlds, and having no hope of a better, take whatever happens, not with resignation, for *that* implies disappointment, but with a smile of some sort, so long as we are not starving, or in physical pain, or the east wind is not blowing. Your out-and-out pessimist is cheerful, even though nature herself plays false, and uses loaded dice against him in the game. Darwinism has helped us a good deal. You expect less of men when you look at them not as a little lower than the angels, but as a little higher than the anthropoid apes. . . .

To Leslie Stephen

CAMBRIDGE, 29 November, 1884.

I wish that we lived within easy meeting distance of each other, not in London, but in some quiet place where there would not be 1001 engagements daily. Whenever a letter from you comes to me I feel how much I lose in not being within call of you. We are very nearly our true selves with each other; about as nearly as men ever are. We know each other well enough to be quite at ease. You cannot surprise me; I believe that I should never surprise you, till, as years went on, you suddenly found what a dull old fellow you had been liking, and how good you had been to him.

Three days ago the rain was pouring down as if this land were England, — a thorough, steady, drenching rain; it was near sunset, and I had just put on my india-rubber coat to go out for a solitary walk, when I saw a respectable-looking man, without overcoat or umbrella, coming toward the house. I had given orders that I would not see anyone that afternoon, but my conscience pricked me a little when the servant brought in word that it was a gentleman, who said he had business

with me and would call again. So I followed him down
the avenue, and found him sheltering himself under
one of the great pine trees. I said "I was sorry he had
been sent away; did he wish to see me?" He was a
worthy-looking man of perhaps 60, with white hair,
neatly dressed, not a tramp, very likely a gentleman.
"Yes," he said, "he knew I had been in Cambridge in
England this summer, that he thought I might perhaps
know some of his friends there, and would for their
sakes lend him a couple of pounds." Imagine my
questions and his answers, or his questions and my
answers. "Did I know Mr. Bradshaw?" Did I know
so and so? His name was B——, I should find it in the
preface to Blades' "Caxton" as of one who had helped
Mr. Blades. So Dr. Grosart had mentioned him
[Heaven help the mark! thought I, remembering my
last news (from you) of Grosart], and he himself had
edited letters of Archbishop Williams and done other
literary work, and had come to this country in hopes of
finding employment, and had been disappointed, and
was now waiting for a remittance which should take
him home, — the remittance was at hand, but he was
embarrassed till it came. Not in distress, oh no! far
from that. There was real (apparently real) simplicity
in the man, nothing of the air of a swindler, a look of
respectability a little hard pressed, the air of a man
who did not mean to be battered down by any foul
blow of fate. So I lent him his two pounds, and put
him into a horse-car to go back to his lodgings in Boston and to get dry.

I wait the event with curiosity, and if the man is not

honest I shall be surprised, and shall not have paid too much for the lesson.

As for Froude, the spirit of truth is not in him. These last volumes [1] are not so openly malignant as the first, but covertly they seem to me quite as much so. Froude's praise generally rings false. I know nothing else so bad against the Sage of Chelsea, as that this man should be his chief disciple and representative. Carlyle is expiating his sins. He, the lover and believer in truth, has "a continental liar" (one of the phrases of our late political campaign) to report him to the world, — this is the penalty of extravagance of speech; and he, the steadfast and courageous man, has a hesitator — "just hint a fault," etc., — and a coward to praise him for not having sold his birthright for a mess of pottage. Ah! dear old Thomas, why did not you know that your exaggerations and outcries were the windy food of humbugs and falsifiers? Well, the poor old Thomas is having a pretty hard Purgatorial experience, and it is n't clear that he will ever get quite into Paradise. I hope so. I fancy Mrs. Carlyle turning to him with a slightly sub-acid smile, and while he is sunk in gloomy patience, whispering to him, a little maliciously, —

"Caina attende chi vita ci spense."

I look forward to your Dictionary as one of the resources of old age. I shall leave my mark somewhere in one of the volumes, about E or F; and my son shall begin where I leave off; and his son shall take it up

[1] Froude's *History of Carlyle's Life in London* was published in 1884.

LESLIE STEPHEN

where he stops and so on. We will be faithful to you. Please tell Mrs. Stephen so with my love.

Ever affectionately Yours,
C. E. NORTON.

To Leslie Stephen

CAMBRIDGE, 6 March, 1885.

It was very kind of you to write me of Mrs. Lowell's illness and of Lowell's condition. I have wanted to hear. Overcome as Lowell may be by the calamity of her death, he must be glad that her life was not prolonged like her sister's, with a shattered mind. But I could wish that he too might die. With all his vigour and force of individuality, he was unusually dependent on his wife; his temperament made her essential to him. I have always hoped that he might die before her. She gone, nothing he cares for is left to him in life. I see no future comfort, or even occupation for him. The best thing, perhaps, would be for him to be left in his present position, and thus compelled to some distraction of mind. I do not see how he can come home to his solitary house, unless for the sake of dying. Before he went away Elmwood was already too full of ghosts for him. His daughter and her children live too far from him to give him daily interest. . . .

Lowell's sister, Mrs. Putnam, and her daughter go to him to-morrow, by the steamer which may take this letter. They are as near him as anyone now, but they cannot help him much. I wrote to him that I would come to him at once if he wished, but I do not believe that he would care for my coming. Indeed my heart is very sore for him.

I am sorry that you have been ill, and sorry that your work is so heavy and continuous. The first volume of the Dictionary seems to me so good, that I cannot but hope that it makes a foundation on which it will be easier to build further than it was to lay the first stones. . . .

Cleveland's inaugural address and his cabinet are entirely satisfactory. He seems to be a man of clear good sense, and solid will.

To W. D. Howells

SHADY HILL, 25 September, 1885.

I am not ungrateful. The gift of "Silas Lapham" from you gave me real pleasure. I had liked the book so much as I had read it from month to month, I had taken such sympathetic pleasure in its excellence for your sake, I had talked of it so often with my girls, with Lowell, with George Curtis, we had all agreed so well about it, — that your gift was welcome not for its own sake merely, but as a sort of friendly recognition and response to all these cordial thoughts and words, — the seal to the long indenture written out in the volume itself. . . .

And now I am enjoying the "Indian Summer" even more. I will not write of it to you as I would to a third person. My only fault with it is that each part ends too soon. You are a delightful benefactor.

Only last night a fair young creature (not from Buffalo) said to me at dinner, "Oh, Mr. Norton, do explain to me the difference between Mr. Howells's realism and George Eliot's! Mr. Howells is so charming, I really want to know about it."

I kept on the surface of the waters, and contented myself with telling her about you, and not about your art. . . .

To Leslie Stephen

SHADY HILL, 4 October, 1885.

I wish you were here that we might have a walk together this Sunday afternoon, or it would be better that I were with you, for the chance of a walk through pleasant country would be greater than in this region of horse-car tracks and suburban "residences." Our friend Benton [1] spent Sunday with me at Ashfield three weeks ago, and we had a long fine walk over the hills, during which he told me much of you. He seemed to think, what I fear is true, that you are working too hard, and carrying too heavy a load with the Dictionary and the Life of Fawcett together. The Life I trust will be soon finished, — but the Dictionary! Do get a sub-editor whom you can trust to lift part of the weight, at least, of this Old Man of the Mountain from your shoulders.

You ask me about the Carlyle letters. It is true that I have undertaken to edit some volumes of them. Mrs. Alex. Carlyle has put all that are in her possession into my hands for the purpose. There will probably be three volumes of letters written before he came to London, to his family and to College friends; another

[1] C. H. Benton, one of Leslie Stephen's company of "Sunday Tramps."

volume of letters to his family of later date, and two or three volumes of letters to Sterling, Mill, Browning and other friends. So far as I have read them they are very interesting, and likely to dispel many of the false notions concerning him which Froude has done so much to propagate. I have all the letters to Mrs. Carlyle and from her, both before and after their marriage, but I hold them too sacred for even my own eyes. I shall not open the packages of them. Of course there is a temptation to print them, to correct Froude's misinterpretations and misrepresentations. But I think it is a less evil to leave these uncorrected than to violate for a second time the confidences and intimacies of husband and wife. At any rate I will not be he who shall do it.

The work of editing is not difficult but it takes a good deal of time, and effectually fills up such leisure as my college work leaves me. Macmillan is to publish them, and I hope to get out three or four volumes in the course of the next twelvemonth. . . .

To G. E. Woodberry

CAMBRIDGE, 30 January, 1886.

. . . The poem as a whole seems to me too absolute in singing the praise of the beloved land.[1] We are men; we know the good and the ill of the world; we love our country, but with keen-eyed and disciplined passion, not blindly exalting her, not feeding our imaginations on unrealities, on what might never and nowhere be. The dreams of a perfecter state are gone.

---

[1] "My Country," published later in the *Atlantic*.

We are awake, and see the shadows as well as the sun-light. To do justice to the America that may be, we must not exalt the America that is, beyond her worth. Moderation is strength. We do not care for a "fourth of July" ode!

I shall send back the poem to-day, or Monday, to-gether with "Marius." I am very much obliged to you for this book, but on the whole you think more highly of it than I. The first half of it deserves your praise better than the last. There is an affectation, a *précio-sité* in it, that sometimes takes from its worth the one thing needful, — sincerity of feeling. . . .

To John Ruskin

SHADY HILL, 8 February, 1886.

DEAREST OLD SAINT AND SINNER!

Here is your birthday once more, and we celebrate it with love and honour for you, and joy for ourselves in the memory of all you have been and all you will ever be to us.

Are you well? and is the day sunny for you? And do you see your image in the sun-lit head of Coniston Old Man across the lake?

And has Joan given you a birthday cake with 67 lighted candles round it? They ought to be at least as big, every one of them, as the biggest on the high altars of St. Anthony at Padua!

What do you say for one more look at Italy to-gether?

Alas! I do not see how we can have it; — but I would like to stand once more with you on the Ponte-a-mare;

and once more in the Duomo, and once more in San Giovanni, "il mio bel!"

This is but to take you what you have long had, — my love. I was just now reading the letters of Marcus Aurelius and Fronto, and the end of one of the letters of Marcus shall serve as the end of mine.

Spiritum vix habeo ita sum defessus. Vale mi magister dulcissime, homo honestissime et rarissime, suavitas et caritas mea...

Ever your loving   C. E. N.

To Miss Sara Norton

SHADY HILL, 10 April, 1886.

... [I found] Mr. Brimmer, who was the only person whom I really wanted to see. At his wish I am going to-night to the dinner of the Merchants' Club, for it appears that they wish to learn something about the Museum, in order to take part in raising the subscription of $250,000 which is required in its aid. I trust we shall be successful in quickening their interest in the work.

We have all been greatly interested in Mr. Gladstone's speech.[1] I have no idea that his scheme can be made to work; and generous as his design is, and powerful as his speech is, the project seems to me Utopian, and the speech an immense added difficulty in the way of a settlement of the Irish question. He has sown the wind, and it will blow a gale before it blows itself out. ...

---

[1] On April 8, 1886, Gladstone brought in his bill for establishing Home Rule in Ireland.

To J. R. Lowell

SHADY HILL, 26 November, 1886.

"Take it by and large, and long and short, and Providence does seem to do about as much harm as good in this world," as the old lady said, and, of all the harm it does, the little needless rubs and worries of life that spoil so many hours are among the worst. How pleasant the world would be if we were all but a grain less self-conscious and self-regardful, a grain more sympathetic with natures different from our own, and if we could but succeed in so expressing our real selves as to make ourselves intelligible! Do you remember Arnold's poem of "The Buried Life?" Your "In the Twilight" is a variation on the same theme. How hard it is to be ourselves! How rarely are we conscious of a true image of ourselves in another's heart! The existence of that image of what we desire to be, and therefore really are, is the blessing of the one and only love, — and when that is gone how solitary we remain, and how empty is life!

Your yesterday's note sets me on this train of reflection, — a familiar one enough, and leading always to one conclusion.

I hope you are in a happier mood to-day. Why should trifles depress us, since we have lost the possibility of being *very* sorry any more? . . .

I am glad that the book of Carlyle's "Letters" has interested you. I knew it would, but it is pleasant to have you tell me so, and pleasant, too, to have the notices of the book from you. Ireland (who bores me) had sent me his articles. The most important notice is that in the "Times"; the "Times" has hitherto supported Froude, but this is a *volte-face.* Indeed it looks as if the "Letters" had dealt Froude a heavier blow than even I expected. . . .

On December 27, 1886, Norton wrote to Mr. Woodberry: "On Christmas eve I gathered a few stray students and we sat down fourteen at table; the party was an interesting one from its representative character; there were delegates from New York, Pennsylvania, Delaware, Indiana, and California; the ancestors of one came from Palestine, the grandparents of another from Scotland, the parents of a third from Germany."

This was the beginning of what became an institution at Shady Hill for about twenty-five succeeding years — the gathering together, on Norton's invitation, of the students of the University whose homes were so far away or whose funds were so limited that they were passing the holidays in Cambridge.

Towards the end of Norton's life when he no longer felt able to receive the students, sometimes one hundred and fifty or more in number, to whom he opened his house on Christmas Eve, he asked President and Mrs. Eliot to invite them to Phillips Brooks House, where he came and read as was his custom at the close of the evening, the story of the Nativity in the Gospel of St. Luke. In 1906, on the last Christmas but one of his life, his voice in the reading was not strong, and when he ended, he turned to President Eliot and said;

Shady Hill. Sunday
December 5, 1886.

My dear James, —

What a pleasant old-
fashioned snow-storm we are
having today! The hush of the
earth is complete as this white
blanket covers it, and it falls
to sleep. We, like you, are having
a quiet day. The pleasantest
incident of the morning was the
coming of your note, with the
five dollars safe within it. No.
the age of a bank-note has
nothing venerable & attractive, like

that of a coin which had passed
through many hands without
being so defiled by them that
it can never be made clean again.
The dirty bank-note typifies the
base used influences of money.
Hawthorne somewhere, in one of his
Note Books, if I remember rightly
hints at its suggestiveness.

I should have written to you
yesterday, had I found your
paper on Landor. I am glad
you found it in the Massachusetts
Review, which I did not think
of looking in when I was at the

College Library I fancy I should have been better rewarded than you, had I found it, and should have descovered more than "one" good sentence in it. As for sentences that I can't understand there is one in your 'Democracy' volume, which I wait for your coming to ask you to explain to me. You will come, we all hope, next Saturday, and stay as long as you can be content. If you do not want to send off the manuscript before then, pray bring what you write

on Landor to read to us. Do
you remember writing
"And Landor's self can Landor's
                    spell undo"?
A various reading, which I would
propose, runs
"And Lowell's voice shall Landor's
                    spell renew."

Good bye, dear boy!
        We all send best love.
        Always your affectionate
            C. E. N.

"Charles, I shall never do that again." In the following year he did not come to the reception.

To J. R. Lowell

ASHFIELD, 24 July, 1887.

... When this shower holds up, I daresay George will come over, for an hour's talk. He is the pleasantest of men. Just now he is busy preparing his discourse for the annual meeting of the Civil Service Reform Association. He has a difficult task; for, on the one hand, he must express the disappointment of the Reformers in the Administration, which cannot longer claim to be a Reform Administration; on the other, to hold the Reformers to Cleveland as a President who on the whole is filling his place so well that he deserves the support of every one who has the best interests of the country at heart. There are doctrinaires among the Reformers, and old dyed-in-the-wool Republicans who will find this hard doctrine.

I think you will have to stay at home next summer to take part in the Campaign! It looks as if the candidates of '84 were to be the candidates of '88, and there would not be much doubt of the result but for the uncertainty of the Labour and the Temperance votes.

I saw your smile at the Pulitzer-Gladstone incident;[1] and I have seen it often as you watched the progress of Col. Cody. London forces you into queer company. We are more select at home. Is a society worth saving,

[1] Apparently a reference to Joseph Pulitzer's presentation to Gladstone of a silver service purchased with funds raised by the New York *World* in recognition of Gladstone's work for Irish Home Rule.

— can it be saved, that has lost its fastidiousness? Alas! — for Venice. I should like to see Leslie Stephen, and get a wholesome growl from him. Pray, give him my love. Five such as he could save even London, — but it would be a tough job.

Ashfield is a sweeter and quieter place, and never was pleasanter in aspect than now. The summer is one of the noblest, — fresh and full at once, with abundant heat and abundant rains, so that all that grows is at its best. . . .

To Leslie Stephen

ASHFIELD, 2 August, 1887.

As I laid down my pen yesterday I said to myself, — "To-morrow I will surely write to Stephen," and so gracious is Providence to the repentant sinner, and with such a reward does Heaven crown even a virtuous resolution, that the evening mail brought to me your welcome letter! It was very good of you to write to me to tell me of my boy's having dined with you, and I am grateful for your kindness to him and to me.

I am glad that you are at the Land's End, where I trust all will go well with you and that you will succeed in getting the vacation you need; that nobody will fall ill depending on Mrs. Stephen to go to nurse him; that she and you and the children may have a good time together. But good Heavens! how have you the energy for a new book? The Dictionary cannot be as bad as you report it, cannot be such a strangling Man of the Mountain as I fancied it if you can take breath enough for any other work! I am glad of it, for

I have begrudged your Dictionary work as keeping you from writing books of your own. One has to read the books of a good many of one's contemporaries (and of some of one's friends), to learn that they really have nothing to say; but there are a few   Interrupted by a carpenter, who came to my window for directions, —I will not finish my sentence, for the conclusion is obvious, and has no novelty for you. You have known for years that I like your books and believe in them, and wish there were a new one every year. Do give us a uniform edition of them, — "Works of Leslie Stephen" in ten vols. post 8vo, —*that* would look well, and the world would be the better for it.

Nobody here seems to be writing for "literature" in these days but Lowell, and his little "Democracy" volume is the only one of the thousands printed this year that seems likely to reach the Fortunate Isles of posterity. It is not altogether bad that printing should by its own excess provide a safeguard against itself, and at the same time help to improve the character of men of letters by reducing their vanity.

I wonder whether you would agree with me that the set of men of letters, and their kindred, whom we have known, is a good deal the best that the world has seen; not the greatest, perhaps, but the pleasantest to live with, the best-intentioned and honestest. Froude for instance is a moral contemporary of Warburton rather than of the men of to-day, — interesting as a survival. But there are no such liars as Pope, or cynics as Swift, or vulgarians as Gay, or sycophants as Young, or mockers as Sterne, — indeed, you and I find it uncommonly difficult to pick our own friends to pieces. We can warrant them to posterity — almost every one of them, — as better than their reputation. The "reporter" sometimes lowers them to his own level, but they do not belong there.

I wish you were here that we could have a walk over these hills.

Ever affectionately yours

C. E. NORTON.

Please give my affectionate regards to your wife, and my true thanks for a lovely little note she sent me in the spring.

To J. R. Lowell

ASHFIELD, 5 September, 1887.

. . . Except for George, I have been very solitary. From year to year I seem to myself to grow more and more silent, and to express less of what is in my soul. I should like to have the power of expression, — at least long enough to give form and utterance to a few of the deepest conceptions of Life and its significance and uses which come to one as one grows old and draws the lessons from his own experience. The whole view of human existence which the world has held up to this time seems to be changing, and the new view is not yet clearly outlined, but enough may be seen to make it certain that it will, in certain aspects, be essentially different from the old. Man will be at once less and more; a poorer creature than of old as regards the glowing illusions to which he has shaped himself; richer by far in self-dependence, at once with a humbler and

a more self-respectful regard of himself and his destiny
— I write on, as if we were talking, — and have come
to the end of my paper. . . .

To Mrs. A. Carlyle

ASHFIELD, 18 September, 1887.

. . . You reproach yourself too much in regard to
your part in confirming the relations between your
Uncle and Froude. Your Uncle's regard for him was
natural enough. Froude is an accomplished flatterer.
His insincerity of nature, and his talent for external
agreeableness fit him for his part. Your Uncle did not
distrust him, did not discover his insincerity, because
such genuine opinions as Froude has were in important
respects derived from him, and Froude played skill-
fully the part of a disciple, with a show of independence. Your Uncle, as I may have told you, asked me
once why I did not like Froude, and when I told him
it was because I thought him lacking in the sense of
truth, he assured me I was wrong, and should like him
better if I knew him better. But Froude's talk with
your Uncle and his manners confirmed my distrust of
him. Still I did not think so ill of him, as he has since
compelled us to think. . . .

To G. E. Woodberry

SHADY HILL, 16 November, 1887.

Your two notes have reached me, — the last one
with its pleasant birthday greeting arriving this morning. For both of them I thank you, — but especially
for the last, which touched my heart.

It is hard for one who is not even a minor poet to put
sentiment into the right words, — but if I could do so I
should try to make you understand that you have
helped me to keep something of the spirit of youth
through the sympathy which you have evoked, and
that your regard has been an encouragement to me to
believe that I might be rendering some service to
others. One can accomplish so little in comparison
with what one desires to accomplish, and in my case
strength so often fails for the doing of what with a
little more strength one would do easily, that there is
need of philosophy not to allow what might be to make
one discontented with what is. Such affection as yours
comes in to reinforce and illumine my philosophy. I
am grateful for it.

I shall try to keep young, and if we both live we shall
be growing, I trust, every day more and more nearly
of the same age! Good night.

Affectionately Yours
C. E. NORTON.

To Leslie Stephen

SHADY HILL, 1 February, 1888.

You are a good man; — and if, when having reached
"S" you are called on to write your own biography,
you will do the world a wrong and yourself an injustice,
if you do not speak of yourself, with great confidence,
as one of the best men in the world. You may say what
you please about wit, good sense, humour, general
superiority of mind, but if you do not set yourself out
well for solid virtue, I (should I be so long-lived and not

quite fallen into dotage) will protest, and bring such
evidence against the writer as shall seriously damage
his credit. I shall have Lowell to back me. You had
better send me proof-sheets in advance to see if I approve. I shall not be content with any half-hearted
assertion.

Here has your letter written after you had been
so kind to Eliot been lying for months on my table and
on my conscience unanswered, when behold comes another, pleasant as the first, as if I had been the most
punctual of correspondents, and had shown my gratitude as well as felt it. The truth is I have not your
powers of work, and the duties of each day leave me
tired and with little energy for even pleasant additions
to them, such as acknowledging the kindness of a
friend. Care and labour do not diminish, as they ought,
as one grows old, — and there is no Switzerland within
reach for me to fly to for change of scene and a week's
forgetfulness of the burden of the days. I hope your
journey has taken the fagged look from your eyes, and
that you have come back refreshed and fit for another
spell of work.

The Dictionary is a source of frequent comfort to
me; this very week it has helped me to answer some
questions that Lowell sent me from Southborough,
where, poor fellow, he has but few books round him.
He is writing on Walton, and he wanted to know the
last word about that creation of Walton's fancy,
John Chalkhill; and where could it be found but in the
Dictionary? He thinks that he has discovered proof
that "Thealma and Clearchus" was Walton's own

composition, from the frequent use of "its" in the poem; a use which fixes the date at least a generation later than that to which any familiar of Spenser belonged. . . .

I have been writing lately a sort of essay, which I am to read as a lecture in a few days, on the Lack of Thought in America. It is a criticism of our social conditions, and will not gain me favour when it is published. Of course now that it is done it seems to me unsatisfactory enough, but I hope that, imperfect as it is, it may open the way to some not fruitless discussion.

The winter has been severe with us of late, and for the last fortnight the temperature has ranged most of the time from 15 above to 15 below zero. . . .

Norton's limited enjoyment of "winter and rough weather" showed itself throughout his life and was closely related to his lack of vigorous health. Writing to Lowell in 1877 he said: —

"To me winter is unwelcome. I like long warm days, — days in which one may feel himself part of a world full of enjoyment of life. In winter the resistance to the cold is wearisome and costly, — and it uses the force that one would wish to reserve for better things. I doubt if winter in New England has had that good effect on the character of the people which poets and moralists are apt to ascribe to it. It was not needed to make the Puritan virtues rugged. We might well be spared half of it without loss of vigour and of goodness. The Romans were not an effeminate race, nor the

Greeks of the generation of Marathon; two months of
mild winter were enough for them."

To Sir John Simon

SHADY HILL, 2 February, 1888.

. . . The last time I saw Emerson at his own house,
as I was bidding him Good-bye, he, pathetically conscious that he was no longer master of his own powers
and sensitive with characteristic sweetness at not being
able to call me by name, said with a sad smile, "Good-
bye, my good friend. Strange that the kind Heavens
should keep us upon earth after they have destroyed
our connection with things." — Kind Heavens! Alas!
for poor Ruskin.

To-day I have been to the funeral of one of my oldest friends, Asa Gray. You have seen a reflection of
him in Darwin's letters to him. There was a Darwinian simplicity and integrity and kindliness in him. His
life had been one of extraordinary tranquillity and enjoyment, and never had he enjoyed it more than during
this last year, his seventy-eighth, which he spent
abroad with old friends and new honours. His mind
was as active and vigorous, and his step as light and
agile as ever. But six weeks ago, without a warning,
he was struck down by paralysis; he was blotted out,
but his helpless body remained and all who cared for
him desired its death. He leaves a great gap here.
He is the last of my own elder Cambridge friends. My
pleasant memories associated with him date back to
my earliest College years. He was one of the few sur-
viving friends of my Father and Mother. . . .

To J. R. Lowell

SHADY HILL, 25 March, 1888.

. . . I read the "Old Téméraire" aloud to the children this evening, to their and to my great pleasure, and great pride in our Uncle! Your hand is firmer than ever at the helm.

"Nothing" has happened this week. I have had too little time either for thinking much, or for reading to any advantage. My best reading has been in Sainte-Beuve, whom I generally turn to when I am tired and want to be interested without effort. One evening I dined at Craigie House. It was a pleasant dinner, but for me it had too many vacant places. The host was not there, and the guests were strangers. I felt as a revenant must do. . . .

To J. R. Lowell

SHADY HILL, 30 March, 1888.

. . . Your last note gave me much bitter-sweet reflection. I could not but think how much more of a philosopher I was than you, about some matters that deeply concern happiness. Here are you depressed because your work is not as good as your ideal, — and yet this (who knows better than you?) is the law of all best work. Perfection would not be perfection could it be attained. You do not do your *possible* best. Who does? Of course such incomparable gifts and powers as yours are constantly suggesting, to you no doubt even more urgently than to me, that your work is never a just measure of them; that you might do a supremer thing than any you have done. But what then? You know that temperament stands in the way of its being done, — and this is something that no artist masters, for it is his unconscious, all-pervading self. No matter! You have done enough for the cheap praise the newspapers can give; and something of what you have done will survive along with the precious rest of the final load of Omar's single camel. I am indifferent about anything but love for my fellow-mortals. I don't even care (except now and then) spite of your teaching, for Quinquennial Catalogue honours. For me this is easy, on the "vacuus viator" principle. When one is as rich as you, no doubt it is harder to be indifferent.

Your loving

C. E. N.

To Miss Sara Norton

SHADY HILL, 18 April, 1888.

... Our hearts have been full of sorrow since Monday, as yours too has been, at the news of Mr. Arnold's death, and full of deepest sympathy with Mrs. Arnold, and their daughters. I am thankful that Mrs. Arnold was with him. The first brief, hard telegram that he had died at Liverpool made us fear that he might have been alone there.[1] ...

He is a great loss, for he was one of the few living thinkers of independent opinions to whose voice men would listen. I had hoped that he might yet live to write for many years. Now that he is dead I trust that a juster opinion concerning him will prevail than has

---

[1] Matthew Arnold died April 15, 1888.

been common during these later years. It is a great
happiness for us that we knew him so well, and had
learned the real sweetness, simplicity, and elevation of
his essential character. We have lost a true and dear
friend, and the world seems emptier for it. . . .

To J. R. Lowell
ASHFIELD, 15 August, 1888.

. . . The days with us run quietly. I have been reading in these last days Church's book on Spenser, a very
good one on the whole, but often ill-written and with
some clerical limitations. It seems to be a tradition
with the deans of St. Paul's to be skilled in writing bad
English. Milman printed some incredible sentences,
and Dean Church follows his example. I naturally
took to reading your essay on Spenser, when I had
finished the Dean's book, and to reading the "Faery
Queen" itself. I like both better than ever. There is
little better reading in these days than the F. Q. It
clears the air of the street-dust of the newspapers, and
the dry light of science. It is the Italy of the lands of
poesy. . . .

To G. W. Curtis
SHADY HILL, 31 March, 1889.

If I had not given all my leisure during the past
fortnight to reading Motley's "Letters," [1] I should
have spent part of it in thanking you for the book, and
telling you with what entertainment and interest I was

---

[1] *The Correspondence of John Lothrop Motley*, edited by George William
Curtis, had just been published.

reading it. The book will have more readers hereafter,
I fancy, than Motley's Histories. The letters raise him
in one's esteem, and those which belong to the time of
the War are of real value as an expression of the sentiment of the time. There is a passion of patriotism in
them that has a noble ring, and touches the heart. It
brings back the emotion of that great moment in our
national life. The foresight that Motley displays is
remarkable; it is the foresight of a student of history.
The lack of humour sometimes makes one smile as
much as a touch of true humour itself would do. But
the general tone of the letters is as honourable to
America as it is to the man who wrote them. There are
two letters of genius in the book, — one of Hawthorne's and one of Carlyle's. And as for Bismarck's,
they are delightful and make one love the old tyrannical
German. It is long since a book so entertaining, and so
varied in its entertainment was published. . . .

To Miss Sara Norton

ASHFIELD, Sunday afternoon, July, 1889.

MY DEAREST SALLY, — Wie geht's? You are missing
some of the loveliest days of the summer. Yesterday
and to-day have been as nearly perfect days as one can
hope for. I walked five miles down the road to the
Falls to meet Aunt Theo,[1] and not meeting her, for she
had taken the other — the North — road, walked the
two miles back, and enjoyed every step of the way, so
fine was the air, so beautiful the summer landscape.
On my way back, just on the border of Buckland, a

[1] Miss Sedgwick.

little boy, perhaps ten years old, came along for a time
behind me whistling and singing. He turned off on a
side road, but as long as I could hear his sweet little
treble he was singing the words

"And the burden on my heart rolled away, rolled away,
And the burden on my heart rolled away"!

. . . I spent the evening at a meeting of the Trustees
of the Academy, at which we fixed the day of dedication for the 24th July.[1] . . .

To-day I have been writing many letters, and reading with great entertainment a volume of Early Letters
of Mrs. Carlyle to an Edinburgh friend, Eliza Stodart,
the great-aunt of the editor, a Mr. Ritchie, who sends
the volume to me.[2] It is a book you will like, for the
letters have the same character as those of Mrs. Carlyle which have been previously published, — as good
letters as a woman ever wrote, so far as sprightliness of
wit, and cleverness of expression, and skill in delineation go. . . .

To J. R. Lowell

ASHFIELD, 8 September, 1889.

If vacation had brought me leisure you would have
had a letter from me before now. . . . The most interesting book — new book — that I have read is Fitz-
Gerald's "Letters," which seem to me among the best
in English, the true expression of a character and a gen-

[1] Through the generosity of Mrs. John W. Field, a new building had
been provided for the Academy, in memory of her husband, Norton's
old friend.

[2] *Early Letters of Jane Welsh Carlyle*, etc. Edited by David G.
Ritchie. London. 1889.

ius both alike rare and delightful. The independence
and sincerity of judgment, the style, the humour, the
taste for the best, fall in with my likings wonderfully.
I have not read a book with more entire sympathy for
years. It is not without its pathos. One wishes that
"Old Fitz" had had experience not only of the best in
literature, but of the best in life also. I think Mr.
Wright might have given us a little more information
about him without harm, and without offence to Fitz-
Gerald's own sensitiveness. "The Parliament of
Birds" was new to me, and seems to me a very striking
and noble poem. . . .

To Sir Mountstuart E. Grant-Duff

ASHFIELD, MASSACHUSETTS, 10 September, 1889.

MY DEAR SIR MOUNTSTUART, — To live in London,
or, still better, near it as you do, is to have a larger
share of the best opportunities of life than can be found
anywhere else. I recognize the fine malice of your
letter. Grillion's, and The Club, and the Dilettanti
Society [1] are truly fit matters of envy. They give you
"society," the very rarest and best thing that the world
proper can give us. It is the thing that our modern
materialism is largely killing out, — that is, in its highest form, the society that bears witness to leisure and
culture, and good breeding, made up of men who
though versed in affairs are still idealists and lovers of

---

[1] Something about each of these "Dining Associations" — of which
"The Club" through association with Dr. Johnson, is best known — may
be found in Grant-Duff's *Out of the Past: Some Biographical Essays.*
London, 1903.

poetry; not all *novi homines*, but men with traditions
and independence. Not much of such society has ever
existed, but now and then, at your breakfast club for
example, there is at least the suggestion of it. . . .

To G. W. Curtis

SHADY HILL, 29 December, 1889.

The old year shall not go without taking you one
more word of love from me, and loving good wishes for
the year that is to come. I had a note from Howells
two or three days ago in which he said: — "Was ever
a man so sweetly and generously praised as I by Curtis?
I could not write him fitly about it, but all the same I
felt it every word; and I was simply amazed at the
magnanimity with which he attributed merit to my
work at the cost of old favourites. There is a man of a
wholly different make from me; he does good because
he loves; I because I hate." What you said of his
book greatly pleased me too.[1] I had just read the book
with the interest and admiration which you had fore-
told to me last summer, and your notice of it expressed
what I felt and could not have said so well. There is
more power in the book than in anything he has done
before. A reader must either be very good or very
unfeeling who is not made better by reading it. It is
a novel in which America finds expression. . . .

---

[1] *Annie Kilburn* appeared in 1889.

CHAPTER XI

THE final decade of the century to which Norton belonged, brought the changes and losses inseparable from advancing years. During its course the country he loved so well made some abrupt departures from policies and standards which had ruled the earlier day. The steady drift in public life — not only in America — toward "jingoism," and in private life toward a more aggressive and more general materialism, were tendencies with which it was impossible that Norton should sympathize; and he would have been unfaithful to the inheritance from his ancestry of preachers if he had refrained from "bearing his testimony" to the truth he saw and the ideals he cherished.

Early in the new decade two heavy losses came to Norton in his personal relations. Lowell died August 12, 1891; Curtis, August 31, 1892. The severing of bonds in which intellectual and political sympathies were closely inwoven with the warmest personal affection, could not but leave him solitary — in spite of troops of remaining friends. Yet the solace he found in direct intercourse and correspondence with those whom the years had proved was characteristically strengthened and increased by a constant extension of friendships in the younger generations. The power of throwing himself heartily into the interests of those in whom he saw the promise of effective devotion to pursuits or ends in which he believed not only contributed much to his own satisfaction in daily life but gave his wide-spread influence a value of exceptional quality. Character, worthy ambition, even in the least distinguished fields of work, could always enlist his help and encouragement.

This identification with the interests of his juniors took many forms. A typical instance of it lay in his relation with the Tavern Club of Boston, an organization formed in 1884 by a group of young men concerned chiefly with the arts and learned professions. In 1890 Norton became its third president. Though not in the accepted sense of the term a "clubbable" person, he brought to the dinners to eminent guests at which he presided, a distinction which made them memorable. It is perhaps one of the charms of such occasions that their flavour can persist only in memory: one holds them more precious in the passing for the very recognition that they must pass. The company, the candle-lighted scene, the intangible *genius loci* bring so much to the total impression that the recalling of the spoken word is at the best a partial process. Yet some suggestion of that which Norton contributed to such occasions may be drawn from the rough notes of what he said — three years before he became the chief officer of the club — at a dinner at which he presided in honour of Edward Burgess, the designer of three yachts which in turn successfully defended the American title to the Queen's Cup. The fact that the dinner, celebrating a victory in international sport, lay quite outside the academic province, is not without its significance as a token of the range of Norton's sympathies.

"A man," he said in this speech, "may have studied the winds and the waves all his life, may have the science of mechanics in all its branches at his fingers' ends, and yet the boat he may build, though a masterpiece of pure science, will not win the race, unless to his calculations and his knowledge be added the spirit of imagination which, in a mode inexplicable to the understanding, enables him to take account of the infinite, incalculable elements involved in a work of poetic imagination.

"For the 'Mayflower,' the 'Puritan,' and the 'Volunteer' are in very truth creations of the poetic faculty — poems shaped in wood and iron and canvas. Their lines as they took form in the mind of the builder matched the flow of the sea, caught their rhythm from the motion and their rhyme from the voice of the waves. . . . Thus the imagination working with the facts that Nature supplies, and under her immutable laws, gradually shapes the instruments by which Nature is conquered into perfect concordance with those facts, into beauty harmonious with those laws. The imagination has thus shaped the ploughshare and the oar.

"Of all the creations of the imagination out of the raw material of Nature, not one is more beautiful and more complete than the fleet white-winged messenger of the sea. The Greek, still our master in every field of creative activity, first shaped the boat to beauty, and the magical ship of the Phæacians which outsped the hawk, swiftest of winged things, was the type and forerunner of the 'Volunteer.' The 'Volunteer' is the embodiment of three thousand years of experience.

"Pindar begins one of his Olympic odes with pomp of eulogy saluting a victor at the games as thrice victorious — τρισολυμπιονίκαν. Thus we hail our guest."

Of the many other Tavern Club dinners at which Norton presided, a few were conspicuous for a special sympathy between the guests of honour and "the chair." One of these was the dinner to Curtis, at which Lowell read a large portion of the "Epistle to George William Curtis" as it appears in his published works. At another, to Lowell, on his seventieth birthday, Dr. Holmes read for the first time one of his poems, "To James Russell Lowell." A dinner to the Architects of the World's Fair afforded an opportunity for the expression of Norton's enthusiasm for the artistic achievement at Chicago. At still another he paid his tribute of personal admiration to Kipling. On all these occasions he committed to a new generation the clear tradition of an older time when the felicities and urbanities of formal speech were more profitably cultivated than they are to-day.

During the years with which the present chapter is concerned, Norton added to the list of the more important publications which he edited, "Letters of James Russell Lowell," in two volumes (1894); "Orations and Addresses by George William Curtis," in three volumes (1894); and a series of School "Readers" for children, in which his wide knowledge of the best pages in English literature was turned to a serviceable purpose, the "Heart of Oak Books" in six volumes (1894–95).[1] The habit of industry was still bearing its abundant fruit.

Again the letters move forward with the progress of his own life and thought. The first of those which follow relates to a gathering in Boston of the "Grand Army of the Republic"; the second is addressed to the old friend in whose company he first met Carlyle.

To Miss Sara Norton

12 August, 1890.

. . . The streets were crowded [yesterday] as I never saw them before, and you met thousands of strangers, women as well as men, and the men with badges bearing the names of the states from which they had come, and the regiments to which they had belonged. It was

[1] Norton's object in making these books is set forth in a preface, from which the following passage is taken: "A taste for good reading is an acquisition the worth of ₁which is hardly to be overestimated. . . . The imagination is the supreme intellectual faculty, and yet it is of all the one which receives least attention in our common systems of education. The reason is not far to seek. The imagination is of all the faculties the most difficult to control, it is the most elusive of all, the most far-reaching in its relations, the rarest in its full power. But upon its healthy development depends not only the sound exercise of the faculties of observation and judgment, but also the command of the reason, the control of the will, and the quickening and growth of the moral sympathies. The means for its culture which good reading affords is the most generally available and one of the most efficient.

"To provide this means is the chief end of the *Heart of Oak* series of Reading Books. . . . The youth who shall become acquainted with the contents of these volumes will share in the common stock of the intellectual life of the race of which he belongs; and will have the door opened to him of all the vast and noble resources of that life."

interesting in itself, it struck many deep chords of memory. On one man's breast I read "Maine, 1st Volunteer Cavalry" and I remembered how in 1861, — Aunt Sara will recall the time, — when I had started to go to the front, with colours for our 20th regiment of Infantry, Col. Palfrey commanding it,[1]— I saw this regiment of Maine Cavalry, superb, 1200 strong, march up Fifth Avenue on their way to the war. It was a magnificent sight of men and horses, and the regiment afterwards did credit to its New England blood. It suffered terribly.

As I went along yesterday I read Pennsylvania, New Hampshire, Connecticut, Dakota, Iowa, Montana, California, and many other names of States on the breasts of the men, and for the time I forgot and forgave the dishonour which so many of these men in their clamour for pensions have done to their own good-name, and the ugly sequel which they are making to the story of the war. . . .

To Sir Mountstuart E. Grant-Duff

SHADY HILL, 1 September, 1890.

In one of his letters, that I was reading lately, Donne, the poet, says: "In such a spiritual thing as friendship time is of no account." And I was reminded of this by the pleasure which your letter gave me on its arrival three days ago. Were the days less full, each of its

[1] On his way to Washington in 1861, bearing the colours to which Norton refers in this letter, he was taken ill, and his address of presentation was read to the regiment by Dr. John Palfrey. The letter of Dec. 19, 1861, to Lowell from New York (see *ante* vol i. p. 247) was written when Norton's journey to the front was cut short by illness.

time-absorbing occupations, the interval between our letters would, I trust, be shorter. I should like to transfer myself for a time into the comparative tranquillity of the eighteenth century, and to draw leisurely breath, and to enjoy a meditative pause out of hearing of the steam-whistle, undisturbed by the fretful interruptions of electric wires, and (to cite Donne again),—

"But suck on country pleasures, childishly,
    Or lie snorting in the seven-sleepers' den."

But since this cannot be, and we must submit to living tired, the best we can do is to try to keep our souls quiet in spite of the rattle and bustle in the intellectual no less than in the physical world, and to write letters when we can! . . .

The two Addresses which came with your letter have interested me greatly. Your judgment of Arnold seems to me wise, though I am inclined to think somewhat more confidently of the permanence of the best of his prose, and I should assert more confidently my conviction that his poetry will, so long as our literature lasts, continue to hold a very high place in the hearts of the best lovers and soundest critics of poetry. His audience may never be large, but it will not be commonplace or inferior. He will have something better than popularity. . . .

Politics on this side of the ocean are not in so heated a term as on yours, but are bad enough. I am quite of your mind in regard to Gladstone. His influence is calamitous. In both countries we go stumbling along, but in neither do we fall. It is an anxious sight, but we may hope. . . .

To Leslie Stephen

ASHFIELD, 25 September, 1891.

I must write a word to you (altho' I have nothing worth saying,) before I go back to the routine of work at Cambridge, and to days in which letter-writing is like the grasshopper in the Psalm. I go back to a changed Cambridge. Before now there have been years enough when Elmwood stood empty, — but never vacant as it is now.

Much work lies before me. I have various things of my own to complete and clear out of the way, and then I have to see what is to be done with the mass of Lowell's papers.

The printers have in hand a little volume of literary essays of his, which will be made up of papers already published in some form or other, but never yet collected. You may know some of these essays, but you will find some that are new to you, and all of them of the best, — for I think I am not wrong in believing that he never wrote so well as in these last years, when his style, scintillating less than of old, has shone with a steadier and fuller light. This volume he himself had arranged for with the publishers.

Then I mean to publish, by and by, a selection of his letters, strung on a brief thread of Memoir. The number of his Letters for fifty years is very great, and the difficulty will be to make a choice among them. Will you let me have such letters of his to you and Mrs. Stephen as you are willing to entrust to me? . . .

What I may find among his mss. that will admit of

publication I do not yet know, but I have a strong hope
of finding his lectures on the Elizabethan Dramatists
in a tolerably complete shape. At any rate he shall not
blame me for printing what he might not wish to have
printed.

I hope you are doing well, and that the summer has
closed happily for you all. "Treat thyself well" as one
of the seven wise men said. . . .

To Miss Sara Norton
SHADY HILL, 18 October, 1891.

. . . The letters in relation to Uncle James's affairs
are numerous, and I have been arranging to bring out
in December a volume of Essays by him, all previously
printed but not yet collected. It will contain that
delightful paper of his on Gray, and the pleasant Walton essay, and that on the Areopagitica, and others
which you will remember when you see them.

Then the first volume of my translation of the D. C.
came out a week ago, and that brings letters; and the
printers are clamorous for completion of the second
volume, and that means many proof sheets and much
time taken in revision.

And beside this I have had to write an Introduction
to the new edition of the "Stones of Venice," and must,
this week, write one for the "Ariadne Fiorentina." . . .

Monday. I was writing those last words, my dearest
Sally, when Mr. Howells came in. He stayed for three
hours and was as pleasant, as interesting, as largely
sweet, humorous, and humane as you so well know
him to be. . . .

To Leslie Stephen

SHADY HILL, 14 November, 1891.

The copies of Lowell's letters to you have reached me safely, and I thank you for them, and for your own letter which came just in advance of them. I have not yet read Lowell's letters, but I shall do so soon, and I am sure that I shall find a great deal of himself in them, — the best thing one could find. In printing (by and by) such of them as shall seem best for publication, I will use the most sympathetic discretion in suppressing everything which you might justly prefer not to see in print. But I should not do justice to him, or to you, or to myself, were I to omit all evidence of the warmth of the affection in which he held you, or the very high and just estimate which he had of your work. You shall not be made to blush, but you shall not be treated as if the regard in which Lowell held you were no more than that in which he held a mere pleasant and friendly acquaintance. His affection for you was a part of himself, — an essential part, necessary for a true likeness of him.

The great mass of his letters which people send to me are of the trifling sort, of which every man of wide acquaintance writes a multitude, distinguished only by some characteristic touch of humour, or trait of kindliness, or grace of expression. They are precious enough to their recipients, but of no worth for publication. So far as I yet know, his letters to you, to Howells, to Tom Hughes, to Holmes, and to myself are those in which there is most interest. Possibly I should include those of H. James. I fancy your wife is right in regarding her letters from him as too personal and private for publication, but I wish she might find one or two which would show how he wrote to a woman for whom he felt so true and deep an affection, and yet were not altogether so private as to require inviolate seclusion.

I should be very glad if you would write "the few words" you suggest about your friendship. Not *too* few. They would fall in admirably with my plan. For, as I think I told you, I do not propose to make a formal biography. I shall state such facts as are necessary for giving the outline of the course of his really uneventful life, — uneventful I mean in the external sense; and for the understanding of his letters. And then I shall endeavour to illustrate his real life by his letters, and by such communications as yours would be.

There is an immense heap of papers to be looked over, and a large work of selection to be done, before I can begin putting the book together; and I have so much other work to do that some time must yet pass before I shall get to the book itself. . . .

Yes, my dear fellow, we will not let the years lay up for us any reproaches as regards each other. There are not many more years for us. All that may be left to us will be the better and the happier that we have loved each other so long.

Always your affectionate

C. E. N.

With love to Mrs. Stephen.

To J. B. Harrison

SHADY HILL, 18 November, 1891.'

. . . Mr. Lowell's loss to the nation is, I believe, the heaviest loss that could have fallen to it. He has done more than any man of our generation to maintain the level of good sense and right feeling in public affairs. He seems to me the best and most characteristic specimen of democratic manhood that New England has produced; an American such as Americans should be, with the rare and exceptional grace and charm of genius added to character.

I do not mean to write a Life of him. His was essentially a private life. I propose to put together a selection of his letters, which may take the place of an autobiographic narrative. . . .

The next letter, to Wendell Phillips Garrison, literary editor of the "Nation," is provided by Mr. W. R. Thayer, to whom as the unknown reviewer of Norton's volume, it was forwarded from the "Nation" office. It illustrates a quality of teachableness which, throughout Norton's life, served him in attaining the ends of high accomplishment.

To W. P. Garrison

CAMBRIDGE, 18 November, 1891.

The reviewer in the "Nation" of my translation of the "Inferno" has done me a real service in pointing out some of its defects; and the justice of his criticism in the particular instance he has selected, gives me a hope, which I should not otherwise have entertained, that his praise may also be trusted. At any rate the article has given me more pleasure than I expected from any criticism, as showing that there is one more competent scholar of Dante.

He has read my book with such care that I cannot but think he must have noted other passages besides those mentioned in the review, which may need correction, or are open to question. If this be so, he would do me a great favour would he take the trouble to point them out to me. I have far too little leisure for that *labor limæ*, on which a great part of the worth of such work as this translation must depend, and I therefore am the more glad to get such help as your reviewer gives me.

To Miss Sara Norton

Sunday, 22 November, 1891.

. . . The great pleasure of the day, my dearest Sally, was the arrival of your letter from Naples, your letter for my birthday, for which I thank you with all my heart. It made me wish more than ever that I could have been with you at Naples. The double stream of feelings and thoughts which has been coursing through your heart and mind while you were there, is one which I fully understand and sympathize with. There are always two aspects of Italy, — the one which appeals to the poetic imagination, the other which appeals to one's immediate sympathies, with a sense of the pathos of the lives of the vast mass of men, women and children, and the contrast between their squalor with the beauty of nature around them, and with the splendour and interest of the poetic and historic associations which add a deeper charm to the beauty of the scene. At the moment, they conflict with each other, each intensifying the other. But in the long run, in memory, the appeal to the imagination proves the stronger and the most abiding. There is hardly a greater delight in life than that which one who comes from a land and life like ours in America, experiences in the sense of the calling forth and growth of faculties of the imagination which find little nurture in our common and familiar experience; in the enjoyment not of imagination through the poets, through literature, but of the very sources by which our imaginations are developed and relieved from their half unconscious, but always pressing thirst. Our sympathies with the universal, continuous life of our own poor race are quickened and strengthened, — with its perpetual longings, passions and emotions, its pathetic joys and sorrows, its mistakes, its aspirations, its failures.

What you say of the conflicting feelings which the Catholic Church awakes in you is most true, and yet the abiding sentiment is what Dr. Johnson so well expressed when he said: "I never read of a hermit but in imagination I kiss his feet; never of a monastery but I fall on my knees and kiss the pavement." I cannot enter an old church, worn by the feet and the knees of generation after generation of those who have brought their cares, and sorrows, and desires there for relief, for comfort, for new hope, but my

heart shares with them in their emotions, and the
tawdry adornments and trifling *ex votos* only add to the
impression; they are the witnesses to the perpetual
incongruousness between the ideal and the realization
of it in expression. I wish I were with you. . . .

To Miss Sara Norton

March 3, 1892.

. . . I hope to get the volumes of Uncle James's
"Letters" published in the course of next winter.
They will make a sort of autobiography, of which the
earlier parts — of the years between leaving College
and his first going to Europe — will be of special
interest, for this was the happiest and most genially
productive period of his life. . . .

Since I began my letter your delightful letter from
the Hotel Mena has come to us. I am glad you stayed
there, and at Luxor, long enough to be filled with the
genius of each place. . . . I have been living there in
fancy with you, though my actual occupations have been
far remote in association. I am very busy with proof-
sheets of the Paradise, for the publishers want to get
the volume out in April. It is far the most difficult
portion of the poem to translate so that it shall be
intelligible to the common reader without requiring
more attention on his part than he is likely to be ready
to give to it, and the revision of the proofs takes many
hours. But it is interesting work. Then, too, I have
had to give a good deal of time to those "English
Readers" which have been so long in hand, and which
are now approaching their completion. . . .

Last Friday night I went to a most unusual, and, as it proved, really interesting entertainment at the Tavern Club, — the performance by some of the members of the Club of a great part of Beaumont and Fletcher's play, "The Maid's Tragedy." The chief parts were taken by Arlo Bates, Barrett Wendell, and Edward Robinson,[1] and the power of the play — it is deeply tragic — was shown in the fact that they were all lifted above themselves in performing it. Robinson, as Evadne the heroine, showed histrionic talent enough to move the feelings. . . . It was, altogether, extremely well done, and it was worth doing. . . .

To S. C. Cockerell [2]

SHADY HILL, 7 April, 1892.

MY DEAR SIR, — I thank you for your kind letter, — and I am much obliged to you for the notes which you have been good enough to send me in regard to some of the drawings of Mr. Ruskin. . . .

I should like to take this opportunity for putting on record a little fact which had fallen from Mr. Ruskin's memory when he wrote in "Præterita" of what he recalled as our first meeting. It was not on the Lake of Geneva that we first met, nor did I introduce myself to him as a stranger. In the autumn of the preceding year, through the intervention of a common acquaintance, Mr. Ruskin had been good enough to show me his Turners at Denmark Hill, and to ask me to come

---

[1] Director of the Metropolitan Museum, New York; one of Norton's earliest pupils.

[2] Since 1908 Director of the Fitzwilliam Museum, Cambridge; in 1892 he became Secretary to the Kelmscott Press.

again to see him on my return to England, which I
was just then leaving. It was natural enough that he
should forget this, for our Lake of Geneva meeting
was the real beginning of our friendship; but I am a
little sorry, for I do not like being represented (even by
his over-partial hand) as trespassing on the privacy
of a gentleman with whom I had no right to speak,
even if he himself did not think the worse of me for
doing so. . . .

To Leslie Stephen

SHADY HILL, 2 May, 1892.

. . . You have had a sad winter and spring. The
death of your wife's mother touches the heart only
with a natural sorrow; and the change in life wrought
by it, and the loss of what was most dear, are tender
and softening griefs. But the death of your nephew[1] is
of a different sort, — hard to bear because so untimely,
because such a bitter disappointment to natural hopes,
because such a breaking of promise. People talk of the
consolations of religion, but they seem generally to be
delusive. You and I, I believe, who have given them
up, stand really upon firmer ground for the meeting of
sorrow. To accept the irremediable for what it really
is, not trying to deceive one's self about it, or to elude it,
or to put it into a fancy dress, is to secure simple relations with life, and tends to strengthen the character
without, I trust, any hardening of heart or narrowing
of sympathies. It should save from cynicism and

[1] James K. Stephen, the author of *Lapsus Calami* and other verses
of great cleverness.

bitterness of temper. Much more might be said, —
but you long since said it.

What you tell me of yourself is good news, — that
you are well, and able to work, and that you find some
of your old essays better than you thought (though
you do not even yet think so well of them as I do, or
as they deserve), and that you will print them in
a volume in the autumn. I don't altogether like the
term "Apology." You remember George III's saying
about Bishop Watson's "Apology for Christianity."[1]
I want some word that shall express confidence, the
Agnostic *contra mundum*, secure on his rock of vantage.
But don't work too hard! I hope you have learned
something by experience, — scarcely any wise man, I
know, ever did learn anything in this way, but you
have the responsibility of being exceptionally wise, and
the author of the science of Ethics!

It seems to me that you have entire reason to be
pleased with the course the Lowell Memorial business
has taken. I think the Dean was right in his decision
that the Abbey itself must be reserved for Englishmen;
and the suggestion of the window, or windows, was
good. If ever any man not native to England deserved
a place in the Abbey it was Lowell, and it would have
been pleasant to read his name among those of the
poets whom he had cared for, and for whose fame he
had done so much. But with the uncertainties of the
future, it was better to let Longfellow alone represent
there the English-speaking race outside of England.

[1] That "he never before was aware that Christianity stood in need of
any apology."

Lowell being excluded, it will be easy to exclude the less fit, — and one can imagine strange figures rising in our democracies that are to be, as competitors for a place in the Abbey. If the Deans to come will be but choice enough in their admissions, they will do good service in thus maintaining the poetic tradition of the place. I would not turn anyone out who is now there, but hereafter I would keep out many better than some who have got in. . . .

I have ventured to give a note of introduction to you to "Joe Choate" as we call him here, — the leader of the New York bar, (or, one of the two leaders, Carter being the other); a man of great ability, and keenness of mind; an excellent wit, a pleasant speaker. . . . He has a conscience as well as a heart, though he does not parade them. He has had hardly a vacation for twenty years; he has had sorrows; he is tired, and he goes to England for refreshment. . . .

To Leslie Stephen

Shady Hill, 3 June, 1892.

. . . There is little news with us. Summer has come, — the season I delight in, wishing that it were longer. The College year is near its end, and brings a good deal of various work. Such time as I have for other things is largely occupied with Lowell's letters and other papers. This month's "Harper's Magazine" contains the first of his lectures on the Old English Dramatists. I hesitated about publishing them, for he did not think well of them, and they need his last revision. They are, indeed, not on the level of his best work, but there is so much excellence in them that it seemed to me on the whole that they should be printed. Next year I hope to bring out some of his earlier lectures on Poetry and the Poets, written in his prime, and crowded with all those fine qualities which were characteristic of his writing at its best. His later years are pathetic to me, as I read them over in his letters and his other writings. His powers were not diminished, but they had become too much dispersed. Could he have concentrated them he would have been as strong as ever. . . .

We are just entering on a Presidential campaign, — not a very good time for an optimist. Human nature is not at its best in a democracy at these periods. I wish I were not to see a newspaper for six months; and yet such inconsistency is mine that I shall read one every day, with ever increasing dislike of my fellow countrymen. Like Horace Walpole, I should love my country exceedingly if it were not for my countrymen. I trust that Cleveland may be nominated and elected; but there is marvellous confusion and uncertainty just now. . . .

To Mrs. Alexander Carlyle

ASHFIELD, MASSACHUSETTS, 17 September, 1892.

. . . I shall never regret the time which I have spent on the volumes that have come out under my editorship. To become intimately acquainted with Carlyle as I have done through reading and reflecting on all the letters and papers which you have entrusted to me is a privilege of no little worth. To come to know his weaknesses and errors as he himself exhibits them is but to learn a higher respect for the fundamental and essential traits of his nature and his character. My affection for him has been steadily confirmed. I owe to him more than ever, — and I thank you for this. . . .

The past summer has been a sad one for me in the protracted illness and the death of a friend who has been very dear and near to me for more than forty years, and who for a quarter of a century has had his summer home close to mine here, — Mr. George William Curtis. He has been "Uncle George" to my children ever since they could speak. No loss outside our own household circle could be heavier to us. He is, too, an irreparable loss to the country. He and Mr. Lowell are the two men who in their time have done the most for the civilization of America. No man was more widely beloved and trusted than he, and the expression of regard for him from all quarters of the land has been striking from its unanimity and touching from the depth of feeling which moved it. . . .

To Leslie Stephen

SHADY HILL, 1 March, 1893.

I have been so busy with proofsheets of Lowell's "Letters" and with putting Curtis's "Addresses" in order for publication that for some weeks I have been forced to give up letter-writing. I have wanted to write to you, to tell you how glad I was to see the "Agnostic's Apology" in a volume, and how good it seemed to me upon second reading. The reading of the volume makes me melancholy, because it compels the conclusion which one would rather avoid, that the

lovers of Truth are a very small band, — otherwise the
Agnostics would be in a majority. There are more of
them, indeed, than openly train in their ranks; and
this also may make a man melancholy, as a sign of the
timidity which rules the lives of the mass of one's
acquaintances. Democracy does not tend to cherish
courage. The independent grows less common. I do
not see how any man accustomed to use his reason can
resist the force of your argument, — unless, indeed,
like Lowell, he reject reason in favour of sentiment, or
of something which he called intuition. Such a position
is possible as we have known, — but as Montaigne
says: "Ces choses-là nous les trouverions autant ou
plus incroyables qu' aulcunes autres."

It is a satisfaction to read (save as it makes one
envious) such writing as yours; — strong, clear, and
with a pervasive humour which must at times compel
a smile even from the horror-stricken orthodox. . . .

In the interval that lies between the date of this
letter to Leslie Stephen and the next to Mr. Henry B.
Fuller of Chicago, Norton visited the Chicago World's
Fair — staying the while with the most hospitable of
friends, Mr. and Mrs. Franklin MacVeagh. Much as
he was impressed by the genius displayed by Daniel C.
Burnham [1] and others in making natural advantages
of lake and shore answer to their purpose, in the great
composition of the "Court of Honour" and its surroundings, it was in the panorama of American life at

---

[1] At the dinner given to Burnham in New York, (in 1894) after the
World's Fair, Norton presided, paying his tribute of admiration to Burnham's work in unstinted terms.

the Fair, and in its significance, that Norton took a still deeper interest.

To Henry B. Fuller

SHADY HILL, CAMBRIDGE, 30 October, 1893.

DEAR MR. FULLER, — It is almost a year since I received a very pleasant and interesting letter from you. I left it unanswered not from any lack of friendliness, but of set purpose, because it seemed to me to show that you were face to face with problems which were to be solved best by yourself, uninfluenced, for help or harm as it might be, by any counsel from another. "The Cliff-Dwellers" affords me the assurance that I was right. You have solved the problem for yourself, and in the best possible way. You have given proof of powers not displayed in your previous books. I do not mean that this new book affords a surprise to a lover of the old, provided only he had critical insight and literary perception. The realism of "The Cliff-Dwellers" was implicit in "The Chevalier."[1] It is the man of imagination, the poet, who alone sees things as they really are; it is the writer who has a natural genius for style who can present with equal worth the charm of Italy, or the repulsiveness of that aspect of Chicago which you depict. It is because Mr. Howells is essentially a poet that he sees and describes our American life with such insight and such worth. I put your work on the same shelf as his.

I said, "that aspect of Chicago which you depict," — because my recent visit there showed me another

[1] Mr. Fuller's novel, *The Chevalier of Pensieri-Vani*, appeared in 1891.

and a better aspect of it. I do not wonder that you detest the Chicago you have drawn, but I think you should have sympathetic admiration, nay, even affection, for the ideal Chicago which exists not only in the brain, but in the heart of some of her citizens. I have never seen Americans from whom one could draw happier auguries for the future of America, than some of the men whom I saw at Chicago. The Fair, in spite of its amazing incongruities, and its immense "border" of vulgarities, was on the whole a great promise, even a great pledge. It, at least, forbids despair.

Your disgust seems to me to have carried you too far in your book for its artistic perfection, and for its moral lesson. . . .

Sincerely yours,
C. E. NORTON.

[P.S. That you are a Chicagoan is one of the strongest grounds of my hope for Chicago, and belief in its becoming what it ought to be.

To Leslie Stephen
SHADY HILL, 13 March, 1894.

I heard last night of your brother's death. Although from what you have written to me I know that you would not have desired that his life should be prolonged, yet I know, too, what a heavy sorrow his death is to you, — all the sadder, perhaps, that it is accompanied with a sense of relief. It is one of those changes which alter the whole habit and aspect of life, — shutting up so many chambers to which nobody else has a key, increasing the solitary and silent part of life which

grows so disproportionate to the rest as we grow old
and lose those who have longest loved us, or been intimate with us. I feel sorry for you.

I recall your brother as he was in 1869, and the
recollections are all pleasant. He seemed to me to have
the most vigorous intelligence I had ever met, the most
capable, and the most typical of the general English
intelligence at its best, — I do not mean of its poetic
and ideal spirit, — but of that intelligence which by its
sturdy insistence on fact, its practical sense, its solid
self-confidence, its independence, its courage and its
honesty have made England what she is, as compared
with the rest of the world, — capable of fulfilling
imperial functions. He was very kind to me that
winter, smiling a little with quite warrantable superiority at my American freshness, amused at my patriotism which was warm then just after the war, but always
pleasant, and very kindly and serviceable. . . .

This is but a word of sympathy. I mean to write
again before very long. I have been busy all winter
with some lectures on Dante that I am to read at
Baltimore in two or three weeks. They have been a hard
and altogether unsatisfactory job. I have neglected
letter-writing, and have an aversion to the pen. . . .

To J. B. Harrison

SHADY HILL, 13 March, 1894.

. . . I agree with your view of the character of
our people, but it makes me less despondent than
it seems to make you. I do not wonder at their
triviality, their shallowness, their materialism. I

rather wonder that, considering their evolution and actual circumstances, they are not worse. Here are sixty or seventy millions of people of whom all but a comparatively small fraction have come up, within two or three generations, from the lower orders of society. They belong by descent to the oppressed from the beginning of history, to the ignorant, to the servile class or to the peasantry. They have no traditions of intellectual life, no power of sustained thought, no developed reasoning faculty. But they constitute on the whole as good a community on a large scale as the world has ever seen. Low as their standards may be, yet taken in the mass they are higher than so many millions of men ever previously attained. They are seeking material comfort in a brutal way, and securing in large measure what they seek, but they are not inclined to open robbery or cruel extortion. On the whole they mean "to do about right." I marvel at their self-restraint. That they are getting themselves and us all into dangerous difficulties is clear, but I believe they will somehow, with a good deal of needless suffering, continue to stumble along without great catastrophe.

The world has never been a pleasant place for a rational man to live in. I doubt if it is a worse place for him now than it has been in past times. . . .

To Leslie Stephen

ASHFIELD, 8 July, 1894.

To-day is Sunday, and in reckoning up my recent blessings, like a good Christian, I count two letters

from you within a month as among the best. But letters after all are but partial blessings and give no full
satisfaction.[1] Yours, which I have just been rereading,
make me wish that you were here this morning, sitting
opposite to me in the easy chair that we might talk at
large of many things, of which there is no room to say a
word even in short-hand within the narrow compass of
a page like this.

I have no one to talk with in these days with whom I
much care to talk. There are no friends to take the
place of those that are gone or are absent, — and, like
you, I feel the solitude stretching around me. The
pleasantest fields lie behind us. The sense of this must
weigh on you as you write the Life of your brother, all
the more because of the large vitality of his active years
and the large space which his figure filled. His big
frame and vigorous form were the fine type and image
of his intelligence. He wielded the broad-sword with
an easy strength and skill matchless in his time. . . . I
am sorry that this biography takes you off from your
own book. Possibly, however, it is a good break, and
you may come back to your own work to find more
pleasure in it than you were having when you wrote
last to me about it.

I came up here a week ago, with Sally as my only
companion, after being in Cambridge for Commencement, which this year was an occasion of unusual interest, because it was turned into the celebration of the
completion of the twenty-fifth year of Eliot's presi-

[1] In a letter to another friend Norton says, "Letters are good, but they
are poor substitutes for the spoken word, and my pen, never very flexible,
grows stiff with age."

dency. There was real warmth in the recognition and honouring of his great services to the University. I had to preside at the dinner (the best sentence in my speech was one I quoted from you) and not being able, as Eliot's cousin, to say what was due of him, I left this to Choate, the most brilliant and effective of our after-dinner speakers. . . .

Your extract from your brother's letter about the dinner at your house in 1868 brought back to me a memory of it, little more than σκιᾶς ὄναρ. The sorrow of my life not many years after blotted out the remembrances of much of the past. I could not have told who was at the dinner, but I recall the pleasantness of it, and the interest to me then a stranger, as it were, in London. . . .

To Nariaki Kozaki [1]

SHADY HILL, CAMBRIDGE, January 22, 1895.

DEAR MR. KOZAKI, — I was glad to receive your letter a month or two since, and to learn that you had a position in the college at Kyoto. The subjects in which you have to give instruction, the History of Philosophy and of Religion, combined with Ethics, are among the most interesting, as well as among those which a good teacher can make most serviceable to his students.

It certainly is a very curious condition of things that these subjects should be taught to Japanese students from Western text-books; it would seem better that

[1] A former pupil.

they should learn the History of Philosophy and of Religion from the Oriental point of view. To an outsider the intellectual condition of thinkers in Japan is somewhat unnatural. There has been nothing like it, so far as I know, in the history of civilization. This introduction of the ideas of other races into the lives of a race, so distinct and with such strongly marked intellectual traits of its own, looks from the outside as if the result could hardly be permanently satisfactory, and as if there must be an inevitable conflict between the long traditional modes of thought and the new teachings.

Another point that is exciting, of course, the interest of the whole Western world at this moment is the change which may be wrought in the Japanese ideals by their success in this war with China. The question cannot but arise as to the staying power of your people, as to whether the extraordinary development of Japan during the last generation is due to widespread national forces, or to conditions limited to a special superior class. If this development really rests upon national character, then it would seem that Japan may have a very large part to play in the world for a long time; but if it be a development confined to a comparatively small upper class, one cannot but ask whether it be not probable that the capacity of progress may be limited by exhaustion. Of course such a triumph as Japan has thus far had in the war is a most dangerous and intoxicating draught for a people. If the Japanese exhibit moderation in proportion to the vigour which they have already displayed, they will give evidence of a character from which very much may be hoped for the future.

> With all good wishes, I remain,
> Sincerely Yours,
> C. E. NORTON.

The work to which Norton refers in the next letter — a by-product of his editorial labours, yet one involving a scholarship the others did not demand —became a great interest with him, and led to his collection of the Donne manuscripts now in the Library of Harvard University.[1]

To Mrs. Alexander Carlyle

SHADY HILL, CAMBRIDGE, 4 March, 1895.

. . . Mr. Lowell left a copy of Donne's poems, (which have never been properly edited,) profusely corrected in regard to punctuation, which was in a most confused state. It seemed a pity that this work of his should not be made available, and a printing society in New York — the Grolier Club— undertook the issue of and edition of Donne's poems for its members, to exhibit Mr. Lowell's corrections. I thought that the editing of it would be a slight task, but I soon found that a minute comparison of all the editions of the poems in the seventeenth century was desirable, in order that the various readings might be given in foot-notes, and that an introduction and explanatory notes were also required. The work has consequently demanded much reading,

---

[1] See *The Poems of John Donne*, The Grolier Club, New York, 1895; also *The Love Poems of John Donne*, ed. by C. E. Norton. Houghton, Mifflin & Co., 1905.

and has occupied much time. I am just now correcting
the last proof-sheets, and am glad to have come to the
end. . . .

To Henry B. Fuller

CAMBRIDGE, 30 May, 1895
Decoration Day.

. . . I am grateful to-day to you for "The Chevalier," and I shall be grateful years hence as I am now
for "With The Procession." It is a painful book,
hardly less so than "The Cliff-Dwellers," but this is at
once evidence of its worth and of its power. It raises a
somewhat serious question, whether such life is fit subject for literary art, and whether the record of it is the
best work which you can do for Chicago — for it is
after all for Chicago that we are all working, — Chicago, or New York, or Denver City, however our
democracy may call its palace-hovels. To be brief, I
hold with the poets and the idealists; not the idealiz-
ers, but those who have ideals, and, knowing that they
are never to be realized, still strive to reach them
and to persuade others to take up the same quest.
I believe that your "Chevalier" has done more for
Chicago than any of the true Chicagoans whom you
have given to us, "twice as natural" as life. . . .

An article on "The Poetry of Rudyard Kipling,"
bearing Norton's signature, in the "Atlantic Monthly"
for January, 1897, speaks indirectly for that capacity
for friendship with younger men which marked his later
years, and directly for an appreciation of poetic meth-

ods strikingly different from those of the earlier time in which Norton's own taste was formed. The nephew of his friend Lady Burne-Jones, had, of course, a special claim upon his heart. The warmest relations followed upon Kipling's coming to America: but Norton could not have written as he did about Kipling's work without a genuine openness to the modern appeal. The words with which his article ended throw light upon both the poet and the critic: "It is enough now gratefully to recognize that he continues the great succession of royal English poets, and to pay him the homage which is his due."

Norton's openness to the modern appeal in literature or art needs in this connection a word more of interpretation. That he greeted such work, as Kipling's, William Vaughn Moody's, Mr. George E. Woodberry's, Mr. Henry B. Fuller's, Mr. Santayana's, Mr. Irving Babbitt's,—it is enough to mention these names,—not only with sympathy born of delight for all that was fine in it, but with genuine liking and understanding of new methods, was not at all to lessen or obscure his dislike of that which savoured of "fad" or insincerity in art. Work undertaken in some sort *pour épater le bourgeois* was in every sense detestable to him. He says characteristically (in July, 1895) in a letter to his eldest daughter: "But the best poem since 'McAndrew' is 'A Fleet Street Eclogue,' by John Davidson, which was privately printed by Mr. Lane, the publisher of the 'Yellow Book,' when he was here a month or two ago, and which now appears alas! in the wretched Y. B. itself,—a vile

place for a manly, hearty genuine-English poem, with
no touch of decadence in it."

During Norton's last illness it was striking to notice
how frequently he recurred to poems he cared for by
some of the writers we have mentioned: as an instance
of this, he repeated a few days before his death
Moody's fine lyric, beginning "Of wounds and sore
defeat," and ending on the note of triumph and confidence —

> "O hearken where the echoes bring,
> Down the grey disastrous morn,
> Laughter and rallying!"

As in literature, so in the visual arts. Norton's
great interest in and admiration for the beautiful work
in engraving done by Cole, Closson, Wolf, Kruell, is a
side-light on this quality in his nature, that his letters
to young writers can but partly illustrate. A passage
from a letter of Lafcadio Hearn's about modern illustration is so descriptive of Norton's point of view that
it may be quoted, since better words could hardly be
found: "I am not of those who can persuade themselves anything is more intrinsically valuable because
it is old. I think I have seen drawing just as fine as
that of Hokusai, Kunisada, etc., made only a couple of
years ago, and merely by way of cheap popular illustration. Nay, I even think much of the drawing now
being done is better than the average of the old drawing. Of course we miss two things, — the ancient
fancy and the ancient colour." These words might
be Norton's own.

To Leslie Stephen

ASHFIELD, 8 July, 1895.

MY DEAR FRIEND, — Your letter, so wholly natural and right, sad as it is, is yet a comfort to me. At least you are not broken down by this heaviest of blows.[1] There is still something left to be done in life, and love for her whom you have lost supplies the strongest and, in a sense, the happiest motive for doing it. If only in her absence you can keep your health! In this matter one must strive against one's own desires, — for one would like to die. But one has to learn to live without joy, and without the hope of it. The hardest time is, perhaps, yet to come, when the excitement of immediate sorrow and the need of constant strenuous effort is past; when the dreary routine of the joyless days begins, and when the sense of solitude and of diminished personality weighs heavier and heavier. The death of her whom one has wholly loved is the end of the best of one's-self. I have often told my children that they have never, since their early childhood, known me. There is no help for this, — after her death the springs of life are fed from the outside, the natural vein ceases to flow.

I do not wonder at what you say of your book.[2] One no longer cares directly for what is said of one's work; it is only as it might please her. I am glad of what you tell me, — that your wife had read it and liked it, and

[1] Mrs. Stephen died May 5, 1895. This letter of Norton's is in answer to Stephen's of June 28, 1895, about his duty to his remaining household. See Maitland's *Stephen*, p. 441.

[2] Stephen's Life of his brother Sir James Fitzjames Stephen appeared in 1895.

been proud of it. I think you may trust her judgment entirely. I finished it last night, and I have read it not only with unusual interest as a biography, but with unalloyed pleasure as a piece of work of the highest quality, every way worthy of you. . . . The race typified by such a man is the best the world has known. The most striking trait in Fitzjames's character is the steadiness of his self-education and self-development. I know no other example of such constancy of progress, of such a process of maturing and enlarging. The pity of it is that it seems so cut short. One can fancy how he would have gone on had his life lasted strong for ten years more. The ripening of his poetic imagination, which had already begun, would have given completeness to his soul, and interpreted and extended the conclusions of his intelligence. It is curious that you had occasion to mention Shakespeare but once. He must have cared for the historical plays, if not for Hamlet. It is a book that cannot but be of service to young men. Your last page will be justified by its effect. . . .

To W. D. Howells

ASHFIELD, 28 July, 1895.

Had I been sure where you were, you would have had a letter from me two or three weeks ago. I wanted to thank you for your "Literary Passions," — a delightful new kind of a book, two sorts of the best mingled in an unnamed better compound, half autobiography and half criticism. The spirit of the little book is as good as its design. It is a genuine human "document" (I would not use the cant term had it not a very special application) and it gives evidence, the worth and significance of which in its testimony for America and for the progress of civilization, you are the last person to appreciate and to believe in.

Every now and then I find myself at serious issue with some of your mature convictions,—but for the sum total I have nothing but sympathy and heartiest acceptance. It is a delightfully sincere, generous, and humane book.

I am sorry for what you say (p. 212) about "the beautiful," — for you mean the sensually or externally beautiful; and yet you include in your condemnation what is really the highest end of life. Beauty seems to me the ultimate expression and warrant of goodness; there can be no ideal aim without it; and the better the ideal, whether shaped in visible form, or incapable of presentation to the dull senses, the more beautiful it is. There is no mysticism in this. It seems to me an ultimate and precious truth. So, too, on the last page I do not like to have you say that the supreme art in literature made you set art forever below humanity. The antithesis is not correct. There is no common measure. Is not Art, properly understood, the expression of humanity? What you mean by it here, I presume, is the technical method which it is the aim of so-called artists to acquire, the "art" to which men devote themselves at the cost it may be of their humanity; but not the art of the great artists through whom Nature has uttered the voice of the world. — But enough.

The book makes me the more sorry for the determination to which you have come about the Life of

Lowell, and of which you tell me in this welcome letter.
. . . I see the force of some of the reasons which have
led you to this conclusion, and in view of them I am
quite ready to give up any formal Biography. There
is, perhaps, no need of one. The biographies of Emerson, of Motley, of Longfellow, of Whittier, depict the
conditions of the times well enough. Lowell's personal
adventures were few, and though, no doubt, an interesting book could be made of his "Life," the man
himself does not require it for his fame, nor does the
country need it for its own good. But might you not
carry out your own suggestion when we first spoke of
the matter, — but perhaps in a modified form, — and
make a volume of mingled reminiscence, criticism, and
narrative, which should serve all the essential purposes
of a biography? I could not write his "Life." Even
if I had "art" enough, I was too near him, and for
many years he made too much of my life for me to
treat him with the detachment required in such a
biography as he deserves. Do think favourably of the
new plan. . . .

To Leslie Stephen

ASHFIELD, 13 August, 1895.

. . . Thus far the summer has been a very quiet one
for us at home. As usual I brought a good deal of work
which had been accumulating on my hands, in the hope
of doing it here in the leisure of vacation; but, as
usual, I have been disappointed in the amount I have
been able to accomplish. The longest summer days are
too short, and too full of temptations. The garden, and

the hills, and the woods, solicit one to leave books and desk,— and I often yield. I have been writing lately a sketch of Longfellow's life, to serve as introduction to an edition of his poems in one volume which is to appear in England. I thought it would be an easy task, but I have not found it so. To write for alien readers about what was so familiar to myself, to give a general outline of what lay in my memory as a series of particulars, not to take too much or too little for granted, made it slow work,— and the result does not please me at all.

While at work I have been living in the past, with innumerable bright and tender recollections. I was about nine years old when he, twenty years older, came to live at Cambridge. He at once became an intimate at our house, and made himself beloved by us children as by our elders, and from that time for forty-five years he was one of the pleasantest and kindest of friends,— one of the standbys of life. . . .

To E. L. Godkin

SHADY HILL, 13 October, 1895.

When I saw, a week or two ago, the announcement of your forthcoming volume, it set me thinking of the time when our friendship began, and of how much I owed to Olmsted for his bringing us together. It was a happy time for us both. And in the thirty years that have passed since then, your friendship has been one of their great blessings. If during late years we have seen less of each other than I could wish, and known less of the course of each other's daily life, I have felt the loss to myself deeply, and at the same time have felt sure that our inmost sympathies remained unchanged, and that, could we be together, we should find our common convictions strengthened by each other's thought, and our affections as warm as ever.

Even when longest silent I have kept in intellectual touch with you, and have often and often wished that I could strengthen your heart and your hands in the work for the nation which you were doing with such unmatched fidelity and power.

I know no one who has better reason to look back on his past life with satisfaction in the use which he has made of it, and in the service which he has rendered to his fellows, than you.

And now comes your note proposing to dedicate your volume to me.[1] My dear fellow, you make me proud and pleased and humble. I feel at once how little I have done to deserve such an expression, and yet in a sense I feel not unworthy of it, for there is no man who would be more pleased, because of his regard for you, to have his name thus associated with your work. . . .

To W. D. Howells

SHADY HILL, 3 November, 1895.

One joy you have in life which cannot suffer change and which has no counterbalancing pain, — that of the good you do and the pleasure you give to others. And this beautiful sad volume of your Poems, which you have sent to me with words very dear to me, touches

[1] Godkin's book, *Reflections and Comments*, 1895, was dedicated: " To CHARLES ELIOT NORTON, to whom the foundation of the *Nation* was largely due, in grateful acknowledgement of a long friendship."

my heart for good, and gives me a pleasure which, if grave and even mournful, is not the less a happiness. These poems of yours "say for me what I could not say," and mostly express my soul no less than yours. But for me they are, as it were, Part I, and in the absence of Part II I recognize the difference in our temperaments, and I cannot but wish with all my heart that I had more of your tenderness, and that you had more of my freedom from trouble in the acceptance of the limitations and the sorrows of life.

Your voice is strangely in harmony with those of the poets who have felt most deeply and suffered most from the riddles and paradoxes of life. One hears in it the tone of the voices of the Greeks, and might match each of its utterances with the sweet verses of the Anthology. Here is one which came into my memory as I read your book: "How can one escape from thee, O life, without dying? thy sorrows are myriad and neither to escape from them nor to endure them is easy. Sweet are thy beautiful things, — the earth, the sea, the stars, the circles of the moon and the sun, but all the rest are fears and pains, and if a good thing befall to one a corresponding Nemesis follows." There are a hundred strains like this.

I cannot read "Change" without tears, — and blessing. . . .

To Sir Mountstuart E. Grant-Duff

SHADY HILL, CAMBRIDGE, 8 November, 1895.

The fault of this section of your Diary, which I herewith return to you with my cordial thanks for the pleasure I have had in reading it, is that of being too short. I ask for more. . . . Do a little for us as Horace Walpole did for Sir Horace Mann. So long as your Journal is intrusted only to prudent persons, pray let them have the benefit of your judgments of men, and of policies. I should, for instance, greatly like to know your opinion of Arthur Balfour, and your auguries concerning him. I find him an interesting subject of speculation, — a curious mingling of the Scotch and the English intellect, an example of inconsistent faculties and dispositions, now a mere theorist, now admirably practical, sceptical, and superstitious, a good logician but often a poor reasoner, half fit to be a professor of metaphysics in a Scotch University, and unquestionably one of the few masterly leaders of the House of Commons. Is the professor or the statesman to grow in him? Which of the traits of his youth is to harden and strengthen in the passage to middle age? Chamberlain is another of the men concerning whom I wish you would speak. I feel less perplexity about him, for he is of a less complex type, and of one more familiar to an American.

Were I to keep a Journal like yours, it would be mainly occupied with public affairs, for social life in America is not rich in memorabilia. The rise of Democracy is for the time fatal to social accomplishments and arts. What its future is to be in these respects cannot yet be prophesied. Even our Universities, as seats of social culture, suffer from the lack of appreciation in the world outside of this special element of civilization. . . .

To Leslie Stephen

SHADY HILL, 8 January, 1896.

. . . The year has begun quietly and happily enough
for us all at home, but the outer world makes a dark
background for the happiest private life. Cleveland's
Venezuela message fell like a thunderbolt out of a clear
sky. It shattered with its stroke his reputation with all
serious and right-thinking men. He had been trusted
to stand firm against the rising tide of Jingoism. That
he should have yielded to it is both a disappointment
and a calamity, —a calamity because it has done much
to encourage the expression, and, by so doing, to increase the force, of the worst spirit of our democracy.
No one can have watched the conditions, during the
last few years, of public sentiment in America without anxiety, because of the manifest growth of a barbaric spirit of arrogance and of unreasonable self-as-
sertion, and especially of a hostile disposition towards
Great Britain. One might cherish a hope, though but
faint, that no opportunity would arise for its display
in overt act; that time might bring a change. I had
looked forward with solicitude to the prospect of
the incoming of a Republican and jingo administration
at the end of Cleveland's term. No one had had a
thought that Cleveland himself would fail, so long as
he was in office, to resist the popular disposition toward
war.

But, there is a deeper consideration. The rise of the
democracy to power in America and in Europe is not,
as has been hoped, to be a safeguard of peace and

civilization. It is the rise of the uncivilized, whom no school education can suffice to provide with intelligence and reason. It looks as if the world were entering on a new stage of experience, unlike anything heretofore, in which there must be a new discipline of suffering to fit men for the new conditions. I fear that America is beginning a long course of error and of wrong, and is likely to become more and more a power for disturbance and for barbarism. The worst sign is the lack of seriousness in the body of the people; its triviality, and its indifference to moral principle. . . .

I had much the same feeling as you in regard to Matthew Arnold's Letters, that there were too many with nothing in them worth printing. Yet when I came to the end of the volumes I could not but wish that there were still more of the book, — it gave such a pleasant impression of him. One needed to see him under conditions of intimacy to know him as he really was, and to know him thus, meant to love him. All the little vanities, all the lack of humour in relation to himself, all the little artificialities, disappeared or changed their aspect, and you found him one of the simplest and sweetest of men, not taking himself too seriously, quite ready to smile at himself, absolutely unpretending, invariably pleasant, cheerful and sympathetic. The freshness of his interest in people and things, his real perspicacity and his essentially generous nature made him a delightful companion; and his poetry added charm to his intercourse. . . .

Your affectionate
C. E. N.

A fortunate circumstance of the final years of Norton's life was the late ripening of a friendship, chiefly expressed through correspondence, with Samuel G. Ward of Washington, the friend and correspondent of Emerson. The intercourse between him and Norton was like that of two seafarers who had sailed in youth from the same port, and, meeting near the end of life, sat down to bridge the intervening years and weigh the new against the old.

To S. G. Ward

SHADY HILL, CAMBRIDGE, 16 February, 1896.

No letter for a long time has given me so much pleasure as yours, and yet it gave me a fresh sense of loss in your being so far away. Years have not filled the gap you left. The younger generation is a good one, but the interests and convictions of most of the younger set are different from those of us who were born in the first half of the century. The change from '46 to '96 is not the natural change wrought by any fifty years, it is the change of an era.

Brimmer's death takes away almost the last of the men who remained to me as real companions. I send you a few words about him which I wrote for the Trustees of the Museum.

Your approval of my paper in "The Forum"[1] is a great satisfaction to me. I might be tempted to write more, if I could convince myself that it would be of service. But work of this kind is like Mrs. Partington's broom. One can note the rising of the tide, and that is

[1] "Some Aspects of Civilization in America." *The Forum*, Feb. 1896.

about all. . . . The one comfort in these last weeks has been the manner in which English public men and the English press have treated our provocation. It is an encouragement as regards the real progress of civilization. But on the other hand it brings home the contrast which the manners and temper of our government and people exhibit to it. . . .

To Leslie Stephen

SHADY HILL, 20 March, 1896.

It is too long since I last wrote to you, but I get no time for letter-writing. Every day my heart bids me write, but the cares of this world choke the word. One of the great evils of Democracy is that everybody thinks he has a right to put what questions he pleases to anybody, and to devastate his day. Here is a man who writes from Osceola, Missouri, on a sheet with a printed heading, *Solum sapientem esse divitem*, asking about Latin versions and comments on the "Divine Comedy"; here is a poor schoolmistress in Texas (perfect strangers both) writing to enquire about the best historical manuals, and the best way of teaching English; and here another woman in Alabama wanting to know the proper pronunciation of Hiawatha, —! and so on *ad infinitum*. As I look up, my eye catches an immense roll of proofsheets, sent to me by my friend Furness, the editor of Shakespeare, which he wants me to look over. I ought to be reading them now, — but they shall lie over.

The days have run quietly with us. For a fortnight in February we had a pleasant, accomplished young

Russian, Prince Serge Wolkonsky, staying with us, while he was giving some lectures at the Lowell Institute and here at Harvard, on Russian History and Literature. He was in America two years as one of the Russian Commissioners at the World's Fair, and he was with us for a few days then. He is one of the finer products of that *terre vierge*, of which a little plot has been highly cultivated while the great stretch of it remains in its native wildness. He is a man of refined taste and delicate perceptions, with all sorts of gifts, a delightful musician, master of half a dozen languages, writing English with a freshness of diction and a sense of the rhythm and intricate construction of the language which excites my envy, a lover of the arts, a writer of stories full of sympathetic insight into the delicacies and reserves of character, a critic with excellent appreciation, — and yet of a type as far removed from any of English or American origin as if he belonged to another century. He has come here to lecture, burning with the desire of a man who has been bred with all the exclusive privileges of the highest aristocracy of his country, to measure himself as man without rank or title with other men. And he has succeeded in winning recognition. His lectures have been as good as if he were a professional author.

He would like to have the chance of lecturing at Oxford or Cambridge, and it would not be a bad thing for the Universities, for he really presents Russia and her literature as nobody has heretofore done it, and his lectures are interesting enough to attract even undergraduates. It is the opportunity and the honour which he wants; a pecuniary honorarium is matter of little consequence.

Public affairs are depressing. I am not cynic enough not to feel sorry, disappointed, and at times disheartened. It is hard to have the whole background of life grow darker as one grows old. I can understand the feeling of a Roman as he saw the Empire breaking down, and civilization dying out. It will take much longer than we once hoped, for the world to reorganize itself upon a democratic basis, and for a new and desirable social order to come into existence. But if we set our hope far enough forward we need not lose it. . . . .

To Sir Mountstuart E. Grant-Duff

SHADY HILL, 19 April, 1896.

I have much to thank you for, — two letters of great interest, your volume of "Brief Comments," and your late Address to your old constituents. As I read your address, distinguished by its judicial temper and its wide and wise survey of existing political conditions, I could not but feel a renewed wish that you were still in Parliament and in office.

Your approving reference to my recent paper in the Forum gave me great pleasure. But, in office or out, you are doing good service. You remember Seneca's fine sentence: "Nunquam inutilis est opera civis boni: auditu enim, visu, vultu, nutu, obstinatione tacita, incessuque ipso prodest." I happened to read it this morning.

The clouds are for the moment less threatening than

when I last wrote to you, but they do not break away. The thunder is muttering all round the horizon, and I do not believe that the storm has blown by for good. The conditions in Germany, in France, in the United States are tending to war rather than to peace. Our generation has been too hopeful. We gave too much credit to the influence of material things in securing a better order of society, — to free-trade, to the increased ease and frequency of communication between nations by means of steam and electricity; and we did not take sufficiently into account the inevitable slowness of the process of civilization of the masses of men who were rising to power. The Democracy has been a disappointment in its incapacity to rise morally in proportion to its rise in material welfare and in power. We ought not to have been disappointed, but there are some excuses for our lack of foresight.

We certainly have lived in the most interesting period of the world's history, — far more interesting than the period into which our children were born; for we had the advantage of knowing the old things before their strength was sapped, and of sharing in the splendour of the poetic and imaginative expression of the mid years of the century. How silent are the fields of poetry now compared with the time when we were young! . . .

Recurring to the death of Martin Brimmer, mentioned in the letter to Samuel G. Ward of which a portion has just been used, Norton wrote, April 20, 1896, to Edward Lee-Childe — in characteristic and significant words: "Brimmer's death is a great loss to me. He leaves no one like him in Boston; few like him anywhere. The true gentleman is as rare as the true genius, and democracy in its present stage is not favourable to the existence of either. There are many excellent and worthy men, but very few who care for, or are capable of practicing, the social art, that finest of the dramatic arts, in which the individual nature expresses itself in modes of ideal pleasantness and refinement."

To Samuel G. Ward

SHADY HILL, 26 April, 1896.

Your very interesting letter of two months ago has given me much food for reflection. I do not know what "apples of gold in pictures of silver" means, but it is a pretty phrase and indicates treasures of some sort, and so it fits your words.

You say that Democracy insures a teachable people; in a sense, yes. But I do not feel sure that it is not becoming less open to any teaching but that of its own experience. The scorn of wisdom, the rejection of authority, are part and parcel of the process of development of the democracy. The rapid growth of its prosperity and power in this country has given to it an extravagant self-confidence, and disposes it to make self-will the rule of conduct. It seems to me not unlikely that for a considerable time to come there will be an increase of lawlessness and of public folly, — and that the calamities resulting from these conditions are to be the hammers by which better dispositions and better conditions are to be slowly beaten out on the anvils of time.

Democracy, ideally, means universal public spirit; practically it exhibits itself in its actual phase as general selfishness and private spirit. Universal suffrage proves not a means of increasing the sense of individual responsibility, but a distinct source of moral corruption. The venal vote in New Hampshire, Rhode Island and Connecticut grows larger every year in proportion to the total vote. Men are not worse than they were, but they are exposed in larger numbers to temptations which they are not prepared to resist, and which are threatening to the public welfare.

At any rate there is one consoling reflection, that there are far more human beings materially well off to-day than ever before in the history of the world; and if you and I could have the choice, there is no period at which we would have rather lived, and none in which we could have lived with so much satisfaction in the condition of the generality of our fellows. I believe, indeed, that the very pleasantest little oasis of space and time was that of New England from about the beginning of the century to about 1825. The spirit of that time was embodied in Emerson, in Longfellow, in Holmes and in Lowell. It was an inexperienced and youthful spirit, but it was a happy one; it had the charm of youth, its hope, its simplicity, its sweetness.

How interesting our times have been and still are! None ever so interesting, or so full of change and of problems!

Let me commend to you Leslie Stephen's recently published volumes on "Social Rights and Duties." The title hardly covers the range of thought in the book. The last essay on "Forgotten Benefactors" is one of the most beautiful and touching personal commemorations ever written. . . .

To Miss Sara Norton

SHADY HILL, 30 October, 1896.

MY DEAREST SALLY, — . . . After you left us yesterday our day was entirely quiet and usual, but the Concert in the evening was out of the common, both for the beauty of the music and the perfection of the performance of it. The familiar Aria from Bach was the best of all. Kneisel took the leading part, and I never heard him play with more complete mastery or more exquisite expression. He was perfectly supported by the orchestra, and to hear such a piece so played was, indeed, a rare pleasure. In sentiment, too, it was not merely appropriate but adequate to express the feeling of the occasion. I wished for you to hear it. The audience felt the excellence of the performance and applauded with genuine heartiness at the close. The Tschaikowski Concerto was one of his pieces of brilliant display and barbaric excess, and the piano part was well played by a performer with fine technique but with a hard, dry touch, a very fit interpreter of music of this sort. . . .

The dogs are well, but when I came from town at two o'clock I found them both almost exhausted and each slightly wounded from a fight, whether with each other or with a strange dog no one knew. They seemed on perfectly friendly terms, so that I suspect they had been fighting with a stranger. It is past six o'clock, and I take this to the post. . . .

To Miss Sara Norton

SHADY HILL, 24 March.

. . . I went last night to hear Mr. Bonaparte on Civil Service Reform. It was an excellent and interesting address, of sound thought excellently expressed, — the work of a gentleman and a thinker. The mere sight of a Bonaparte in such a position is interesting, and suggests a thousand associations, and curious interweavings on the loom of time. And this Charles Jerome B. looks enough like his mighty great-uncle to be his son, — the build of his head and body are Napoleonic, and so are his unconscious attitudes and holdings of himself. . . .

To Miss Sara Norton

SHADY HILL, 30 May, 1897.

MY DEAREST SALLY, — Your letter from Brantwood came to me at sunset yesterday, a fit close to a beautiful day. Your account of my dear old friend touched my heart deeply, and brought tears to my eyes. I am thankful that you have seen him. . . . I had been afraid lest you might find him in a condition which it would have been painful to you to witness, but your description of his peacefulness of mind, and of his capacity still to take some pleasure in the beauty of the world, of his sweet recognition of you, and of his half-dreamy but tender remembrance of the past, and of his fidelity to old affections, gives me a sad but not sorrowful content, and these days which you have passed at Brantwood will leave for me, as well as for you, lasting memories which will associate themselves naturally and sweetly with all that is happiest in our recollections of the great spirit and generous heart which are now but shadows of their former self. . . .

That the days at Brantwood should have been sun- shiny, after such cold bleak weeks as you have had, adds the crowning touch to them. The lake, the mountains, the moors, the trees in their loveliness of the colour and growth of the Spring season, the prim- roses, all make up quite a perfect landscape and setting for the rare human experience. . . .

To Goldwin Smith

ASHFIELD, 14 June, 1897.

You gave me a great pleasure in sending to me two or three months ago a copy of your book on the "Riddle of Existence." It was a great satisfaction to me to find myself in entire agreement with you on every main point, and to have my own convictions set forth with such lucidity, temperance, and force. Pos- sibly I regret less than you do the giving up of the old faith, and the being compelled to renounce as hopeless every attempt to solve the problems which excite our curiosity. The position toward the universe in which we find ourselves seems to me on the whole the manliest which has been attained. We are thrown back on our own resources to make the best of our lives. A new

sense of responsibility is aroused in us, and, by the
narrowing of the limits of our hopes and expectations,
we find ourselves more capable of using our faculties
for legitimate and rational ends. I do not find it hard
to quench the eagerness of curiosity about the unknowable, and to accept as sufficient this brief, incomprehensible existence on earth. Man seems to me to be
for the most part in a very early stage of development,
and the loss of religious faith among the most civilized
portion of the race is a step from childishness toward
maturity. That it will have many sad results I do not
question, that the progress will be very slow and irregular is certain, but in the long run I have no fear in
regard to improvement in the general morality of the
race. Our morals seem to me the result and expression
of the secular experience of mankind. As such they
have a solid foundation. The doctrine of love is the
one ultimate achievement in this field. And the
validity of that doctrine as the rule of life is but
confirmed by such convictions as you and I have
reached.

The progress of freethinking seems to me, in spite of
ecclesiastical reaction and resistance, much greater in
England than America. I was interested in seeing in
the last sheets of Grant Duff's "Diary" (which I
suppose he sends to you from time to time as he does to
me) what he says of your book, — to the effect that its
conclusions are sufficiently familiar to all educated
persons, implying that they are also accepted by them.
Now that is certainly not true as regards educated
persons in America. No doubt many such persons have

reached similar conclusions, but the timidity which seems to be one of the intellectual conditions of the present stage of democracy, prevents them from giving expression to their convictions. In my own circle I find myself almost solitary in my open profession of free-thinking. . . .

I hope the years go well with you. They treat me kindly for the most part, but they leave me solitary. Child was the last of my near friends to be taken. His loss makes a great change in life for me.

I am, as of old,

Affectionately yours,

C. E. NORTON.

To Leslie Stephen

ASHFIELD, 19 June, 1897.

. . . I am just finishing the "Life" of Jowett. I have been much interested in it. I knew Jowett just enough to have a personal impression of him, in the main a very pleasant one, and to be curious to know more of him. The biography, especially the second volume, seems to me very good, for it gives a clear image of a most paradoxical character, of which his face and head were the type, in their combination of strength and weakness, of simplicity and subtlety, of openness and of reserve. His intellectual and moral nature was a strange compound of clearness and confusion, of cour-age and cowardice, of honesty and self-deception. The ecclesiasticism of Oxford was his ruin. If he, like you and Goldwin Smith and Clough, had broken loose from the bondage, it would have been well with him.

It is striking to see the evil wrought on a man's soul by being forced to justify his position by sophistry, of the sophistical nature of which he is himself conscious. Carlyle's saying, which Jowett naturally found objectionable, went to the root of the matter, "The sentinel who deserts should be shot." Jowett's plea of reform from within was only specious; it was revolution, it was destruction in which he was engaged, — and yet he signed the Articles.

Nothing has pleased me more in the book than Jowett's feeling toward modern metaphysics. They exercise the same allurement and produce the same evil effects here at Harvard as they have done at Oxford. There is no worse school for the training of the intelligence, if metaphysics be taken, as it is commonly accepted, as *la recherche de l'absolu*, and the investigation of the unknowable. At the close of his life he had not much left of the old-fashioned religious faith. He was like an old dowager who has found out that her heirloom diamonds are after all only paste, yet still goes on wearing them to make a show in the world, which has begun to suspect them, and because she herself is fond of them from old association. When he comes to writing of God as "the great overruling law of progress in the world, whether personal or impersonal," he does not differ much from Mat Arnold.

If you write anything about the book or about Jowett, do not neglect to tell me of it or to send it to me.

Another interesting book which I read lately is Goldwin Smith's "Guesses at the Riddle of Existence,"

— which, I take it, you have read also. It contains little or nothing new, but it defines with great clearness the positions which are held by thoughtful men who do not shrink from admitting the consequences of their convictions. . . . I am pleased that Oxford should have given an honorary degree to Godkin. He deserves more public recognition than he has had. His virtues as well as his defects have made him unpopular. The Overseers of Harvard refused some years ago to sanction his receiving an honorary degree from the University, when it might have done him service. The English degree will not add to his popularity here. . . .

Always affectionately yours,

C. E. NORTON.

On reading over my letter I think I have been too hard on Jowett. In his biography as in real life, he inspires one on the whole with a warm feeling of regard, and great respect for some of his qualities.

To Edward Lee-Childe

ASHFIELD, 28 June, 1897.

It was very good of you to write to me again after so long a silence on my part. Almost two years ago a bent twig switched back across one of my eyes as I was walking in a wood, and gave it such a blow as left it weak for many months, and compelled me to humour it. I had to take to dictation and to employ a typewriter. But I do not like to send to a friend a typewritten letter, and so my proper correspondence fell greatly into arrears. My eye is now almost as strong as ever, and I am taking again to writing with my own hand.

These years have gone quietly and quickly with me. I do not resent the approach of old age. Old age has, indeed, its advantages, provided the mind remains vigorous, and the body be free from pain. One gathers in the late harvest; there is the calm and the clear light of evening, the winds have sunk, and the sun does not dazzle as at mid-day. There is, indeed, one irremediable sorrow — the narrowing of the circle of the friends who have given support and charm of life. A year ago the last was taken of those friends who had been dear to me and intimate with me from boyhood — almost the last who called me by my Christian name. You knew him of old, I think, Child, the most learned of the scholars of English, the most faithful of Professors for fifty years, one of the sweetest and soundest-hearted men, a lover of all good things, a humourist, genial, original, excellent in talk, a most constant friend. I can meet with no other such loss. Fortunately he had completed his great collection of the "English and Scotch Ballads," — a work of immense research, and of widest range of learning. Only the general introduction remained to be written: he was just beginning upon it when death stopped his hand.

If you have seen Brunetière since his return home you will have heard much of America, and, perhaps, something of Cambridge from him. It was a pity that he could not speak or readily understand English, — but, in spite of this drawback, I am inclined to believe that his impressions of America were more just than those of most travellers. His insight is less penetrating, and his perceptions less quick and delicate than Bourget's, — but his keen and clear intelligence, his intellectual principles and discipline, his strong moral convictions, would give value to his estimates of the significance of conditions so novel to him as those in which he found himself here. His lectures on Molière which he gave at Cambridge were excellent, but I wished that he had taken a topic of the day. Any accomplished man can lecture well on Shakespeare and Molière. I saw him often while he was at Boston, and should have been glad to see more of him. He is of a type of Frenchman whom one rarely meets, but who are of more interest and importance than the commoner sort.

There is nothing good to say of public affairs. I fancy that it will be long before a thoughtful man, a lover of his kind, will find the time in which he is living other than disappointing. I should like to be sure that the world were growing a happier place to live in. . . .

To S. G. Ward

ASHFIELD, 14 July, 1897.

Undoubtedly you are right. Men are not worse than they have been; and if we could reckon the gain and loss in our time, the sum of gain would, I believe, be the larger. But then there are many incommensurables in this reckoning, and the gain and the loss are not evenly distributed. You and I, and men like us, have experienced some losses which nothing can make good, — mainly losses to be classed as disappointments, but others of actual blessings. There was great truth in Talleyrand's saying, that no one had had experience of the best of life who had not lived before the French Revolution. So we might say, *mutatis mutandis*, of those who have not known the New England of our boyhood. There were fine ideals partially realized then, of which scarcely a trace remains. I fancy that there has never been a community on a higher and pleasanter level than that of New England during the first thirty years of the century, before the coming in of Jacksonian Democracy, and the invasion of the Irish, and the establishment of the system of Protection. It is a fortunate thing for America that that time was productive of Poets, and that its spirit has found expression in their verse. Longfellow, Emerson, and Lowell show what it was, and their verse eternizes its spirit and its influence, each expressing a different element in its composition. Such homogeneousness as existed in New England then exists nowhere in the United States now. Are we too big territorially, and too various in blood and tradition ever to become a nation? I should like to come back some centuries hence and see. Meanwhile I believe in the law of general, but not particular, compensation. As Stendhal says on one of his title-pages, professing to cite from Shakespeare, "J'ai connu la beauté parfaite de trop bonne heure." . . .

To S. G. Ward

SHADY HILL, 28 November, 1897.

Your letter of two months ago was very interesting. It has been much in my thought. My days, like those of most Americans, are too full of occupation to leave much time for the quiet and continuous thought which takes account of what has been going on in the subconscious regions of one's own mind. Still, I manage, from time to time, to take new bearings, and plot my course over the uncharted sea. The further I sail, the less I have to do with any of [the] metaphysical systems of navigation, or of explanation of the marvels which daily meet me. Prince Kropotkin has lately been here, the mildest and gentlest of anarchists, and one day, talking of metaphysics, he said, "Yes, your metaphysician is a blind man hunting in a dark room for a black hat which does not exist." We have had George Darwin, too, an admirable Darwinian, . . . who has made one of those big generalizations in regard to gravitation, as exemplified in the action of the tides, by which our knowledge of the structure of the stellar universe is indefinitely increased. He told a story of his own boy of eight years old who asked him what Metaphysics was. He tried to explain to the child, who, after listening to him, said, "Yes, papa, I understand; you think, and you *think*, and you THINK, and then you say that two and two make about five."

I grow more and more contented to accept the fixed limitations of human nature, and find room enough for the highest and longest flight of human wings within the vast spaces legitimately open to man. What you say of our real existence being in our relations with other men, seems to me admirably true. It is the achievements of good men that give shape to our own ideals, and the little which anyone of us can do for his

fellows (that is, the true end of life) consists in his
attainment of such relations to them as may enable
him to contribute his mite of individuality to the
improvement of the common ideals. It is the poets who
help us most, through the arts; their contribution is the
largest and the best. . . .

To Leslie Stephen

SHADY HILL, 20 December, 1897.

The time is too long since I last wrote to you, but, as
usual, the days are too short for the doing of half what
one intends and desires to do. The main difficulty lies
in the multitude of unauthorized letters which inter-
rupt with pertinacious insistence, . . . Against the letter there is no protection; it invades privacy, it dis-
turbs work, it spoils leisure. . . . Against the living bore
there may be defences, but when he incarnates himself
in a letter there is no escape. Forgive me for this dia-
tribe. The mail has just brought me five letters, all of
which I must answer and no one of them need have
been written. And so it is every day. But "Silence!"
as the great Thomas says.

My last missive from you, I think, was the "National Review" with your excellent article on Jowett. I
found it extremely interesting, — altogether fair in its
estimate, and full of insight into a perplexed and complex nature. . . . I was reading the other day in
Luther's "Table Talk," and in what he said of Eras-
mus was reminded of Jowett, and of Carlyle's saying
about him. "I regard not his words, indeed they are
well adorned, but they are merely Democritical Epi-

curian things, for he speaketh of every matter doubtfully with diligence and of set purpose; his words are
wavering, or (as wee use to say) screwed words which he
may construe as he pleaseth, which beseemeth not a
Christian, yea such words, equivocating, beseem no
honest, humane creature."

23d. I forget what interrupted my letter the other
day. I am not sorry for the interruption, for it is
pleasant to talk with you, as it were, from day to day.
Since I wrote last to you I have passed my seventieth
birthday. It surprises me to find myself so old in
years. And I am surprised, too, with so many years to
my count, to feel still so young. To be sure at times I
seem to myself older than Methusaleh. I suppose the
paradox is to be explained that each year but increases
the sense of ignorance, of the little that one knows compared with the vast sum of the knowable; one is still
sitting on the schoolboy's bench. While, on the other
hand, one seems to have gone the whole round of experience, so that there can be nothing novel, nothing
strange in the course of the days. One has lived the
full circle of life, — per tutto il cerchio volto. I do not
regret the approach of the end. I am not impatient for
it; I do not care whether it come soon or late, — provided only it come before I become a burden to others.
There is a good deal which I should like to do, but I
shall not be much disappointed if I have not time to do
it. At seventy one must begin to furl the sails, and I
have just resigned my Professorship. I am to be made
Professor emeritus, and I shall keep up my relations
with the University by still carrying on, at my will, a

class in Dante. This is interesting work, for I get ten or
twelve youths of the better sort round a table two or
three times a week, and the study of Dante becomes a
study of literature, of poetry, of religion, of morals,
and to some of them it is a service.

Send to me another paper of yours. What you write
for the public always has a special address to me. I
hope that all is going well with you, and that your
young people are good and well and cheerful, and will
have a pleasant Christmas. I share your grave
thoughts, — and your thankful ones. The blessings
and joys we have had are blessings and joys still, and
will be as long as life lasts.

                    Always your affectionate
                                        C. E. N.

To Moorfield Storey
                    CAMBRIDGE,   26 December, 1897.

One of the first pleasures which the comparative
leisure of the Christmas holidays has brought me has
been the reading of the two addresses which you were
good enough to send to me some weeks ago. Your
speech as Chairman of the National Democratic Convention I had read with great satisfaction when it was
originally published in the newspapers. It is an admirable statement of the position and principles of those
who cannot enroll themselves in the ranks of either of
the great parties. Our hope must be that our numbers
may become such as may enable us to exert a powerful
influence by exciting the desire in the leaders of each of
the parties to obtain our votes. If only, for example,

Mr. Lodge should consider it as well worth while to bid for our votes as for those of the Jingo or Irish section of the community! . . .

The words with which you end this address reminded me of a passage in one of Carlyle's Letters written in 1831 from London, in which he speaks of the prevailing temper of the men whom he was seeing, as that of deploring the prevalence of stupidity and dishonesty in public and in private life, but not resisting it, not believing that it must and should be resisted. I suppose all present times to be much alike to the thoughtful lover of his kind, in the contrast they afford between the actual and the ideal conduct of men. For such a man no present time ever has been or ever will be a happy time.

But I wish you a happy New Year! I have no space left in which to tell you how much I liked your Annapolis address.

I am glad that you are coming to the Tavern Club dinner on the 30th. You know that the dinners are absolutely private, and that you will be expected to speak.

The foregoing letters will have expressed Norton's attitude towards public affairs quite inadequately if there can be any doubt on which side his sympathies would be found, in the course of events that led to the declaration of war between the United States and Spain in April, 1898.

The war appeared to him the expression of the very tendencies in American life, which, as a lover of his country, he most distrusted, and to which, in the capacity of a private citizen, he was opposed. That popular sentiment was against him in no wise affected his feelings or the utterance of them, on private or public occasion, both before and after the declaration of war. If he had needed reassurance, the character of the minority in which he found himself would have provided it.

What his exact position was at this time, his own words — in an address on "True Patriotism" — will best prove.

This address,[1] following a few weeks after some informal and ill-reported words of Norton's to undergraduates in regard to the War, and their duty to their country, created a storm of public feeling — of sympathy with Norton's views (small in proportion to the abuse poured out upon them) and bitter antagonism. For days the arrival of the post, at Shady Hill, meant the arrival of many letters, anonymous and signed, from strangers — a few from acquaintances — of varying intensity of feeling. Newspapers from Maine to California — not those, however, ready to support an anti-Imperialist — expressed their opinion in terms often as abusive as the anonymous letter. Senator Hoar in public, attacking Norton, added his word of denunciation.[2] This was fuel on the public's fire.

After several months the letters of abuse — and of agreement — ceased to arrive with the morning paper. The incident had, however, made a deep impression

[1] Delivered on June 7th to the Men's Club of the Prospect Street Congregational Church, Cambridge.

[2] See Appendix D.

on the mind of the public. It was not forgotten. Norton had been pilloried as a "traitor" to his country. In some minds he remained one; for others the courage and patriotism of what he had said grew clear, and they acknowledged the truth in his words.

Where there is no vision, the people perish.

It seems desirable to quote in full the address to which reference has been made, since it gives expression, as no separate letters can, to Norton's views regarding the Spanish War, and war in general: —

"Gentlemen — There are moments in every man's life, in the life of every nation, when, under the excitement of passion, the simple truths which in common times are the foundation upon which the right order and conduct of life depend are apt to be forgotten and disregarded. I shall venture to-night to recall to you some of these commonplace truths, which in these days of war need more than ever to be kept in mind.

"There never was a land that better deserved the love of her people than America, for there never was a mother-country kinder to her children. She has given to them all that she could give. Her boundless resources have lain open to them, to use at their will. And the consequence has been that never in the history of man has there been so splendid a spectacle of widely diffused and steadily increasing material welfare as America has displayed during the last hundred years. Millions upon millions of men have lived here with more comfort, with less fear, than any such numbers elsewhere in any age have lived. Countless multitudes, whose forefathers from the beginning of human life on earth have spent weary lives in unrewarded toil, in anxiety, in helplessness, in ignorance, have risen here, in the course of even a single generation, to the full and secure enjoyment of the fruits of their labour, to confident hope, to intelligent possession of their own faculties. Is not the land to be dearly loved in which this has been possible, in which this has been achieved?

"But there is a deeper source of love of country than the material advantages and benefits it may afford. It is in the character of its people, in their moral life, in the type of civilization which they exhibit. The elements of human nature are indeed so fixed that favourable or unfavourable circumstances have little effect upon its essential constitution, but prosperity or the reverse brings different traits into prominence. The conditions which have prevailed in America have, if broadly considered, tended steadily and strongly to certain good results in the national character; not, indeed, to unmixed good, but to a preponderance of good. The institutions established for self-government have been founded with intent to secure justice and independence for all. The social relations among the whole body of the people, are humane and simple. The general spirit of the people is liberal, is kindly, is considerate. The ideals for the realization of which in private and public conduct there is more or less steady and consistent effort, are as high and as worthy as any which men have pursued. Every genuine American holds to the ideal of justice for all men, of independence, including free speech and free action within the limits of law, of obedience to law, of universal educa-

tion, of material well-being for all the well-behaving
and industrious, of peace and good-will among men.
These, however far short the nation may fall in expressing them in its actual life, are, no one will deny it, the
ideals of our American democracy. And it is because
America represents these ideals that the deepest love
for his country glows in the heart of the American, and
inspires him with that patriotism which counts no cost,
which esteems no sacrifice too great to maintain and
to increase the influence of these principles which
embody themselves in the fair shape of his native land,
and have their expressive symbol in her flag. The
spirit of his patriotism is not an intermittent impulse;
it is an abiding principle; it is the strongest motive of
his life; it is his religion.

"And because it is so, and just in proportion to his
love of the ideals for which his country stands, is his
hatred of whatever is opposed to them in private conduct or public policy. Against injustice, against dishonesty, against lawlessness, against whatever may
make for war instead of peace, the good citizen is
always in arms.

"No thoughtful American can have watched the
course of affairs among us during the last thirty years
without grave anxiety from the apparent decline in
power to control the direction of public and private
conduct, of the principles upon regard for which the permanent and progressive welfare of America depends;
and especially the course of events during the last few
months and the actual condition of the country to-day,
should bring home to every man the question whether

or not the nation is true to one of the chief of the ideals
to which it has professed allegiance. A generation has
grown up that has known nothing of war. The blessings of peace have been poured out upon us. We have
congratulated ourselves that we were free from the
misery and the burdens that war and standing armies
have brought upon the nations of the Old World.
'Their fires' — I cite a fine phrase of Sir Philip Sidney
in a letter to Queen Elizabeth — 'Their fires have
given us light to see our own quietness.' And now of a
sudden, without cool deliberation, without prudent
preparation, the nation is hurried into war, and America, she who more than any other land was pledged to
peace and good-will on earth, unsheathes her sword,
compels a weak and unwilling nation to a fight, rejecting without due consideration her earnest and repeated
offers to meet every legitimate demand of the United
States. It is a bitter disappointment to the lover of his
country; it is a turning-back from the path of civilization to that of barbarism.

"'There never was a good war,' said Franklin.
There have indeed been many wars in which a good
man must take part, and take part with grave gladness
to defend the cause of justice, to die for it if need be, a
willing sacrifice, thankful to give life for what is dearer
than life, and happy that even by death in war he is
serving the cause of peace. But if a war be undertaken
for the most righteous end, before the resources of
peace have been tried and proved vain to secure it, that
war has no defence; it is a national crime. And however
right, however unavoidable a war may be, and those of

us who are old enough to remember the war for the Union know that war may be right and unavoidable, yet, I repeat the words of Franklin, 'There never was a good war.' It is evil in itself, it is evil in its never-ending train of consequences. No man has known the nature of war better than General Sherman, and in his immortal phrase he has condensed its description — 'War is hell.' 'From the earliest dawnings of policy to this day,' said Edmund Burke, more than a hundred years ago, 'the invention of men has been sharpening and improving the mystery of murder, from the first rude essays of clubs and stones to the present perfection of gunnery, cannoneering, bombarding, mining, and all these species of artificial, learned and refined cruelty in which we are now so expert, and which make a principal part of what politicians have taught us to believe is our principal glory.' And it is now, at the end of this century, the century in which beyond any other in history knowledge has increased and the arts of peace have advanced, that America has been brought by politicians and writers for the press, faithless to her noble ideals, against the will of every right-minded citizen, to resort to these cruel arts, these arts of violence, these arts which rouse the passions of the beast in man, before the resources of peace had been fairly tested and proved insufficient to secure the professed ends, which, however humane and desirable, afford no sufficient justification for resorting to the dread arbitrament of arms.

"There are, indeed, many among us who find justification of the present war in the plea that its motive

is to give independence to the people of Cuba, long
burdened by the oppressive and corrupt rule of Spain,
and especially to relieve the suffering of multitudes
deprived of their homes and of means of subsistence by
the cruel policy of the general who exercised for a time
a practical dictatorship over the island. The plea so far
as it is genuine deserves the respect due to every humane sentiment. But independence secured for Cuba
by forcible overthrow of the Spanish rule means either
practical anarchy or the substitution of the authority
of the United States for that of Spain. Either alternative might well give us pause. And as for the relief of
suffering, surely it is a strange procedure to begin by
inflicting worse suffering still. It is fighting the devil
with his own arms. That the end justifies the means is
a dangerous doctrine, and no wise man will advise
doing evil for the sake of an uncertain good. But the
plea that the better government of Cuba and the relief
of the reconcentrados could only be secured by war is
the plea either of ignorance or of hypocrisy.

"But the war is declared; and on all hands we hear
the cry that he is no patriot who fails to shout for it,
and to urge the youth of the country to enlist, and to
rejoice that they are called to the service of their
native land. The sober counsels that were appropriate
before the war was entered upon must give way to
blind enthusiasm, and the voice of condemnation must
be silenced by the thunders of the guns and the hurrahs
of the crowd. Stop! A declaration of war does not
change the moral law. 'The ten commandments will
not budge' at a joint resolve of Congress. Was James

Russell Lowell aught but a good patriot when during
the Mexican war he sent the stinging shafts of his
matchless satire at the heart of the monstrous iniquity,
or when, years afterward, he declared, that he thought
at the time and that he still thought the Mexican war
was a national crime? Did John Bright ever render
greater service to his country than when, during the
Crimean war, he denounced the Administration which
had plunged England into it, and employed his magnificent power of earnest and incisive speech in the
endeavour to repress the evil spirit which it evoked in
the heart of the nation? No! the voice of protest, of
warning, of appeal is never more needed than when the
clamour of fife and drum, echoed by the press and too
often by the pulpit, is bidding all men fall in and keep
step and obey in silence the tyrannous word of command. Then, more than ever, it is the duty of the good
citizen not to be silent, and spite of obloquy, misrepresentation and abuse, to insist on being heard, and
with sober counsel to maintain the everlasting validity
of the principles of the moral law.

"So confused are men by false teaching in regard to
national honour and the duty of the citizen that it is
easy to fall into the error of holding a declaration of
war, however brought about, as a sacred decision of
the national will, and to fancy that a call to arms from
the Administration has the force of a call from the lips
of the country, of the America to whom all her sons
are ready to pay the full measure of devotion. This
is indeed a natural and for many a youth not a discred-
itable error. But if the nominal, though authorized,

representatives of the country have brought us into a war that might and should have been avoided, and which consequently is an unrighteous war, then, so long as the safety of the State is not at risk, the duty of the good citizen is plain. He is to help to provide the Administration responsible for the conduct of the war with every means that may serve to bring it to the speediest end. He is to do this alike that the immediate evils of the war may be as brief and as few as possible, and also that its miserable train of after evils may be diminished and the vicious passions excited by it be the sooner allayed. Men, money, must be abundantly supplied. But must he himself enlist or quicken the ardent youth to enter service in such a cause? The need is not yet. The country is in no peril. There is always in a vast population like ours an immense, a sufficient supply of material of a fighting order, often of a heroic courage, ready and eager for the excitement of battle, filled with the old notion that patriotism is best expressed in readiness to fight for our country, be she right or wrong. Better the paying of bounties to such men to fill the ranks than that they should be filled by those whose higher duty is to fit themselves for the service of their country in the patriotic labours of peace. We mourn the deaths of our noble youth fallen in the cause of their country when she stands for the right; but we may mourn with a deeper sadness for those who have fallen in a cause which their generous hearts mistook for one worthy of the last sacrifice.

"My friends, America has been compelled against

the will of all her wisest and best to enter into a path
of darkness and peril. Against their will she has been
forced to turn back from the way of civilization to the
way of barbarism, to renounce for the time her own
ideals. With grief, with anxiety must the lover of his
country regard the present aspect and the future prospect of the nation's life. With serious purpose, with
utter self-devotion he should prepare himself for the
untried and difficult service to which it is plain he is to
be called in the quick-coming years.

"Two months ago America stood at the parting of
the ways. Her first step is irretrievable. It depends on
the virtue, on the enlightened patriotism of her children whether her future steps shall be upward to the
light or downward to the darkness.

"'Nil desperandum de republica.'"

The letters of the spring and summer throw a more
intimate light upon the passing conditions.

To Herbert Welsh

CAMBRIDGE, 30 April, 1898.

I thank you for your interesting letter.

My words to the students in regard to this abomin-
able war, and their responsibilities as educated youth,
were spoken without notes and were not reported in
full. They were cordially responded to by a great
majority of the young men to whom they were addressed, but they are bringing to me a vast amount
of, mainly anonymous, abuse and denunciation. One
eloquent Irish orator, a man not without standing in

our local politics, the Hon. Thomas J. Gargan, has gone so far as to suggest that I deserve *lynching*.

Your report of Mr. MacVeagh's [1] conversation is of great interest. I trust that you have made a full record of what he said. His words confirm what was reported to me of the talk of Mr. —— during a visit to Boston two or three weeks before the declaration of war. I was told that he said that, in order to secure the next Presidential election, the Republican party must either declare itself for free silver or make a war; that the first of these alternatives was impossible, but that the second of them was to be adopted. . . .

To Leslie Stephen

ASHFIELD, 24 June, 1898.

I have been silent too long, — partly because this iniquitous and perilous war has made me averse to letter-writing. The days are grave and disheartening, and the prospect is dark. We have been living in a Fool's Paradise, hoping that in the long run the better elements in our national life would get the upper hand, and that we should stumble along, with many a slip indeed, but on the whole in the right direction. But the war has suddenly roused us from this dream. America has rejected her old ideals, turned her back on her past, and chosen the path of barbarism. All the evil spirits of the Old World which we trusted were exorcised in the New, have taken possession of her, and under their influence she has gone mad. A mere accident, — the report of some words which, at the mo-

[1] The Hon. Wayne MacVeagh.

ment of the declaration of war, I spoke to my class on
the nature of true patriotism, brought me into transient prominence and made me the subject of a good
deal of newspaper obloquy. I stated my opinions more
fully in a speech to a young men's club, and unexpect-
edly found myself in the position of representative of
the rights of independent individual judgment and
expression. The attacks made upon me would have
been simply humorous, had they not been indicative
of the blindness and despotism of popular passion. One
of our Irish patriots, a man prominent in politics, in a
speech in my own native Cambridge, intimated that
a coat of tar and feathers would be a proper suit
for me, and the suggestion was repeated in a Chicago
newspaper! My mail was loaded down with letters
and post-cards full of abuse, mostly anonymous, some
of them going so far as to bid me look out for a stray
bullet! But the storm is ceasing and will soon die
wholly away. It has not disturbed me, — and here at
Ashfield life is as tranquil and the days as fair, as if
no war or battle's sound was heard the world around.

But we have had a real sorrow, since Sally and I
came here ten days ago, in hearing of Burne-Jones's
death. He and I have been close friends for more than
forty years, — very close for more than thirty, with a
friendship which did not depend on frequency of intercourse, but which was so firm-knit that when we met
or interchanged letters there was no need to link a
broken chain, for we were at once as familiar and intimate as if we had lived side by side. My children and
his were much together when they were little things,

and from that early time he has been "Uncle Ned" to Sally and Lily. The Grange has been a home to them when they have been abroad, and last year Sally was there and at Rottingdean for three months, and learned to love him more than ever. He was one of the sweetest-natured of men, one of the pleasantest companions. I don't know whether you knew him well enough to have seen his humorous side. He had a charming humour, the best possible set-off to the poetic sentiment which is manifest in his pictures. I do not believe that there has ever been a painter of richer poetic gift than he. I had never thought of his dying before me. He is a great loss out of my life.

How full our letters to each other of late years have been of the death of friends! and how solitary we are left! Your last letter told of two of them. . . .

To Edward Lee-Childe

ASHFIELD, 26 June, 1898.

MY DEAR CHILDE, — Your letter of six weeks ago gave me much pleasure, and I should have thanked you for it before now, but for the fact that owing to the position I have taken in regard to this wretched, needless and, consequently, iniquitous war, I have been burdened with letters which demanded immediate attention, from a great number of known and unknown correspondents, more of them denouncing my course than expressing sympathy with it. . . .

The old America, the America of our hopes and our dreams has come to an end, and a new America is entering on the false course which has been tried so often and which has often led to calamity. This war will in the long run result in far more evil to the United States than to Spain. We shall nominally win, but at the cost of what infinite loss!

The world is uglier physically, and in part morally, than when we were born, — but I believe that in the portion of it which we call civilized there is less misery. At any rate, I comfort myself with what may, after all, be a delusion. . . .

To Charles Waldstein

June 27, 1898.

MY DEAR WALDSTEIN,— . . . I trust that your work on the "Heraion" will go on prosperously. I cannot help you as I once might have done, for I have left the management of the Institute and of the School wholly to other hands. Still if there should arise occasion, I may have power to promote your wishes. You will write to me if I can serve. The publication of the "Heraion," and of the great work on Assos, will be the fulfilment of one of the chief wishes and hopes which I indulged when the Institute was established twenty years ago,— that it might promote the production of work of this order by American scholars, — real and original contributions to the general stock of knowledge of Greek antiquity. . . .

To C. C. Stillman[1]

ASHFIELD, 4 August, 1898.

I thank you for your cordial note. It gives me great pleasure.

[1] A former pupil.

The recent attacks upon me have not disturbed me. It is, of course, unpleasant to be misunderstood and misjudged by large numbers of one's countrymen, who know nothing of one but what they see in the newspapers. But it is a matter of no essential consequence. I feel as the poor old poet, George Wither, did:—

> "Let men without me keep what noise they will,
> So I within be still."

I want you to fulfill your promise of coming over to see me at Ashfield. I shall be glad to welcome you at any time this month. . . .

To S. G. Ward

SHADY HILL, 10 October, 1898.

. . . You say that your interest in public affairs in this wonderful year has rejuvenated you. I am glad of it, but I cannot detach myself sufficiently from the crowd, to look on at its performances as at a spectacle in which I have no part, and I am so sorry for the course which the crowd is taking that I feel worn and tired.

It is easy enough now to see that we have all (or shall I say except you?) expected too happy a result from the fortunate conditions of America; that we looked for too great an effect upon human nature itself, and were too confident that in the long run the good would prevail over the evil elements in society. And it is easy enough now to recognize our early divergence from the true path. I trace a great part of the *corruptio optimi* to the adoption of the Protective policy. Its effect in lowering the moral tone and weakening the character of the nation can hardly be overestimated. It has brought us at last to this disastrous war, in which we have made jettison of all that was most precious of our national cargo. The future for America looks to me very threatening. But calamity may do more for our improvement than prosperity has done. . . .

You tell me that you have got Frazer's Pausanias. I, too, look forward to reading it this winter, in the leisure which my giving up of College work will afford me. I have lately been reading much in one of my favourite books, — Plutarch's Lives. They are full of comment on passing events. . . .

To Leslie Stephen

SHADY HILL, 22 October, 1898.

. . . Dicey[1] has been with us for a week past, and leaves us, I am sorry to say, on Tuesday. . . . He is excellent company, and his mental vigour and animation, his solidity of judgment, his active intellectual interests, make his abundant flow of talk both pleasant and profitable. He and I find ourselves in close agreement upon most questions; while in regard to most matters of opinion, our judgments so nearly coincide that there is little chance for discussion. You would doubtless smile, with a semi-cynical but pleased amusement, at what you would regard as our delusion,

---

[1] Professor A. V. Dicey, of Oxford — a cousin of Leslie Stephen's, and for many years Norton's friend — then delivering a course of lectures at the Harvard Law School.

could you hear the amœbæan strains with which we celebrate you and your work!

He is having a "good time" in this country. His lectures are received with great approval, and he likes his audiences. Everybody is cordial to him. He is lunching and dining out almost every day, and I should wonder at his capacity to do so much and endure so much, were it not that he is entertained by the variety of experience, pleased by the warmth of the regard expressed for him, and taken care of most watchfully by his devoted guardian niece. He went on Friday to Princeton to receive an Honorary Doctorate, and returned this morning none the worse for a long night-journey in the train, and with a splendid yellow and black hood.

The news this morning from Europe is black and ominous, but I still believe that war will be averted. The situation is perilous enough, and it may well be that France will drive on to war, in order to force the Dreyfus iniquity into the background. Nor do things look well on this side of the ocean. . . .

I have never thanked you for sending to me your "Studies of a Biographer," — delightful volumes, and worthy continuation of your "Hours in a Library," good for many readings, — wise, acute, humorous, sensible and altogether pleasant. And now, by all means, follow them up with a reprint of your longer contributions to the Dictionary. It would not give you much trouble, and these "Lives" of yours ought to be accessible to a multitude of readers who cannot have the Dictionary. If you don't want the trouble, slight as it would be, let me have the pleasure of it. I can promise you more careful proof-reading than your own! I am in earnest about this. Let me hear soon that you are sleeping well, and going on prosperously with your difficult task.

Affectionately always yours,

C. E. N.

CHAPTER XII

ACTIVITIES OF RETIREMENT

(1899-1907)

"So it has come to pass that the American is a marvel who lives as an old man in the house in which he was born, who inherits and transmits hereditary acres, who, like Claudian's Old Man of Verona,

> A neighbouring wood born with himself he sees,
> And loves his old contemporary trees;

and who closes his eyes at the end of life on the same landscape which they beheld when they first opened."

Thus Norton, writing of "The Lack of Old Homes in America," [1] described his own situation, for life as it drew to its close found him where childhood, boyhood and manhood had known him.[2] Changed was the Cambridge about him, but not his own spirit; for he was ready, while strength lasted, to march with the advance guard, provided it bore the standard of what he conceived to be true progress. And to the very end, "like all citizens of high public ideals" — as Curtis said of Lowell — he "was inevitably a public critic and censor."

Released from obligatory college engagements, when

---

[1] *Scribner's Magazine*, May, 1889.

[2] Mr. C. F. Adams, writing to Norton in 1907, expressed one of many beliefs which they shared: "We in America, I am continually made to realize, give no weight to the traditional element which ought to figure so largely in the education of each rising generation. It is the root of all true patriotism, — that sentiment attaching to localities and the soil!"

in 1898 he became Professor emeritus, he was the freer through the remaining ten years of his life to observe and to reflect, to occupy himself with such congenial labours as the revision and improvement of his translation of the "Divine Comedy." And through these latest years he continued to give time, generously as of old, to friends and students. The habit of many a year was still unchanged in his having almost always on hand the proof-sheets of some book which, as with "The Oregon Trail" in 1848, he had gladly undertaken to read for the sake of helping the author.[1]

Though the official bonds of teacher and pupil were now severed, Norton maintained to the end, through personal intercourse and correspondence, those relations with younger men which enriched his old age. Presiding in June of 1899 at the dinner of the Harvard Chapter of Phi Beta Kappa, he addressed the newly elected members of the Society in words that well illustrate the nature and force of his influence: "For you, young brothers, just entering on the perplexed paths of actual life, we elders, about to leave them, have no counsel more practical, no command more absolute than that you be true to those generous ideals which now lift your hearts and shape your hopes. Follow their gleam; pursue, never to overtake; the pursuit is all, for by fidelity in it you become masters of fate and leaders of mankind. And we, your elder brothers, obeying the

---

[1] Writing in 1901 to the Rev. Charles A. Dinsmore, Norton says, "In reading the proof I have found your little book very interesting [*The Teachings of Dante*]. You have penetrated deep into Dante's meaning, and I have gained much from your interpretation. . . . Let me thank you for the pleasure and instruction I have gained from your work." Such phrases as these are the man himself.

voice at eve obeyed at prime, to-day renew our youth with you at the fountain of those ideals which are the source of vital strength for youth, for manhood, and for age."

This faith that younger men would continue the eternal pursuit must constantly be borne in mind while noting Norton's realizations of the troubled process of what he liked to call the old world's "stumbling along." Two years after the Spanish War he wrote to Leslie Stephen: "The condition of the world in these days (which are, indeed, not much worse than ordinary) might make a pessimist of the most shallow and smiling saint. The old century is flickering out in a very ugly fashion." Yet in August, 1900, he wrote to Mr. Ward: "There is no reason why we who feel the present darkness, should not use every effort in our power to dispel such part of it as our poor torches can light up" — and, a little later, to Mr. Moorfield Storey: "The refuge from pessimism is the good men and women at any time existing in the world, — they keep faith and happiness alive." What they gave to Norton he gave — if only through a knowledge of his expectation of the best — to a multitude of others.

To Miss Sara Norton

SHADY HILL, Wednesday evening, 8 February, 1899
Ruskin's 80th birthday.

. . . I had yesterday another interesting, but not *so* interesting, and very long letter from the soldier in Co. E of the Colorado Regiment at Manila. He must find it hard to shoot at those poor Filipinos. He did not

SAMUEL GRAY WARD, 1881

enlist for that, and he must feel with Birdofredum
Sawin that,

"Ninepence a day for killin' folks
Comes kind o' low for murder."

It is all a miserable affair, a kind of world's comi-
tragedy, — with a beginning of fine humanitarian
pretensions under which could even then be seen grin-
ning the sardonic features of the old enemy who
brought death into the world.

To-day I have been lunching with Admiral Sampson
at the Hollises. They had a pleasant little party of six,
— Dr. James, Mr. Shaler, etc. The Admiral is a very
quiet, silent gentleman, — quite simple and pleasant
but entirely lacking in social animation. He has a very
fine forehead, a dark brow and deep-set dark, almost
black eyes. . . . His nose is small and refined, the nose
of an artist, not Dante's *naso maschio;* the mouth and
chin are hidden by a well-kept, well-trimmed beard,
under which one can make out that the chin is not
broad and solid enough to be in fine proportion with
the forehead. The poor man looks thoroughly tired out,
and his eyes have a pathetic look of weariness amount-
ing almost to sorrow. His bearing is eminently that of
a gentleman who means to do his part well, but has no
zest in doing it. . . .

To S. G. Ward

SHADY HILL, 6 April, 1899.

You have given to me a great pleasure. These letters
from Emerson [1] which you have confided to me are of

---

[1] Published in August, 1899, as *Letters from Ralph Waldo Emerson to a
Friend, 1838–1853.* Edited by Charles Eliot Norton.

quite exceptional interest. None, I think, of his letters which have been printed afford such illustration as these of his intimate nature. From most even of his nearest friends he held himself somewhat aloof, owing to incomplete or imperfect sympathy. With you he felt essentially at one, and to you he expressed himself with easy openness. With you his originality, which often operated unconsciously to make him reserved, was not shy, and these letters consequently reveal him to a degree in which he seldom revealed himself. This makes them precious. No other American has approached him in the absoluteness and purity of his originality.

Your scheme for printing the letters seems to me excellent. . . . I will see to it at once, and when I have written what brief introduction and notes they may require, I will send the manuscript to you for revision. . . .

To C. C. Stillman

CAMBRIDGE, 10 April, 1899.

. . . You ask me, what is the best service which you can render to your generation? And is the life of a business man the highest that you can live? The greatest service which any man can render to his fellows consists not in any specific, and may be rendered in any profession. It consists in the influence, direct and indirect, which he may exert by force of character. Let him possess himself not merely of the common moral virtues of industry and integrity, but let him steadily aim to acquire open-mindedness, independence of judgment, generosity, elevation of purpose in his dealings with men, and keep himself simple, pure, tender-hearted and sympathetic in relations with those nearest to him, and whether he be business man or clergyman, he will be doing the best service to his kind.

The extent of this service will depend, indeed, greatly on matters not wholly under his control, — on his intellectual ability, on the chances which circumstance affords, on health.

He may shape and develop his character while sealing packages of bonds to as good purpose as if he were ministering in a hospital. In the long run, if circumstances are not adverse, the bent of his nature, whether to business activities, or to preaching, or to writing, or to whatever else, will probably assert itself. But even if he be confined to uncongenial tasks, he need not fail of the highest ends of life.

All these thoughts need development, but you will give this to them. One thing is to be added — that the service which a man may render to his fellows will depend largely upon the woman whom he loves. A true wife more than doubles her husband's virtues and power. Love is the fulfilling of life.

Whenever you come to Cambridge, be sure to come to see us, and believe me always,

Sincerely your old friend,

C. E. NORTON.

To Leslie Stephen

ASHFIELD, 8 July, 1899.

I have no valid excuse for not writing oftener to you. . . . The months since I last did write have gone by quickly and easily with me as a private man, but have been dreary enough for me as a lover of the old American ideals. This miserable war in the Philippines, this bastard "imperialism," this childish temper of the people, this turn of affairs toward barbarism, do not help to make one light-hearted. I cannot be cynically indifferent to what is going on, and that philosophical indifference which is perhaps the acme of wisdom, (if it do not interfere with the energy of our opposition to evil), is far removed from joy. How much I should like a good solid talk with you! It would be a comfort. . . . If I had assurance of another twenty years of capacity to work I should like to write a history of man from my point of view! Somebody will do it by and by.

The chief event of these months for me has been the return three or four weeks ago of my boy Richard, after a stay in Rome of nearly two years. He comes back as pleasant as when he went away, and happy in having just been chosen Director of the School of Classical Studies at Rome, for a term of five years. This is really a great honour for such a youth. He is, I am glad to believe, capable of filling the place serviceably and creditably. The separation from home is a serious drawback, but if he should stay out his full term, he may during its course take a summer vacation at home as he is doing this year.

For myself, I have been busy with many transient things, and with one steady piece of work, — the revision of my translation of the "Divina Commedia." You do not care much for the poem, but I am interested always in it as a man gets interested in whatever he really pursues, — even in mathematics. And then, one of the secret thoughts common to us is, of the essential relative unimportance of any work of man, even of "Hamlet" or the "Midsummer Night's Dream."

I was thankful that you could tell me in your last letter, now three months old, that you were sleeping again, — and another comfort was, that your book was complete, needing only the final revision. I trust that that has been given to it and that you are taking a genuine vacation in some pleasant place, and that you are well, and the children all well and doing well. I wonder sometimes if the youth of these days has really as good a time in life as we used to have. He (and she) seems to me to live with too little in life of what we used to get from poets and story-tellers.

Sally and I are alone here just now. . . .

To S. G. Ward

ASHFIELD, 16 July, 1899.

. . . To your three elements of Genius I want to add one more, for which I can find no more satisfactory word than comprehensiveness, — the faculty of reconciling divergences and contradictions in the shows of things, of bringing unity out of variety, of grouping things in right relations, of seeing the whole in its parts, and of —

I was interrupted here and cannot take up my dropped stitch. I have just been reading the "Life of William Morris," whom I knew well. Here was a man who had passion, insight and will, the first and last in great force, but his genius lacked something to make it absolute and conclusive. He failed, it seems to me, to see things in their due relative importance. He had the narrow view of the world of a thirteenth century artist. The later centuries said nothing to him, and he preferred the rude barbaric elementary passion and art of Iceland to all that Italy affords. . . .

To Moorfield Storey

ASHFIELD, 31 July, 1899.

I was on the point of writing to you when your note came to me to-day. . . .

As for the Dinner, its object is to increase the funds of our Academy, which is the most important and unifying institution in the town. The Dinner is held in the Town Hall; it is supplied and served by the village people, and is a good New England feast. On a fine day there are two hundred people, more or less, present at it, — a small half of them the town's people, the rest summer boarders and visitors from neighbouring towns. It is a pleasant audience to speak to. We have never made the speaking merely amusing; the national tendency of such an occasion is to degenerate into an entertainment, and the fault of our dinners here has been, perhaps, that they were too serious. But there is often some good humour and good fun intermingled with the sober talk. Curtis was the most accomplished master in the art of saying serious things in a way to charm as well as to inspire. Every man talks as he will, on any subject on which he wishes to be re-

ported in the "Springfield Republican," the "Green-
field Gazette," and more briefly in the Associated
Press.

I have always to begin with a little local talk, but
after that I am thinking of saying something on the
settlement of the Philippine troubles as a test of national character, as an opportunity for the American
people.

I thought the Φ. B. K. performances as a whole uncommonly good. Parts of Bonaparte's address were of
a very high order of political satire and warning. I did
not like his talk about supporting the war. It seemed
to me that he had forgotten that we once settled the
question of the Higher Law. . . .

To E. L. Godkin

ASHFIELD, 2 August, 1899.

Your letter from Vichy, which came to me a fortnight ago was a great pleasure to me. I trust that . . .
Vichy is not the most intolerable of frequented water-
ing-places. Perhaps, indeed, you find some good company among your fellow-rheumatics. One agreeable
man, still more, one agreeable woman would make any
place endurable; — but pleasant people are rare, and
grow rarer as we grow older, for those of our own generation naturally fall away, and those of the new generation have a new order of pleasantness which is not
quite sympathetic to us. Half the pleasantness of a
companion lies in the common stock of things taken
for granted, the broad basis of natural understanding. The lack of this among people who move in the

same circles in America is what makes society in the higher sense impossible. Not even in Cambridge can I now get together half a dozen men or women round a table, who have a large common background for their thoughts, their wit, their humour. Literature in the best sense used to supply a good deal of it, but does so no longer. My fair neighbour asks, "What are Pericles?"

But as Emerson says in one of his letters which I will tell you of, "I find I am writing sentences, not a letter." Let me stop. A month or two ago Sam Ward sent to me copies of some of Emerson's letters to him and asked me about publishing them. They were, as I thought, full of Emerson at his best, and so they are to be published in a little volume which one may read through in half an hour. It is to be issued at the end of September; but you may like to read it now in advance, and so I send to you a set of the proof-sheets. Ward does not want his name to become known to the public, so that not even the publishers are aware who the friend is to whom the letters were addressed. Of course it will leak out. . . .

The actual condition of our affairs is as bad as can be, but the signs of discontent and reaction increase, and I am not wholly without hope that we shall stop fighting the poor Filipinos. But we are such a new thing in history that prediction is more difficult than ever. Just now we are getting hysterical, and mock-hysterical, over Dewey. And who is Dewey, and what has he done for a nation to go wild about him? . . .

E. L. GODKIN, 1889

To S. G. Ward

ASHFIELD, 21 September, 1899.

I am sorry that your summer is over, — mine too is near its end, and in a few days I shall be again in Cambridge, more solitary even than I am here, for in the crowd of men few old friends are left, and there are no new ones to take their places. . . .

You ask me about accounts of the great Unitarian movement in the early part of the century. There are two books which treat of it and I believe, for I have read neither of them, treat of it well, one by Octavius Frothingham, the other by J. H. Allen. I do not recall the exact titles of them; I will send the titles to you when I get to Cambridge, but if you are in haste for them, an enquiry at the Library of Congress would be readily answered. You will find a good deal bearing on the matter as seen from the Orthodox side in the "Life of Lyman Beecher," a very interesting book in its presentation of a strong character, and of a condition of society which has wholly passed away. Something there is too in Weiss's "Life of Theodore Parker,"and perhaps in the "Life of Channing."

Your little volume of "Letters" will be published, I suppose, on Saturday. I have written to have five copies sent to you. I hope that it will please you. I do not believe that you will find yourself in the papers, though unquestionably some of the writers for them will get hold of your name. Nothing now-a-days is secret or sacred to the purveyors to the press. . . .

To Charles Waldstein

CAMBRIDGE, November 18, 1899.

I have read your little volume on the "Expansion of Western Ideals and the World's Peace" with great interest. As you are aware, your position and my own differ widely on the fundamental question which underlies your essays. But I read with genuine sympathy your very able statement of your own views. I do not think that you do quite justice to the opinions of the men who regard the present policy of America as a misfortune. It is not that we would hold America back from playing her full part in the world's affairs, but that we believe that her part could be better accomplished by close adherence to those high principles which are ideally embodied in her institutions, — by the establishment of her own democracy in such wise as to make it a symbol of noble self-government, and by exercising the influence of a great, unarmed and peaceful power on the affairs and the moral temper of the world.

We believe that America had something better to offer to mankind than those aims she is now pursuing, and we mourn her desertion of ideals which were not selfish nor limited in their application, but which are of universal worth and validity. She has lost her unique position as a potential leader in the progress of civilization, and has taken up her place simply as one of the grasping and selfish nations of the present day. We all know how far she has fallen short in the past of exhibiting in her conduct a fidelity to those ideals which she

professed, but some of us, at least, had not lost the hope
that she would ultimately succeed in becoming more
faithful to them.

There are many points in your two papers which,
were you here, I should be glad to talk over with you.
But it is hardly worth while to write of them. Your
presentation of the Imperialistic position has this great
value at least, that it shows that men who hold it are
cherishing ideals which, if they can be fulfilled, will
make the course on which America has entered less
disastrous than we who do not hold them now fear. . . .

To Leslie Stephen

SHADY HILL, 28 March, 1900.

. . . Perhaps I may see you before long, — *that* would
be a pleasure, however sad. I expect to spend June in
England, compelled to be there for a very little while
to attend to the matters which Ruskin by his will put
partly in my charge. I do not think there is much for
me to do, and I leave home reluctantly, and only for
the sake of fidelity to an old friendship. I mean to get
to England about the first of June. . . . For two or
three weeks I expect to be at Brantwood, and for a
week in London. That will be all. I dare say that
Sally will accompany me. If it depended upon me,
there would be no further word of Ruskin or about
him given to the public. Enough is known. He printed
or allowed to be printed far too much. I have never
known a life less wisely controlled, or less helped by the
wisdom of others than his. The whole retrospect of it
is pathetic; waste, confusion, ruin of one of the most

gifted and sweetest natures the world ever knew. He was a kind of angel gone astray; meant for the thirteenth century, he got delayed on the way, and when he finally arrived was a white-winged anachronism.

The days of the winter have gone quietly enough with me. I have been revising my translation of the "Divine Comedy," a quite endless work, a pleasant and harmless occupation. . . . Our chief external interest, as for everybody, has been the war in South Africa. It was doubtless, in a sense, inevitable, but it is none the less hateful. It has no good side. Of course all our immediate sympathies are with the English. I long to hear of the relief of Mafeking, and long still more to have the whole thing over, not merely that its miseries may end, but that its baleful effect in stimulating the popular spirit of militarism may cease. Lord! send peace in our time.

Well, dear old fellow, keep up your heart as well as you can. Cultivate your garden, and continue to care for

Your affectionate

C. E. N.

To S. G. Ward

Shady Hill, 8 April, 1900.

. . . I had a letter to-day from an old friend of mine, a very "unusual" person, whom I fear you never fell in with, J. B. Harrison by name, the most complete and genuine product of American institutions that I have ever known. He tells me that he is just recovering from an attack of "the grip," and says, "Fifty

years ago the people on the Wabash, when suffering
from malarial fever, said they felt 'powerful weak,'
and I feel so now." — Harrison is a Western man by
birth, of poorest stock, a Methodist by inheritance,
and with traits that remind me of Lincoln. He worked
himself out of Methodism finally into Emersonianism,
that is, by means of Emerson's help, into intellectual
independence. He fought in the war, was desperately
wounded, came back to Illinois to continue fighting by
means of a newspaper, and his articles caught my
attention in the early days of the Loyal Publication
Society. They were admirable in spirit and in expression, and a good many of them were reprinted in our
broadsides. After the war he gave himself to serving
the country in all sorts of ways till at last he broke
down his health by overwork, and for ten years past
he has lived, cultivating his garden, very poor, very
thoughtful, in Franklin Falls, New Hampshire. You
may have seen at the time a paper of his published
perhaps twenty years ago in the "Atlantic" on "Certain Dangerous Tendencies in American Life." It
contained some remarkable forecasts which events
have justified. . . .

To E. L. Godkin

ASHFIELD, 21 July, 1900.

. . . My weeks in England were full of interest, and
would have been altogether pleasant and prosperous
but for two grave drawbacks, — the missing of old
friends, and the very sad condition of William Darwin,[1]

[1] Mr. W. E. Darwin (Norton's brother-in-law) had had a serious accident while riding; his recovery was retarded by long and grave illness.

which caused us great anxiety. My last intelligence concerning him was a cable message from Sally consisting of the single word "Satisfactory," . . . He has borne himself through all his trials with most admirable patience, self-control and courage. . . .

There was one other drawback to enjoyment in England, — the condition of public affairs, and the deterioration of public sentiment since I was last in the country fourteen years ago. The same evil influences have been at work there as in America, and with the same ill results, — the materialisation of the public temper, the vulgarisation of society, and the increase of jingo militarism. . . .

I saw many interesting people, — Morley, Leslie Stephen, Acton, Reay, Lecky, Frederic Harrison, Choate, etc., etc. At Oxford I saw no one of special interest but Dicey. . . .

To S. G. Ward
                                   ASHFIELD, 23 July, 1900.

. . . I am glad to be at home again, though England was beautiful in June, friends very kind, and London crowded with interests and far more stately and superb and spectacular than when I saw it last fourteen years ago. The changed aspect of the great town shows how rapid has been the advance of democracy, and how great is the effect of its wide-spread wealth. Vast hotels of American style, built with designed picturesqueness to advertise themselves from afar, and furnished as lavishly and sumptuously as if they were in New York; tall apartment-houses, many of them of showy and fantastic architecture and of enormous extent; great new public buildings, ugly, irrational in design, but striking and impressive from their mass and costliness; the superb embankment, — all these have made the London of to-day practically a new city. Its old charm has disappeared, — all the West End is mainly as fresh as Chicago or Denver. Society too has changed. There is no longer a distinctively literary or intellectual group uniting the fashionable world with the world of ideas. There are plenty of able men, but they are separate figures. Society has taken to advertising itself, and even the aristocracy have fallen into the habit. Advertising is the key-note of the hour. . . .

I lived for the few days which I spent in London close to the corner of Piccadilly and St. James's Street; — the most entertaining, the most interesting street corner in the world. I should have much to tell you if we met. . . .

To Leslie Stephen

ASHFIELD, 3 August, 1900.

A month has passed swiftly since I bade you good-bye.[1] To have seen you even for the little that was possible during my few days in London is a lasting happiness. As I sit here, in the familiar quiet of these country days, solitary for the most part, and living much with the past, the pleasant recollections of my recent visit to England connect very naturally with

[1] Leslie Stephen wrote in a letter to Mrs. Fisher on July 3, — "To-day Norton came in the afternoon to take leave. He goes back to America to-morrow and I shall never see him again. It was a sad parting, for I have no better friend."

those of the past, adding new light and colour to them.
The part of life in which you have a share seems larger
and fuller than ever before. Common interests and our
common sympathies seem stronger than ever, and our
late meetings only make me wish more than ever that
such meetings could be frequent and that the merciless
sea did not divide us. The friends whom we have loved
in common, now that they are gone, draw us the more
closely together, — and even those who were yours
and not mine or mine and not yours exert similar
influence.

One great advantage of old age is that it helps us to
see things in their true proportions and quickens our
sense of humour. We see ourselves objectively, and
smile at ourselves, and are indifferent about ourselves,
as we smile at other men and are indifferent about them.
I care to have you honoured; I liked to be at the Lord
Mayor's banquet for your sake, but I believe that both
you and I are quite honest if we say that the only
pleasure we take in honours that may fall to ourselves
is in the pleasure they may give to the few who love us.
To be sure, like Lowell, (I dare say I learned it from
him,) I like an Oxford degree for the sake of the entry
on the Harvard Catalogue, our chief New England roll
of fame; but this liking is altogether humorous. . . .

The world is raging after its own wild way, but
though it makes me very sorry for its folly, it does me
no other harm. My days are passed in absolute tranquillity here, where my daughter Margaret is now my
only companion. I read and write, and play piquet with
her in the evening, but I have not followed your exam-

ple yet in taking to solitaire. I spend more time over Dante than over anything else. . . .

Give my love to your girls and boys. I am glad I saw them, and I am always

Affectionately Yours

C. E. N.

To S. G. Ward

ASHFIELD, August 8, 1900.

. . . With your philosophy of old things and new I am in entire agreement, but my application of it may, very naturally, be in some respects different from that which you would make. I have no doubt, for instance, that many of the new things, which are raw and disagreeable to us, will by degrees take their place as natural and wholesome facts in the slow evolution of civilization; but, at the same time, I believe, that in every generation, in every year, every day indeed, new things present themselves, which are undesirable, socially ugly and evil, and to be resisted, even though their force seem irresistible. There will be new, horrible, inevitable wars to be striven against with all the force that good men can bring against them. I dare say that a hundred years hence, people will look back on these days which seem dark to us, as being brighter than those in which they are living, but this is no reason why we who feel the present darkness, should not use every effort in our power to dispel such part of it as our poor torches can light up.

To this, doubtless, you would agree, but I wonder whether you feel the doubt which often assails me, as to the advance of mankind, — whether the increase in knowledge and the mastery of nature is to be counted as true progress. There can be no question that in our time a greater proportion of mankind are physically comfortable, than has ever been the case in the past, but even this is not unmixed blessing. Is there a moral advance at all in proportion to the material? There is a wider diffusion of virtue, morality has become democratic, more men and women are controlled by right principles, but better men and even women than there were two thousand years ago are not easy to find. That book of Dill's which you were reading some months ago, suggests a good many questions of this sort. All life is made up of a series of compensations for which there is no quantitative balance. . . .

You mention Ruskin in your letter. His was essentially one of the saddest of lives. His feminine nature needed support, such as it never got. . . . Ruskin wrote and printed far more than he should have done, and there is nothing left among his papers for future publication; nothing, unless, perhaps, some years hence, a selection be made from his journal and letters, to form as it were, a supplement to his own "Præterita."

That book is the most characteristic of him of all that he wrote; delightful for the most part, exhibiting the sweetness, the generosity, and charm of his nature, and the power of his genius, yet, at the same time, the feebleness of a distracted mind. His home at Brantwood is one of the many in England which nature has done everything to make lovely. . . .

9 August.

Since what precedes was type-written I have had the pleasure of receiving your letter in which you bestow on me far too many thanks for the little service which I can render you in the reading of your proofs. The obligation really is on my side, for what you have written is of great interest to me, and I am glad to read it more than once.

But how long this retrospect makes our lives seem! In fifty years what enormous changes! in seventy years what changes which would seem incredible had they not occurred! No other generation has had, or is likely to have, so long a date as ours, if measured not by years, but by change in the spiritual and intellectual, as well as in the material conditions of the world to which we belong. . . .

To S. G. Ward

ASHFIELD, 19 September, 1900.

. . . I have been busy with the revision of my translation of the "Divine Comedy." It is an engrossing and endless task, for it has to do with the choice and aptness of words, "the subtlest and delicatest instruments," as I think Donne calls them, with which the spirit of man has provided itself to give form to immaterial things, the words themselves being *forma e materia congiunte.* I dare say that you have noticed that the chief verbal difficulties in the poem are in the rhyme-words. Dante's boast that no word had ever compelled him to say aught but what he wished, but

that he had often compelled words to say other than
they were used to say, is quite legitimate if it be rightly
understood. Many of his strained metaphors, of which
there is abundance, are due to the exactions of the
rhyme.

My summer is nearly at its end; I go back to Cambridge on Monday, and leave the country reluctantly.
Cambridge is not what it once was for me; not a single
one of my near friends is left, and among the younger
men there are very few with similar tastes and interests. There is no atmosphere of letters. Our scholars
are men of learning in the modern sense, and of very
little literature. . . . No, the Cambridge of to-day is a
town of prose, and the College is given over to science
and athletics. . . . I quite agree with you that this is
the best century to have lived in since time began; if
for nothing else, that all of us who have lived in it
have lived much longer lives in the same space of
years than any men before us could do, our range of
thought has been wider, our interests more various,
our resources of all sorts indefinitely increased. How
ignorant, how immature the world was a century ago,
compared to what it is now, at least for the men —they
are, indeed, very few, — who know what this century
has potentially secured for mankind. "Primum
Graius homo," secundum, homo hodiernus! But the
man of to-day is less independent than the Greek; he
cannot get along alone, he is more helpless by himself
with every new advance of our complicate civilization.
Will he finally succeed in so adapting himself to these
new conditions, as to master them,—and, "with many

wants," still find opportunity for great thoughts and
great expression of them?

Do you see the English weekly called "Country
Life"? If not, let me commend it to you. Every week it
gives many illustrations of some one of the great country places in which the genius of England has found its
most characteristic visible expression. The pictures
are full of a charm quite peculiar to England. . . .

To Leslie Stephen

SHADY HILL, 21 December, 1900.

I wrote a long piece of a letter to you some days ago,
but I was interrupted before finishing it, and now, on
reading it, it does not please me. How speedily a letter
of one's own grows stale, if it lie on one's hands. Your
last letter was not altogether satisfactory. I trust that
you have not had more of those fainting fits of which
you told me, and that they proved to be nothing worse
than "stomachic vertigo." Since reading your "Utilitarians" — I finished the first reading of it night before
last — I do not wonder that your stomach should give
you trouble. It is an amazing book! with more, and more
various, hard thinking in it than any book which I have
read for years. Political theory, political economy,
logic, metaphysics, theology, and what else, each seems
your peculiar province, and you pass from one to the
other with firm mastery, exposing one after another the
fallacies of the ablest thinkers in each special department, — and with such clearness, wit, humour and
sound sense, and such characterisation of the thinkers
as well as of their thought, that the book is as entertain-

ing in its exhibition of the reaction of life upon thought,
and thought upon life, as it is interesting in the general view which it presents of the course of the chief
intellectual currents of the century. It is, in truth,
an amazing book! It is not strange that you are tired,
and disposed to damn the "Utilitarians."

Parts of the book are by no means easy reading. I
can find no celestial juice which will so clear my eyes
that I can see the ontologists and the transcendentalists otherwise than all "translated" like Bottom, and
my unpurged eyes loathe the vision. But you have
done me immense service, for which I am correspond-
ingly grateful, in coördinating for me a multitude of
facts which were lying disorderly in my mind, in supplying many a lamentable gap in my information, in
guiding me through maze after maze of speculation,
and above all in setting me a lesson and example in
candour, clarity and vigour of thought. Your book indeed is far too good to find many readers capable of ap-
preciating it at its worth; it requires more effort from
those who read it than many in this lazy age of ours
will be ready to make. I rejoice with you on the completion of such an enormous task. You yourself cannot estimate its worth yet. By and by, when you are
as old as I am (!), you will think better of it than you
do now, and agree with me as to its merit.

Such a book cheers one a little in these dark days,
when one is tempted to exclaim, "Lord! what fools
these mortals be." It affords a good argument against
such black pessimism as Goldwin Smith's in the last
"Contemporary." In spite of the loss of supernat-

uralism, the old world will stumble along not much more clumsily than it has done in the poor past centuries. . . .

Write soon. I hope for a good report of yourself. Give my affectionate good wishes for the new Century to each of your young people. May it bring good to you!

Always affectionately yours,

C. E. N.

To S. G. Ward

Shady Hill, 20 January, 1901.

. . . How impressive to the imagination is the passing from earth of the great figure of the Queen! She dies at the right moment, the end of the Century which will bear her name. . . .

To S. G. Ward

Shady Hill, 13 March, 1901.

. . . Besides the usual hindrances to writing, your letter itself deterred me. It contained so much for reflection, so much for discussion which cannot be carried on in writing unless one have vast leisure; so many striking generalisations, most of them convincingly true, some of them questionable. I hesitated to begin to debate them with you, — I hesitate now. I reach one conclusion — that I have been too much of an idealist about America, had set my hopes too high, had formed too fair an image of what she might become. Never had nation such an opportunity, she was the hope of the world. Never again will any nation have her chance to raise the standard of civilization. My error was a natural one for a New Englander born when and where I was: —

me non riprendo,

.   .   .   .   .   .

Poich' era necessario, nè commendo.

You were exposed to the same error, by temperament, perhaps, even more than I, but you were saved from it by more intimate and instructive acquaintance with the "business" of the nation, and the moral forces at work in shaping its destiny. I saw mainly the good, I did not recognize how strong were the bad.

I have been reading Barrett Wendell's "Literary History of America," and commend it to you. It is far the best book on the subject, full of excellent literary criticism, and with some admirable and novel points of view. . . .

To S. G. Ward

Shady Hill, 14 April, 1901.

. . . Certainly the religious, the political, the financial conditions of our country are extraordinary, and I am at a loss as to the proportion of the good and evil auguries to be drawn from them. Such wide-spread and immense material prosperity is a novelty in the world's history. . . .

There is no force to counteract its influence; for Protestantism as a religion has completely failed. It is not the mere breaking down of its dogma, but the fact of its having become, with the progress of science, vacant of spiritual significance, and a church of essentially insincere profession, that is the ruin of Protestantism. It has no spiritual influence with which to oppose the spirit of materialism. If Rome were but a trifle more enlightened, and, instead of opposing, would support and strengthen the American Catholic interpretation of Romanism, the Catholic church in this country would rapidly gain in spiritual power, and would render an enormous service in standing against the anarchic irreligion of the unchurched multitude. In spite of Roman obscurantism, it seems to me likely that Catholicism will gain strength among us. For science has obviously nothing but a stone to offer to the ignorant and dependent masses who are always longing for bread, and the Roman church offers a convenient and, for those who like it, a wholesome substitute for bread. . . .

To Alain C. White [1]

SHADY HILL, CAMBRIDGE, 18 April, 1901.

I am truly sorry to learn that you are ill again, and I hesitate to comply with your request for advice as to reading for fear lest you ought to be desisting altogether, for the present, from study. . . . So, take the rest of this note as advice as to what you shall do when you are running no risk of hurting yourself by doing it.

As for passages in the "Divine Comedy" to be learned by heart, (not committed to memory, which is very different,) take as much as you like from the thirtieth and thirty-first cantos of the "Purgatory,"

---

[1] A pupil in Norton's small Dante class. The letter affords a single example of the kind of helpfulness the teacher was constantly showing.

and of the last canto of the "Paradiso." There is little poetry in any language of nobler quality than these cantos, or better worth making a part of one's possessions.

You would find Villani's "Chronicle" well worth reading in, not perhaps reading through; and the little chronicle of Dino Compagni is an exceedingly interesting account of affairs in Florence at the beginning of the fourteenth century. The book is subject of much controversy as to its genuineness. I am inclined to think that it may be like Defoe's narrative of the Plague, not literal truth, but more true to the conditions of the times than if it were an absolutely exact statement of facts.

If you have not read Dante's "Letters," you should do so, with the help of Mr. Latham's translation; and so, too, the "Convito," with Miss Hillard's version.

I hope that you will soon be well, and with sincere good wishes I am

Very truly yours,

C. E. NORTON.

To S. G. Ward

CAMBRIDGE, 17 May, 1901.

. . . I have been having of late read to me the manuscript of Mr. Scudder's forthcoming "Life of Lowell." . . . The times have changed so rapidly, and conditions are so widely different from what they were during the period of Lowell's greatest influence and activity, that it has become difficult for anyone who was not familiar with them by actual experience to understand the true position and relations of things at that period. But what has been most striking to me in the rapid review of Lowell's life has been the fact that the conditions of his youth were both favourable and unfavourable to the development of his character and genius. We have had no man of such a large stock of native gifts as he; but the soil of this "uncouth corner of the world," as Governor Belcher called it some hundred and fifty years ago, was not favourable for the free and full growth of his powers. His gifts would have flourished better in a richer soil; but his character perhaps gained as much from the New England tradition as his genius suffered from the limitations of the New England life. There was a steady development in him from boyhood to late manhood; but he never succeeded in giving full expression to his extraordinary powers, and his work leaves one with the sense of its not doing complete justice to the potentialities of his nature. It would have been well for him if he could have gone abroad earlier, and come into fuller relations with the great world. I think he never was completely at ease in the society of that world, — never completely at ease even in that little fraction of the society which we have here; and although his brilliant gifts made him a delightful guest, yet his want of ease sometimes resulted in a lack of amenity and in a display of the brilliant rather than of the genial side of his nature. Still, as one looks back over the whole life, one cannot but take delight in such splendid achievement and in such admirable traits of character as he exhibited from the beginning to the end. . . .

What you wrote to me in your last letter in regard to Roman Catholicism in America was of great interest to me. When I get back the full use of my eyes, I shall have something to say to you in relation to it. I am inclined to think that the Church will be strong in America, not because its adherents will adopt all its doctrines, but because they will find in its services a satisfaction for their sentiment which no other ecclesiastical organization offers. . . .

P.S. I have not yet learned to dictate with ease. In what I have said above of Lowell I was thinking of him only in relation to the outside world. His virtues as a friend, and his delightfulness in intimate relations were more than all else in him, and to them I owe a great part of the happiness of life.

To S. G. Ward

SHADY HILL, 29 June, 1901.

That I have not written to you during these last weeks has been due to the fact that my "Spirits of the sight," as Dante calls them, have been resting, and gradually getting over the fatigue which too hard use of them in the winter had brought to them. . . .

I do not recall what I said two or three months ago which has led you to write more or less about the Roman Church and its influence. My own personal experience of it is, of course, far less intimate than yours, yet I accept and agree with all you say of it, and all that your words imply. I fear I must have expressed myself imperfectly if you received the impres-

sion from my words that I thought better of the
Church in such relations as those concerning which
you speak, than you do. No, surely not. But I do
find the Roman Church in this country, in its relations
to the poor and ignorant and suffering, an organization
which is rendering more direct and constant service
than any other. One of its greatest services during the
past sixty years has been the control it has exercised
over the Irish immigrant. The Irish, both men and
women, have become inmates of our houses to a degree
of intimacy which would have been absolutely impossible if it had not been for their pecuniary honesty and
their chastity. These two virtues have been largely
maintained by the influence of the priests through the
confessional.

For some years past I have been pretty thoroughly
acquainted with the management and interior working
of a Hospital for Incurables,[1] which stands about half-
a-mile from my house. It is in charge of the Gray
Nuns, and it would be hard to find any women giving
their lives to the most exhausting and painful charities,
with a sweeter spirit, with simpler feeling, with more
entire devotion and good sense. There is no limitation
of sect, colour or locality as regards the patients. One
could not tell, so far as the treatment of the patients is
concerned, whether the Sisters were Catholic or Pro-
testant. The Hospital is open to the clergy of every
denomination, and if a dying girl wants her Methodist
minister to pray with her, he is as welcome as if he
were a priest.

[1] See *ante*, page 141.

We have a priest in Cambridge who is a great character, full of force, and of bigotry modified by Americanism. He has his separate parish schools, his separate Gymnasium for Roman Catholic youths, etc., etc. But his influence against intemperance and hoodlumism is probably the strongest individual influence in the city. He is doing more to civilize our semi-barbarians than any one else, — and this is the good work which I think the Church is accomplishing throughout the land. As the people become civilized, the Church more or less loses its hold on them.

Anyhow I should prefer to see the Roman Catholic Church grow, — in spite of its obscurantism, and its elevation of itself above the State, — than to see this rapid growth of the most vulgar and debasing of modern sects, that of Christian Science, with its Mother Eddy and her fatuous inanities, and the superstitious delusions of its votaries. The Roman Catholic Church has at least dignity, and splendid ceremonial, and noble traditions, and secular sympathies, — and Christian Science is ungrammatical, unpoetic, absurd to the last degree, yet possesses the immense power which low ideals dressed up pretentiously have over the multitude of the commonplace, prosaic, superstitious souls. Mother Eddy is the most striking and ugliest figure in New England to-day.

She is an illustration of the mediævalism, of which you speak, in its least attractive aspect. It is not only a few but the vast mass of the people even in New England, who are living in the Middle Ages. . . .

To S. G. Ward

ASHFIELD, 30 August, 1901.

. . . I feel entirely with you about England, about her present aspect of feebleness and decline. But I have faith in her recuperative force. She still has the best select breed of men, and if at times, as now, there seems a dearth of those competent to do her work well, a new generation is fast coming on. Did you see Rudyard Kipling's fine poem "The Lesson"? The newspapers have sneered at it, but it has the soundest English ring, and it is by a man who understands versification better than most of his critics do. . . .

To S. G. Ward

SHADY HILL, 7 October, 1901.

Here is a letter from Japan which will interest you, and I send with it the little book to which it refers, and which touches one's sense of humour by the poignancy of the contrasts which it evokes. Mr. Tokutomi was in America four or five years ago, and spent an hour with me, and since then he has from time to time sent to me some pleasant token of remembrance. He seemed to me one of the Japanese marvels, with a keen, ready, assimilating intelligence, an exquisitely refined taste, and an inscrutable soul, as distinct from us spiritually as physically. I used to tell my classes that civilization was a purely relative term, meaning the sum of the acquisitions of a race at any given time, and not as white people are apt to assume a possession exclusively theirs. If the Chinese and Japanese civilization were in one scale, and the British and American in another, it is likely that they would more nearly balance each other than the missionaries and the Christians generally have supposed. I have no such liking for our civilization that I want to see it prevail in Asia, and I cannot but hope that the Chinese have drawn back only *pour mieux sauter.*

I am more and more obliged to you for directing me to Pasteur's "Life," and giving me the opportunity to read it. As a piece of literature the book is full of faults, but as a record of the life of one of the greatest of men of science there are few books of deeper interest, for it is the record of a life of a man whose genius was not a mere superiority of intelligence, but a superiority of character. In this respect Pasteur reminds one of Darwin, and their two "Lives" might well be set side by side. Such contemporary men as Pasteur and Littré make one hope for France, while her men of mere letters . . . might make one despair. . . .

I think you may have gone back to Washington. I take the chance, and send this letter and book there. We left Ashfield on Saturday, though the fine autumn days tempted us to stay, and here we are immersed in collegiate suburbanism. . . .

To Frederic Harrison

SHADY HILL, 31 October, 1901.

Your letter and your book came to me last week, and I thank you cordially for them. I am glad to hear that Mrs. Harrison is improving and likely to improve still further in health, and I hope that before long you will be able to tell me that she is really strong, and her heart as sound physically as it is spiritually. I am glad too of your good account of yourself. You tempt me to competition in regard to eyesight. "Without glasses and without trouble," I write my compliments to Frederic Harrison. Charles Eliot Norton.[1]

I resume my glasses, and wait to be beaten by you when you are 74 years old, as I shall be on the 16th of November!

I have read with great pleasure, but with sad reflections, your fine address on "Washington and the Republican Ideal." The descent from Washington to McKinley is as from Gabriel to Lucifer, and to-day McKinley is the more "popular" of the two. He would carry a general election by a vast majority of voters "rejoicing in their matchless chief." Roosevelt is a better man, but he has not equally the art and the craft by which popularity is to be gained. I met him last week at New Haven, at the celebration of the 200th anniversary of Yale University. Almost his first words to me were of you, as the only man who could talk intelligently with him of the Invasions of the Mongols! He appeared well on the whole, simple and without conscious effort to assume an artificial dignity. It is barely possible that his accession to the presidency may result in a change in our detestable policy and proceedings in the Philippines. He is not pledged to the subjugation of the Filipinos, and he is not hard-hearted nor possessed with the cruel spirit of

[1] These names are written in the clearest and smallest of characters.

Christian self-righteousness. . . . This war of ours is even more criminal, and in a profound sense more disastrous than the war in South Africa. The lesson administered to England was needed by her, and if she learn it, (and she may do so), you and I may live long enough to cherish once more our old pride in her, and renew our hopes for her. . . .

To S. G. Ward

SHADY HILL, 5 November, 1901.

. . . The celebration at Yale [1] was a great success as an advertisement, and interesting in many ways, especially in the evidence it afforded of the astonishing change in the temper of the governors of the University during recent years. It would have seemed incredible twenty-five years ago that Yale should give her highest degree of honour to a Catholic prelate [2] and to a popular novelist,[3] and that, on the chief day of commemoration of her founding, the warmest applause should be bestowed on the Archbishop, on a Japanese statesman,[4] and on Mark Twain! — warmest, with the exception, of course, of that which greeted the Harvard graduate, President of the United States. By far the most interesting figure on the platform crowded with notorieties was the Marquis Ito. He looked like a Buddha in his passive serenity. His tranquil, wrinkled face had the wisdom of the ages in its look, in striking contrast to the smug modern visages of the men who sat near him, the politicians of the passing day. . . .

[1] The bicentennial; at which Norton received the degree of LL.D.
[2] Archbishop Ireland.   [3] Thomas Nelson Page.   [4] Marquis Ito.

The celebration had many pleasant and picturesque aspects, but it afforded one more illustration of the fact that we have no genius for ceremonial pomp, and no appreciation yet of its value in touching the poetic imagination. There was a total lack of splendour; there was no dignity or stateliness in the arrangements. But the most serious lack was the absence of any presentation of the true ideal of a great University, and of its supreme function in a modern democratic republic. . . .

It was a disappointment to me that you had to give up your proposed visit to Boston. I should have been glad to see you once more, but I do not doubt that you were right in not attempting the journey. The death of your sister [1] has removed what I presume to have been one of the strongest motives of your coming. Her [death] deprives me of a very kind friend, and almost the only one who had many familiar memories in common with me of persons and places dear to us both in childhood and youth. I was very much at the Ticknors' and the Guilds' in those days, and your sister's intimacy with my cousins led to our meeting frequently. She was a grown girl, I a little boy, but she treated me so pleasantly that I became much attached to her. What a worthy set of people lived on Park Street then, before Abbott Lawrence disturbed its tranquil dignity with his big new house! There is no room in Boston now, with all the magnificence of its new palaces, and with all the costly splendours with which they are adorned, to compare with Mr. Ticknor's library, and no man to compare with him, in social

[1] Mrs. Charles H. Dorr.

experience and in culture, and, when he was at his best, in refined and genial hospitality. There is no such good talk now-a-days, as there used to be at his table, with Frank Gray and Prescott and Allston, and Everett and my father taking part in it. They were gentlemen of a breed never common, and now rare.

What you tell me of your recent reading is very interesting, or, I should rather say, your reflections on it are very interesting. The truth of what you say about the prevalence and evil of caste in England is strikingly illustrated by the Buller incident. But the war in South Africa is doing much to undermine the system.

My reading of late has been mainly in Shakespeare, — but I read last week with some interest Maeterlinck's book on Bees. Everything in the study of Nature now-a-days tends to the lowering of human conceit, *incuora buona umiltà, e gran tumor appiane.* . . .

To S. G. Ward

SHADY HILL, 6 December, 1901.

To-morrow I mean to return to you the "Life" of Pasteur. I thank you for it, and especially for commending it to me, for very likely, had you not done so, I should never have come to know the man who alone suffices to redress for France the balance of judgment, weighed down on the wrong side by her contemporary novelists, poets and anti-Semites. I say "alone," but such a man could not exist unless there were others like him, and the Life shows that this was the case. And yet how little there is of superior thought in his record. He seems to have deliberately narrowed his

view, and to have refused to consider what lay outside
of it till, at last, he became incapable of being an intelligent sceptic in regard to the deeper problems of existence. I doubt if the word "evolution" occurs in its
wider application on any page of the great volume, and,
as for the meaning of the universe, he does not seem
to have done other than accept the traditional creed
which he had been taught in infancy. He is a disciple
of the Aristotle concerning animals, not of the Aristotle
concerning the soul. He was Greek in curiosity concerning what lay around him, but — . . .

I have been kept in the house all day by a heavy
cold, and have been reading "The Taming of the
Shrew," which I had not read for many years. I had
forgotten how little of Shakespeare there is in it, and
how that little is scattered through the clever extrava-
ganza in brilliant touches which flash "Shakespeare"
in a single word, as in such a verse as this: —

"Your ancient, trusty, pleasant servant Grumio";

or this: —

"Sacred and sweet was all I saw in her."

The longer one lives and the more one learns of men
and of books, the greater grows the wonder of Shakespeare. No poet is more open to the carping criticism
of pedants, but his superb indifference to long-sus-
tained perfection is one of his most engaging qualities.
His very defects but show his mastery. . . .

So far as I personally am concerned I am altogether
indifferent as to the time when death may come. In a
sense it must always come too soon, before one has

finished what he would like to do. I have work laid
out which would take up many more years than can
remain to me, and so it would be were I to live to be as
old as Methusaleh. A little more done, or a little less
is, however, of no consequence. The balance-sheet of
life was practically made up long since. I hope only
that death may come before decay, — nothing else is
of much concern. . . .

To S. G. Ward

SHADY HILL, 2 March, 1902.

. . . I have been reading of late a good deal in
Donne's Sermons. They are as unlike any other sermons as his poems are unlike any other poetry. In
sermons and poems the same temperament is manifest,
and in the sermons are passages of fine imaginative
conception, and of passionate emotion expressed in
that noble Elizabethan mode which was the appanage
of even inferior men in those days. And, as for learning, Donne hardly has an equal among English men of
learning. I cannot read a modern sermon with patience,
and I find even Jeremy Taylor tedious, but Donne
is interesting in spite of his theology, the superfluity
of his citations, and his long-winded subtleties. . . .

To S. G. Ward

SHADY HILL, 10 March, 1902.

Mrs. Gardner knows what I think of her achievement,[1] but I owe you no grudge for letting her know
what I had said of it to you.

[1] In Fenway Court.

A work of another woman of genius has been exciting my admiration during these last days, and when
you read Mrs. Wharton's "Valley of Decision," you
will not, I believe, wonder that it has done so. She
calls it "a novel," but it is rather a study of Italian
thought and life during the latter part of the eighteenth century, in the form of a story. The material and
spiritual scene and its significance are more interesting
than the individual characters of the personages who
are the actors in the drama. These are, indeed, not
without interest, but they are not convincingly alive.
The intellectual element in the book is stronger than
the emotional and passionate, and Mrs. Wharton's
imagination has fused her material of reflection, learning, and personal experience into a wonderfully complete and vivid picture of the Italy of the period, and
exhibits its power in this more than in the creation of
the men and women whose conditions and characters
are the result of the long course of Italian history. Her
knowledge of Italy is that of a scholar and a lover of
"that pleasant country," and her book is one to be
prized most by those who know Italy best and most
love it. It is a unique and astonishing performance, of
which the style is not less remarkable than the substance. It is too thoughtful and too fine a book to be
popular, but it places Mrs. Wharton among the few
foremost of the writers in English to-day.

Harvard did so well by Prince Henry that it seems a
little hard that her reward is to be a great herd of white
elephants, presented by the Emperor, in the form of five
hundred thousand marks worth of casts from German

sculpture! Where are they to be housed? Where are keepers for them to be found? If the Germans had ever produced a beautiful work, either of painting or sculpture, the prospect would be less distressing. But the rich German dealer in bric-à-brac and works of art whom I met in Venice and complimented on his taking the ugliest things he could find, was quite right when he replied to me, "Aber, mein Herr, die Schönheit ist ein Schimpfwort in Deutschland." A colossal statue of the Great Elector! ten heroic statues of German heroes!! What are we to do with them? We cannot even burn them for lime as the Barbarians burnt even greater masterpieces! The invasion of German erudition is bad enough, — but of German art —! . . .

To W. D. Howells

SHADY HILL, 26 March, 1902.

Mr. Hurlbut,[1] one of the pleasantest and most helpful of the younger generation of our College teachers and officers, tells me that he is in correspondence with you in regard to supplying —— College with the young instructor for whom Mr. R—— applied to you. He is more likely than any one else to know of the youth fitted for the place, and longing for the opportunity it might afford him for starting on his career in life and making his Amanda happy with the prospect. But in this changed America such simple hopes and

---

[1] Byron S. Hurlbut, appointed Dean of Harvard College in 1902. Norton's correspondence with his fellow officers of the University was almost wholly in regard to the detail of common affairs and interests; but as Carlyle said of his relation to Norton that it was "very human," so one might say of Norton's intercourse with his colleagues.

prospects seem unnatural and out of fashion. Do you recognize your own country any more? I feel myself a stranger, an exile in my own home. Yesterday there was a meeting before a Legislative Committee in the State House of a crowd of advocates of a statue of General Butler, to be erected in the grounds of the State House, which have lately been enlarged till the top of Beacon Hill is beyond recognition. He was celebrated as the best of Americans, one of the greatest men of the century, and so on! And I see that an Aaron Burr Legion (of Honour?) has been started in New York. The great American drama has turned into a tragedy under the guise of a Comic Opera! What is the next scene to be? "When the Thing that Could n't *has* occurred" one knows not what to expect. . . .

To W. D. Howells

SHADY HILL, 2 May, 1902.

"The Kentons" have been a great comfort to me. I have been in my chamber, with a slight attack of illness, for two or three weeks, and I received them one morning. I could not have had kinder or more entertaining visitors, and I was sorry when, after two or three days, I had to say Good-bye to them. They are very "natural" people, "just Western." I am grateful to you for making me acquainted with them.

"Just Western" is the acme of praise. I think I once told you what pleasure it gave me as a compliment. Several years ago at the end of one of our Christmas Eve receptions, a young fellow from the West, taking my hand and bidding me Good-night, said with great cordiality, "Mr. Norton, I've had a delightful time; it's been *just Western*"!

"The Kentons" is really, my dear Howells, an admirable study of life, and as it was read to me my chief pleasure in listening was in your sympathetic, creative imagination, your insight, your humour, and all your other gifts, which make your stories, I believe, the most faithful representations of actual life that were ever written. Other stories seem unreal after them, and so when we had finished "The Kentons," nothing would do for entertainment but another of your books: so now we are almost at the end of "Silas Lapham," which I find as good as I found it fifteen or sixteen years ago. As Gray's idea of pleasure was to lie on a sofa and have an endless succession of stories by Crébillon, — mine is to have no end of Howells! . . .

To Leslie Stephen

SHADY HILL, 3 June, 1902.

. . . I do not grieve for Godkin's death; the sorrow came almost three years ago, when he was struck down by the blow which left him shattered and disabled. No one who loved him could desire that his life should be prolonged. The fatal final stroke was a mercy. His death increases my solitude. He was a friend of more than forty years standing, and for a great part of that time, especially during the years when he lived in the house at the foot of my old avenue, we were on terms of the most familiar intimacy. In later years, after his second marriage, when he returned to live in New York, we did not meet very often, but we still shared in each other's interests, and always when we met, it was on the old terms of mutual sympathy and understanding. He has not had so wide a reputation as he deserved, his influence on public opinion was much wider than his reputation. He did more than any other writer of his generation to clarify the intelligence and to quicken the conscience of the thoughtful part of the community in regard to every important political question of the time. But the strongest forces in the immediate development of national life were against him. He fought them with matchless courage and resource. He recognized that his work often seemed of little avail, but he was too well read in history to expect other result. There is no one living to take his place, no one whose death would be so serious a loss to the country.

We mean to go to Ashfield about the middle of the month. May made me doubly a grandfather, my youngest boy Richard having a daughter born to him in Rome, my eldest boy Eliot having a son born to him in New York. Happy but grave events!

Do not keep me long waiting for a letter.

Affectionately Yours,

C. E. NORTON.

To Sir Leslie Stephen[1]

ASHFIELD, 27 June, 1902.

MY DEAR STEPHEN, — Day before yesterday brought to me your long-desired letter. I am most grateful to you for writing with such frankness of your

---

[1] Created K. C. B., 1902.

condition. Your account is not such as I hoped for. I am sorry with all my heart that you have such bodily trouble. I can only hope that, under your present regimen, it may not increase, and that, at worst, it will not bring you any greater suffering than you have now to endure. . . . Your description of your mental condition is curiously similar to my own. I look forward to the end of life with entire tranquillity; with hope only that it may arrive before I become a burden to those who love me, and that the body may give way before the mind fails. I don't want to lose consciousness of the joy I have had; that joy remains joy still, and will do so as long as memory lasts. May it do so to the end!

And yesterday came the news of the honour done you. I am heartily glad of it and pleased by it. My next letter shall begin: "My dear Sir Leslie!" I could not give up the old form to-day. I believe you will not have as much pleasure in this honour as you ought, because you do not know your merit as we do. And besides, any honour now comes too late to you and me; for those who would have taken most pleasure in it, and for whose sake we might have cared for it, are gone. There is a certain sad happiness in dedicating it to them; any tribute to us is theirs by right.

We have all been sorry for the postponement of the coronation, because of the confusion, loss and calamity which result from it to so many people. It is a striking event, so unusual is it that any great national ceremony is so sharply prevented. One has sympathy, too, for the poor King as for any other fellow-mortal in distress, but he does not evoke any warmth of affectionate or admiring regret.

I am grieved at Acton's death, for though he and I had never been on specially intimate terms, we had been in very friendly relations ever since we were youths, and whatever intervals there might be between our meetings, we always met as if no long time had elapsed since the last. His genius for the acquisition and retention of knowledge from books was far beyond that of any other man whom I have known.

I am here at Ashfield with Sally. Our days are tranquil, and we are busy with pleasant occupations. At this moment Phil Burne-Jones is spending some days with us.

Good-bye for today, dear old friend. . . .

To Eliot Norton

ASHFIELD, 30 June, 1902.

MY DEAR ELIOT, — Just a word of remembrance and love and hope for to-morrow.

May your little boy make your life happier than it has ever been! and on his thirty-ninth birthday may you write to him with as much affection as I write to you to-night! My blessing to you both, and to his mother.

Your loving
FATHER.

To Goldwin Smith

ASHFIELD, 10 July, 1902.

It would give me the greatest pleasure were I able to accept your affectionate invitation and go to see you,

and renew old days in talk of things of deepest concern. . . .

The greatest spiritual change in ourselves which
the past forty years have wrought is, I take it, the
change in our conceptions of the relation of man to
the universe, and of the possibility of knowledge of
anything whatsoever that lies outside the narrow limits set for us by our senses and by the constitution of
our mental powers. For us at least, faith in human
fancies about invisible things long since died away,
and, for my own part, I have no sentimental regret at
its vanishing. Without it, I find myself more in harmony with that exceedingly minute section of the universe to which I belong; not, indeed, in closer intellectual agreement with most of the good men and women
my contemporaries, of whom all but an insignificant
fraction are still living under the Ptolemaic dispensa-
tion, undisturbed in their practical conviction that this
earth is the centre of the universe, and man the chief
object of creation. Even when their religion has gone
as a controlling force, their superstition remains
affecting their imaginations.

Our talk would be less hopeful than in the early days,
but, I trust, not less cheerful. But alas! there is to be
no talk, for although old age treats me kindly enough,
it warns me that to stay at home is best. I wish with
all my heart it would let me free for a visit to you, to
celebrate your eightieth birthday. I shall celebrate it
here, with honour for a life well spent in the best service of man, for powers nobly used, for an example of
intellectual vigour, honesty and independence, and with

NORTON IN HIS GARDEN AT ASHFIELD

this honour affection will be so mingled that the two will be indistinguishable.

Affectionately Yours,

C. E. Norton.

To S. G. Ward

Ashfield, 19 August, 1902.

Your letters are wonderful and a source of great pleasure to me, alike in what they contain and in what they give proof of. If I sometimes seem remiss in acknowledging them, it is not that I am ungrateful, or unmindful of you, but the remissness is due altogether to the inertia which results from having too many letters to write to people toward whom I am indifferent, and on matters of merely transient or remote interest. To-day, for instance, I have had to write a long letter concerning the care of the fund of our little Academy here, of which I am one of the Trustees; another to a boy who was fitted for College at the Academy (a great feat for such a little country high-school) and is now working his way through Amherst. The old type of the poor New England student, such as was familiar to us in our College days, still survives, in spite of the changes in the ambitions of youth and in the general standards of living. This boy — one of the State-boys so-called — without known parents, writes to me: "Last year my expenses amounted to $160. I earned my board by washing dishes. This year my expenses will probably amount to $100, as I shall earn my room and board." Of this sum he tells me that he has already earned during the summer more than half.

He stands well in his studies. Here is Spartan iron against the Persian gold—(*Persicos odi apparatus*)—of the many boys at Harvard and Yale spoiled by the money which they squander. . . .

August 25.

I was interrupted here the other day, and had no chance to resume my letter before the arrival of three interesting guests who came from Colorado Springs, from Chicago, and from Alabama (by way of Cambridge) to take part, on last Thursday, in our Annual Dinner. I have sent to you a report of the speeches on that occasion, and, though you will not approve altogether of their doctrine, you will be interested in the manner in which it is set forth, and especially in the substance of the speech (which was not delivered) of my young friend, Mr. Garrott Brown, of Alabama. Perhaps you have seen some of his recent articles in the "Atlantic" and other magazines, or his lately published volume on "The Lower South in American History," a volume well worth reading. . . .

He is a man of refined nature, sensitive, modest, of high character, and a strong and cultivated intelligence. His studies of the South have special value from his intimate knowledge of the field, from his inherited sentiment for the old conditions, and his clear appreciation of the new. He is greatly hampered in social relations by deafness, but he is so entirely a gentleman that his disability stands little in his way. I commend his book to you. . . .

Another of my guests was a man whom I had never before seen, and of whom I knew little save as the banker and broker in Colorado who had stood alone there in resistance to the silver craze, and had maintained his position not only with courage but with unusual ability. This was Mr. L. R. Ehrich. . . .

My third guest, Mr. Burritt Smith, is of a different order — an excellent specimen of the best class of "self-made" men of the Middle West, beginning life as a poor boy, a Methodist, and now at fifty, one of the leading lawyers of Chicago, the President of the Chicago Literary Club, the head of their Civic Reform Association, interested in all good things, a freethinker, large-framed, tall, simple in heart and manner, a true democrat, a sort of man whom Lincoln would have trusted and Theodore Parker liked. He had come a thousand miles and more to make his speech at the Dinner, and yesterday afternoon he left us to go back. That shows the kind of man. . . .

To S. G. Ward

SHADY HILL, 18 December, 1902.

. . . You have a precious possession in your Greek, — but what a rare blessing to recover it for easy and delightful use after years of infrequent enjoyment of it! There is no later poem to compare with the Odyssey in healthiness of spirit. Have we gained in our modern civilization an equivalent for what the Greeks possessed and what is not ours? We seem to have eaten of the fruit of the Tree of Knowledge, and to have lost Paradise thereby. And, worse than this, the apples of the Tree are no better than apples of the Dead Sea. They turn to dust and ashes in the mouth. The knowledge we acquire gratifies curiosity, but answers none of the deeper questions which perplex the souls of most thoughtful men. Here for instance is Herbert Spencer whose last word, at the end of his long life, is of shrinking, appalled and troubled, at the conceptions of Space which the advance of knowledge opens to us. This strikes me as an example of the common experience of men who have for a time advanced before their fellows, and who have set up their pillars with the *Ne plus ultra* upon them. . . .

While you have been reading the Odyssey, I have been reading "Paradise Lost," with renewed admiration of Milton as poet, and wonder at him as theologian. I cannot agree with Leslie Stephen that "the first book of P. L. holds the very first place in English, if not in all existing, poetry"! I am surprised that so excellent a critic should ever make this sort of assertion. He should leave it to the penny-a-liners. In its kind the first book may have no superior; but there are other kinds. . . .

To W. L. Mackenzie King [1]

SHADY HILL, 26 January, 1903.

Your long and interesting letter of three weeks ago gave me much pleasure. I am much obliged to you for it, and for the volumes of your "Labour Gazette" which you were good enough to send to me, and which I have looked over with great interest. You are engaged in

[1] Canadian Deputy Minister of Labour, 1900–1908. Minister of Labour in the Laurier administration, 1909–1911. While he was a graduate student at Harvard, 1897–98, Norton had come to know him, and to have the highest regard for him.

work than which there can be little doing in the world
of greater concern in itself, or of more interest to one
who is engaged heartily in it. The questions with
which you have to deal are perhaps the most important
with which this generation has to occupy itself, and it
is plain that on their satisfactory solution depends the
welfare of our great modern industrial and commercial communities. The methods that you have put in
practice in the settlement of labour disputes seem unquestionably the best yet devised, but their successful application depends largely upon the character, the
judgment, and the tact of the adviser, or arbitrator,
as he may be. Knowledge of men, judgment and tact
are not so frequently combined that we can hope that
what might be called individual arbitration would generally be successful, as in the cases in which you have
dealt. On the whole, no method of dealing with these
labour disputes seems to me to promise better than the
plan urged by Mr. Charles F. Adams in a recent
address, a copy of which, I am glad to learn from him,
he has sent to you.[1]

Whatever may be the evils attending the great coal
strike, it was almost worth while that the community
should experience them, for the sake of the increase of
interest and of knowledge concerning the matters in
dispute between the workers and the operators which
the community have been forced by the strike to acquire. The discussion which has been actively going
on now for many months concerning the rights, the

[1] On Dec. 8, 1902, Mr. Adams read before the American Civic Fed-
eration a paper on "Investigation and Publicity as opposed to 'Compulsory Arbitration.'"

duties, the advantages, and the limitations of the unions, the rights of non-union men, the relation between the unions and employers, is leading to the formation of clearer opinions and of better relations on both sides than has ever before been the case. With the public there can be little doubt, I believe, that the cause of the unions has greatly gained, and that the conviction of their usefulness has become general; but, at the same time, the sense has grown that the very grave evils connected with them must be abated, if they would gain the real confidence of the community. Those evils have long been familiar to you. It is not that you and other men who have attended to these questions will have acquired new views from the discussions which have attended the strike, but that the views which you and others who have studied the questions with open minds have long held will have become more widely diffused, and have more power in the shaping of that public opinion which is the ultimate source of power of such institutions as the unions, and which must be the ultimate determining force in the relations between employers and employed. If the committee of investigation, whose sessions are stretching out to a length which cannot but be regretted, — if this committee should make such a report, or reports, as may be hoped, dealing with the questions in a large and intelligent manner, with suggestions for the remedies of the evils which their investigations have brought fully to light, it will have a great effect, not merely in the coal industry, but on the relations of employers and employed in every branch of trade.

Your "Labour Gazette" shows, I think, that in many particulars of the labour question you in Canada are in advance of us in the United States. It is perhaps not strange that this should be so. Your Canadian system of administration has the advantage of being comparatively unhampered by legislative acts and purely political considerations. . . . If in the higher regions of civilization there be little improvement, if a commercial aristocracy with low ideals is taking the place of the aristocracy which, whatever its faults, cherished or pretended to cherish respect for intellectual and spiritual things; if vulgarity is taking the place of refinement among the upper classes, yet we may be content in reflecting that these upper classes are but few compared with the multitudes of the lower class that are rising from degradation into comparative civilization and comfort.

The comparison is not infrequently made between these days of wasteful and vulgar luxury and those of the decline of Rome, but the comparison fails in justice, because at the period of the decline of the Roman Empire the poor were growing more wretched in proportion as the rich grew more extravagant; but to-day, in spite of the enormous inequalities of wealth, the distribution of it still continues to be wider than in any preceding time. . . .

To S. G. Ward

SHADY HILL, 9 March, 1903.

I hope that the last five or six weeks have gone well with you. For most of them I have been shut up in my

chamber. . . . I have had recourse to the friend of
mankind, Sir Walter, and have read and heard read
one after another of his novels, — not the best among
them, for with those I was too familiar, but the next
best, like "The Pirate," "Quentin Durward," and now
"Redgauntlet." I accept much that our dear Howells
says in criticism of them; the new "realism" has antiquated them as "psychological documents"; there is
hardly a truly natural conversation in a dozen of them,
there is no subtle analysis and well-considered development of character; but admitting these and whatever
other faults, they are yet so full of dramatic incident,
their plot and scenery are so excellent as play, their
picturesque variety is so great, and the spirit which
animates them is so fresh, generous, and wholesome,
that I am in full sympathy with FitzGerald and bare
my head to the great and gallant Scott in devout
gratitude and admiration.

I received a gift the other day which I was really
pleased with, — a cast from Saint-Gaudens's medallion
of you. As a work of art I should value it as I should
value a fine Renaissance medal, but its chief worth for
me lies in its excellence as a portrait of you. I see the
family type in it very distinct, even stronger than in
real life. In memory I see you generally as you were
in the war days. We were all immature at that time;
enjoying our Emersonian June.

I wish, by the way, that you would write to me your
thought of Emerson, — a little sketch of your intellectual relation to him and estimate of him. No one
else could write so intimately and so wisely as you,

looking back across the years that have divided you so
far from the Dial which marked the hours of youth.
How different is the spirit of this football generation!
of this generation without a poet! nay, it has Kipling,
and he is its true voice, expressing its good and its bad
as few poets have ever expressed their age. . . .

To Moorfield Storey

ASHFIELD, 29 August, 1903.

MY DEAR STOREY, — I thank you for your letter of a
week ago; it gave me great pleasure. I am sorry to have
the Ashfield Dinners come to an end, but my seventy-
sixth birthday comes next November, and at such an
age it is hardly safe for anyone to engage in undertakings which, if he fail to carry them out, may involve
many others in needless trouble and disappointment.
If there were any lieutenant to whom, in case of need,
I could surrender command, the Dinners would have
gone on.[1] At any rate if there be occasion, I shall easily
make opportunity here to speak my mind in the future
as in the past.

What you say of your getting comfort from Emerson's "Diary" interests me much. I doubt if such
comfort as one may derive from such faith as his and
such doctrine, is other than a modified Stoical attitude
of mind, at least for one who does not, like Emerson,
indulge in an optimism that rejects the evidence of

---

[1] The last "Academy Dinner," to which Norton refers in this letter, was
striking to those who had been present on former occasions, and were once
again, for Norton in a few simple words took farewell of his audience, commending the Academy — for which so much had been accomplished — to
the continued interest of its friends.

facts. In one of the recently published letters of Darwin he says, "What a book a Devil's-chaplain might write on the clumsy, wasteful, blundering, low and horribly cruel works of nature." It is plain, I think, to the student of history, that the same principle holds in the world as in the material universe. "This is a moral world and eternally destroys what is not moral" may be accepted as a truth, but the root of "what is not moral" is as vital and everlasting as the root of what is moral. And though we may be sure that retribution is always certain as a consequence of error and crime, the retribution is often so remote, often falling on the innocent, often taking the form of new error or crime, that the criminal, be he man or nation, does not recognize its connection with his sin, and in many instances seems to his own view to escape altogether from punishment for it. In a large sense the moral law prevails in the long run, and man, perhaps, slowly improves, but how "blundering, wasteful and horribly cruel" seems the process!

The refuge from pessimism is the good men and women at any time existing in the world, — they keep faith and happiness alive. . . .

To Nariaki Kozaki

CAMBRIDGE, February 10, 1904.

DEAR MR. NARIAKI KOZAKI, — Your interesting letter of the 28th of December gives me pleasure as a token of your kind remembrances, and comes to me at a time when we are anticipating with anxious interest news from Japan. I sympathize fully with your anxiety in regard to the issue of a struggle between Japan and Russia. Should it come, I believe public opinion generally in America and England will be upon your side; but, even should Russia be worsted in the struggle, I dread the consequences of war for you. Its best issue cannot but bring many evils in its train. When you say that "we do not wish to fight if we can possibly avoid it," you show that your nation is inspired with the right sentiment in regard to war. It would be an immense triumph for civilization could the questions in dispute between Russia and Japan be referred, even at this last moment, to The Hague Tribunal. If war must come, Japan will at least have the satisfaction of knowing that it has been forced upon her in the defence of her national existence.

I am greatly in accord with the views expressed by Mr. Spencer, in his recently published letter, in respect to the importance to Japan of resistance to the invasion of Western ideas and of Western people; but under the present conditions of rapid communication and the general shrinking of the size of the world by the effect of steam and electricity to its needs, it is vain to hope that any nation can maintain the isolation requisite for the preservation in their purity of those national and racial distinctions which have existed during the past centuries. I have no such liking for our Occidental civilisation as to desire to see it extended over the East. We have as much to learn from the East as you of the East have to learn from the West, and I am not sure but that the lesson the East has to teach is the more important. In a letter which came to me from an American friend, the Editor of a local newspaper in one of the smaller New England cities, on the same day on which your letter reached me, are the following words: — "I do not feel certain that our civilization (that is, the civilization of Western Europe and America) is the *right* civilization. Contemplation, which is associated with the East, looks to me as worthy an occupation as ' hustle '; and is it not conceivable that some race in Asia is developing a form of civilization that by and by would prove as precious as that which Greece left us, if the Persians of Modern Europe could be kept from crushing it back into conformity?" Japan has already taught much to the Western world, and the lessons she has to teach are by no means yet completely learned.

I am glad to hear of the welfare of your household, and of your interesting occupation. In order to fit yourself for your duties as Professor of English, the course upon which you have entered, of reading Shakespeare, Milton, and the nineteenth century poets, is excellent, if at the same time you are pursuing a favourable course in English history. From Shakespeare you will naturally go back to Chaucer, who more than any other poet represents the healthy and solid qualities of the English race in the fourteenth century, and whose work, delightful as poetry, is not less instructive as illustrating the character of English genius.

With kind remembrances and all good wishes, I remain,

Very sincerely yours,

CHARLES ELIOT NORTON.

P.S. The preceding pages were dictated just before the announcement of the declaration of war between your country and Russia reached us. You will have seen that the sympathies of America generally are with your people and their cause. I have great hope that the war will not be so protracted as to become exhausting of the strength and resources of Japan, and that peace may be arranged upon terms which shall admit of the natural development of your country and of her assuming that hegemony in the East which she seems capable of holding, to the advantage of other Oriental races. . . .

To S. Weir Mitchell

SHADY HILL, 5 March, 1904.

MY DEAR MITCHELL, — It was a pleasant deed of yours to write to me of your seventy-fifth birthday, and to give me a chance (though belated, but none the worse for being so) to add my good-wishes and congratulations to those of the friends who have a special and private right to celebrate it. It is a good age to which to have lived, with all one's faculties alert and vigorous and obedient as ever. And the seventy-five years over which your life extends have been on the whole the most interesting and the most important period in the whole history of man. The changes in the material and in the moral world alike have been far greater and more essential than in any corresponding period in the past. While the limits of the Universe have been inconceivably extended, this little trifle of a world of ours has been steadily shrinking in size. There never was such a breaking down of old creeds, such a dispelling of the phantom army of the gods, and such a generally agnostic regard toward the great Unknown and Incomprehensible. The discovery of America, the invention of gunpowder, the printing press, wrought no such effect upon the lives and thoughts of mankind as the compelling of steam and electricity to man's use have done. And so on, — but how about the individual man? It seems to me that but a few have been able to take advantage of these changes and make the best of them, — and that the many have suffered morally for the time being.

But all these thoughts require expansion, and are fitter for an essay than for a birthday letter. What should the good wishes be for his seventy-five-years-old friend of one who is himself seventy-six? They should be what he would wish for himself, — first, health; second, freedom from heavy sorrow; third, life, so long as the grasshopper does not become a burden; fourth, a painless death and a happy memory in the hearts of a few friends.

If you have any other wish for yourself, I wish it for you. . . .

Norton's reference to "a painless death" among the good wishes for old age leads to the introduction here of a letter in answer to a request — from a stranger — for his opinion on the subject.

DEAR MADAM: — You ask me to express my opinion in such form that it may be given to the public concerning the prolongation of life by medical or surgical science when it can be prolonged only at the cost of misery. I have no objection to doing so.

The matter has of late acquired new claim for consideration, owing to the rapid advance in knowledge and in skill alike of physicians and of surgeons, and to the application of this increased knowledge and skill to the lengthening of wretched lives.

The principle that it is a duty to prolong every human life so long as possible, at whatever cost, has hitherto been generally accepted.

Its main support has been the doctrine of the sacredness of human life, and this has been reinforced by two practical considerations of great weight. One, the freedom of physician, surgeon or bystander from all responsibility of decision of a question grave in any case, and in which a mistake in judgment might be severely blameworthy. The other, the natural desire on the part of members of the medical and surgical profession to exhibit the resources of their art in mastering extreme difficulties.

The doctrine and the practice have both been pressed too far.

There is no ground in reason to hold every human life as inviolably sacred, and to be preserved, no matter with what results to the individual or to others. On the contrary, there are lives to which every reasonable consideration urges that the end should be put. . . .

It is not to be hoped that a superstition so deeply rooted in tradition as that of the duty of prolonging life at any cost will readily yield to the arguments of reason, or the pleadings of compassion, but the discussion of the subject in its various aspects may lead gradually to a more enlightened public opinion, and to the consequent relief of much misery. . . .

To S. G. Ward

SHADY HILL, 4 March, 1904.

. . . The days have gone very quietly with me of late. I have been touched deeply by Leslie Stephen's death.[1] He is the last of the men in England with whom I have had a long and more or less intimate friendship. He had a delightful heart and an admirable mind. If you have not read his autobiographical papers which have been lately appearing in the "Atlantic," pray do not fail to do so. They are like good talk, — simple, animated, the narrative of his own experience and observation, without the slightest touch of egotism. . . .

To S. G. Ward

CAMBRIDGE, 26 March, 1904.

The ham which you were good enough to send to me was most excellent. The Virginia pig seems to be as superior to his New England brethren as the Virginia statesmen used to assert themselves to those of the North. The breed of statesmen has perished; may that of the pig survive! Is there a statesman in the high sense left anywhere? Roosevelt would assure us that his Cabinet is full of them. But his best examples do not seem to me the genuine thing. . . .

[1] Sir Leslie Stephen died Feb. 22, 1904.

"I sent into the lists," said Alcibiades, "seven chariots, — no other private man ever did the like. The general sentiment honours such magnificence, and the energy which is shown by it creates an impression of power." — "I have established seven great yellow journals" says Hearst, "no other private man ever did the like." κ. τ. λ.

I have not read any new books of late, unless Boissier's "Tacite" may be called so. It has the usual merits of his writings, merits of his own as well as of his race. Would that the Germans could take example by him! for he is as learned as any of them, but carries his learning lightly and makes use of it for the pleasure as well as the information of his readers, and persuades them that his judgments are sound by the evidence he gives of acquaintance with a wider world than that within the immediate field of his studies.

I have had occasion to look up one or two matters of the *rinascimento* in Italy, and have recurred to two excellent books by Voigt, which some of our younger scholars have been pillaging. I dare say you know them, but if not, I commend them to you, his "Enea Silvio," and his "Wiederbelebung des klassischen Altertums." They —

I am interrupted. Good-bye for to-night! . . .

To Edward S. Morse

CAMBRIDGE, 27 May, 1904.

I am much obliged to you for sending to me a copy of your paper in regard to the evil of needless noise, an evil which is one not only in our cities but in many country districts. I cannot but believe that if you would have a proper bill drawn for the suppression of the needless steam whistling and of other similar noise, it would be widely supported and might be carried through our legislature.

I am sorry, indeed, to hear that you have been driven from your home by the excess of needless noise around you, for it implies much suffering and disturbance for a long while past.

I have just been writing to the University Club in Litchfield County, Connecticut, which had invited me to speak to them next week in regard to the proper modes of celebrating the Fourth of July.[1] The manner in which our country generally has recently celebrated it is of a piece with the evil which you are attempting to correct.

We must begin everywhere, as regards the Fourth, to insist that our town authorities should suppress the use of cannon crackers and other similar explosives, of toy pistols and other instruments of like danger, and the ringing of bells, and other noise in the streets before sunrise. If we can secure this, we can then go on to provide the means for a rational and civilized celebration of the day.

With great regard, sincerely yours,

C. E. NORTON.

---

[1] In 1911, it was pointed out in the "Official Program of the Independence Day Association of Springfield, Massachusetts," that "the movement for a safe and sane Fourth in Springfield to a certain extent received its inspiration from the late Professor Charles Eliot Norton." In 1903, Norton had already begun to interest himself actively in this important matter.

To Charles Moore[1]

CAMBRIDGE, 3 June, 1904.

Your question is not easy to be answered. There are few artists concerning whose work more qualifications are required in a correct estimate than is the case with Whistler. Some of his gifts were quite exceptional and gave to his work a distinguishing individuality of genius which will render it permanently interesting, but the greater part of his work, as it seems to me, would not hold a high place were it not for the extraordinary and even supreme excellence of a certain fraction of his production. Were it not for his best things the great mass of his work, while distinguished, indeed, above that of most of his contemporaries, would soon be likely to sink into oblivion. In the matter of etchings, the same statement might be made in respect to Rembrandt. It is a comparatively small number of his etchings which give value to the great mass of them. At his best, in etching, Whistler seems to me to have had no contemporary rival. There are exquisite refinements in his work which display a sensitiveness to delicate impressions of nature and a capacity of rendering them quite beyond the range of any contemporary.

Of his pictures, so far as I know him, there are but few which seem to me to possess extraordinary merit. Most of them, as I have just said about his other work, become interesting because of their relation to these greater works; but even if one take the finest of

[1] Mr. Charles Moore of Detroit, Michigan, who studied Fine Arts at Harvard in 1877–78, and was led by Norton's influence to interest himself in architecture and in city-planning.

Whistler's portraits, that of his mother and that of
Carlyle, it will not do to set them side by side with the
great portraits of the Venetian artists or with those of
Rembrandt and Velasquez. "Why drag in Velasquez?" I imagine that Whistler asked that question
not so much out of conceit, as for the sake of scoffing at
those who were praising him extravagantly. He had
too keen an eye and too clear a judgment not to recognize, at least in his sane moments, his position
in regard to the supreme masters of the arts. His best
work, whether in black and white or in colour, of whatever mode, will, I believe, hold a high place and possess
a real value in the future. It has the indefinable charm
of genius, the peculiar stamp of special artistic gifts
which no artist has possessed in larger measure than
Whistler, but they are gifts not of the highest order, —
gifts mainly of the outer eye, not of the inward eye of
imagination. The poetic element in Whistler's work is
comparatively small; but it is by the measure of the
poetic element contained in it that the position of a
work of art is finally determined. I am tempted to
run on with these desultory thoughts, but perhaps
what I have written will give you what you desire, —
the estimate which I set upon Whistler as an artist. I
could not decline to comply with your request, and yet
I fear that without a much longer statement I should
fail to give a satisfactory reply to your question. . . .

To William Roscoe Thayer

ASHFIELD, 29 July, 1904.

. . . What you say of the connection between physical health and mental serenity or distress in giving up

NORTON'S HOUSE, ASHFIELD (THE LOCUSTS)

the hereditary faith, and finding one's-self incapable of forming any rational theory of the universe and of one's own relation to it, is undoubtedly true. But the mass of men, even of those called civilized and intelligent, really take little heed of these things, living by the day, and content to live without other faith than that the course of things, so far as they are concerned, will not undergo any startling change in their time. Natural motives are taking the place of supernatural, — with considerable damage to the morality of common men, and with a need for a fundamental revision of ethical theories, and legal systems. The process is slow and revolutionary. It will work out, in the long run, in a better order than that of our chaotic civilization, based as that is very largely on unstable foundations.

The sentiment of "Vanity of vanities, all is Vanity" has its source, it seems to me, in exaggerated expectations and illusory hopes. When men learn that the mystery of the Universe and of their own existence is insoluble, that this life is all, they will perhaps find that with the limitation has come a new sense of the value of life to the individual, and of his infinite unimportance to the universe. He will learn that he can be a help or a harm to his fellows, and that is enough.

I am glad to hear of your Venice work.[1] Venice is the one city that acquired the art of self-expression in a noble and beautiful communal life. She had twelve hundred years of it!

No more to-day, not even of the beauty of the sum-

[1] Mr. Thayer's *Short History of Venice* was published in the autumn of 1905.

mer or the hopes of the Democracy, or the pluck and splendid capacity of the Japanese. . . .

From May to September of 1904, Norton printed in the "Atlantic" some of the letters from Ruskin which made up the two volumes of "Letters of John Ruskin to Charles Eliot Norton," published that autumn. On June 30, William James wrote: "Dear Charles, — I have just read the July 'Atlantic' and am so moved by your Ruskin letters that I can't refrain from over-flowing. They seem to me immortal documents — as the clouds clear away he will surely take his stable place as one of the noblest of the sons of men. Mere sanity is the most philistine and (at bottom) unessen-tial of a man's attributes. . . . Do you suppose that there are many other correspondents of Ruskin who will yield up their treasures in our time to the light? I wish that your modesty had not suppressed certain passages which evidently expressed too much regard for yourself. The point should have been *his* expression of that sort of thing — no matter to whom addressed!"

The editorial reticence to which William James thus referred was recognized not only by Norton's friends, but — from a somewhat different angle — by himself. On September 6, 1904, he wrote to Miss Gaskell: "I shall send you before long two small volumes of Rus-kin's letters to me, which I have been compelled to print much against my will, by the urgency of the editors of the new edition of his Writings. It is so much against my taste to give such letters to the public that I wish now that I had burned the letters as they came." One need only add that it is fortunate that he did not.

To James Ford Rhodes

SHADY HILL, 21 November, 1904.

One of the pleasant results to me of Morley's visit to Boston has been the frequent interchange of notes with you, or let me say, with more precise truth, the frequent receipt of a note from you, — for I am a candidate for membership in the club which Darwin wished for, in which everyone should receive pleasant letters and not have to answer them! Yet even if this ideal club were in existence there would still be some pleasant letters which one would like to answer, — such, for example, as yours of yesterday.

Although I did not see Mr. Morley during his too short stay as often as I should have been glad to, our single meeting was full of pleasure to me, — for it showed that, though we had had but one chance meeting and that only for a moment during the past thirty years, our old friendship remained firm.

You asked me about Nordhoff. I never knew much of him, but on the few occasions when I had talk with him he impressed me as truthful and trustworthy. . . . You speak of his account of Southern affairs in 1875. This reminds me to ask you if you know a remarkable series of letters on the South which appeared in the "Nation" before 1868, — I cannot fix the exact date. They were written by a very remarkable youth, John R. Dennett, a graduate of Harvard in 1862. He died too soon, in 1874 if I remember rightly. Godkin never had a lieutenant whom he estemed more highly, not merely for literary gifts, but for judgment of men and affairs. I remember a letter of his from South Carolina, describing an interview with Governor Chamberlain, which did not leave a favourable impression of the Governor upon me. I have learned since then to esteem him highly, and I am truly glad that your investigations have convinced you that the imputations upon him were groundless.

I dare say you know another very remarkable series of letters on the South, of a somewhat later date, 1881, published in the New York "Tribune." They were written by Mr. J. B. Harrison, of whom, I think, I must have at some time spoken to you. If not, I must tell you his story some day. The "Tribune" collected his letters in one of its "Extras," under the title of "The South of To-day." Probably few copies still exist, but I have one which is at your service if ever you should care to see it. . . .

To S. G. Ward

SHADY HILL, 15 December, 1904.

I hesitated as to having a copy of Ruskin's "Letters" sent to you, for I doubted if you would care for them, but at last I had them sent on the chance that you would have some curiosity about them, and also because, fragmentary as they are, they suffice to give a clear impression of the man with his brain and heart all aflame and Clotho always spinning thread to supply the fire. . . . He had the stuff of a saint in him, and should have been a contemporary of St. Francis and

SIR EDWARD BURNE-JONES
From a photograph by Hollyer

an earlier Fra Angelico. There are pleasant glimpses
of him in the "Memorials" of Burne-Jones which I
have been reading with the greatest interest in the last
two or three days. The book is every way remarkable.
I do not know a more intimate and frank biography.
It is as if his wife had written it for their children and
close friends. Intimate as the book is, there are no reve-
lations in it of the sort which have made so many biographies an offence not less against good breeding and
good morals than against good letters. Burne-Jones
was a delightful man. I have never known anyone in
whom there was a finer mingling of the poetic imagination and the artistic temperament with the traits
of a large, generous, deep nature. He was in this akin
to Shakespeare. He had a noble and perennial gift of
humour, and the tenderness of heart of a woman.

The book shows him as nearly what he was as a
book could well do, but the likeness is imperfect, for
the thing which cannot be told, the evanescent expression which cannot be fixed in words or on canvas, the
originality which made him distinct from other men
and which yet cannot be defined, — all these have to
be taken for granted and sympathetically imagined in
order to make the portrait representative of the living
man.

Morris, Ruskin, Carlyle are far easier figures to draw
correctly. But there is enough in the passages of his
letters printed in the volumes to give you a fair impression of him.

I hope that the winter has begun well with you. I
have no reason to complain of the burden of years.

But length of life has brought me bitter disappointment in regard to the country that I have loved and hoped for. I admit that had I been wiser I should have expected less and been less disappointed. The substitution of Roosevelt as an ideal in place of Washington and Lincoln is not encouraging. . . .

Among many expressions called forth by the publication of the Ruskin letters, one — from Horace Howard Furness of Philadelphia — was peculiarly fortunate in its consequences, for it led to active correspondence with a friend valued not only for himself, but also as the son of an older friend [1] of Norton's and of his father's. In the letters written during these last years to Mr. Furness one finds, as in the correspondence with Mr. Ward, a grateful sense of falling back, at the end of life, upon mutual comprehensions and sympathies.

To H. H. Furness

SHADY HILL, 22 December, 1904.

DEAREST FURNESS, — It is a red letter day with me when the morning postman brings me an envelope addressed in your noble handwriting. The day may be cold and gray, but your letter makes it warm and fills it with sunshine.

What you say about Ruskin and his "Letters" gives

---

[1] When on the 20th of April, 1892, the ninetieth birthday of Dr. Wm. H. Furness was celebrated, Norton sent him these lines: —

"Honour to him who, for full ninety years,
Walking through what men call the Vale of Tears,
Finds it the garden of perpetual Youth,
All redolent of joy and love and truth!"

me special pleasure by its sympathetic insight and appreciation. They need to be interpreted sympathetically if they are to be rightly understood, — and imaginative sympathy is one of the rarest graces of man or woman. You will not wonder that I hesitated and was reluctant to print these letters which expose themselves so often to being misread, — but which, if read as you have read them, give entrance to the heart of —

I was interrupted last night (it is now Friday) by the coming in of an old pupil who has become [one] of the physically big and mentally optimistic men whom the West breeds. He is one of the chief lawyers in Chicago, and the sort of man who makes one hopeful of the issue of the hard struggle between Ormuzd and Ahriman in the vast dark valley of the Western rivers of wealth. Jeshurun often recurs to my thought in these days, and I turned the other day to see what was said of him in the Vulgate, and was delighted with these words, which roll out like crashing thunder: — Incrassatus est dilectus, et recalcitravit: incrassatus, impinguatus, dilatatus, dereliquit Deum factorem suum. . . .

Your affectionate

C. E. N.

To L. P. Jacks [1]

CAMBRIDGE, MASSACHUSETTS, 29 April, 1905.

DEAR MR. JACKS, — Six months ago I had the pleasure of receiving from you a copy of the "Hibbert

[1] When the editor of the *Hibbert Journal* spent the year of 1886–87 as a student at Harvard University, he was strongly influenced by Professor Norton. Mr. Jacks, since Norton's death, has made warm acknowledgments of this influence.

Journal" containing a more than usually interesting article by Mr. Edmund Gardner upon Dante, and I ought long since to have thanked you for it. It gave me much pleasure to receive such a token of your remembrance.

I should be glad indeed, if, instead of such a token, I could have the greater pleasure of seeing you here once more, and of learning from you concerning the course of thought in England in regard to the topics of highest permanent interest. The "Hibbert Journal" affords me, indeed, from time to time the measure of the current of the stream of thought. Both in England and in this country the disintegration of the old foundations of faith proceeds steadily until no part of them seems to be secure. But, although this has proceeded so far, there is a very general refusal to recognize the fact on the part of those who through temperament or position are disposed to maintain, so far as may be possible, the old order. The whole condition is novel. Never before has there been such a widespread actual skepticism combined with so much external regard for traditional beliefs.

The effect of this conflict cannot but be injurious to the finer moral sense of those who recognize the difference between their actual and their professed beliefs, and the effect upon the great mass of the mere conformists without conviction is, I believe, to produce a condition of moral indifference to which we may ascribe a considerable part of that reaction against the best results of our civilization which has of late years been so conspicuous. . . .

To S. G. Ward

ASHFIELD, 19 June, 1905.

. . . After all, our meeting would be but for a moment, for the sake of the touch of the hand and of an affectionate glance. We have no special message, one to the other, to communicate by word of mouth. We have no new thought about the *quatuor novissima,* no explanation, or expectation of explanation, of our whence and wherefore. On the whole, as, soon to quit the scene, I look back over the vast stage of life on which we have played our little parts, the futility of the whole drama is what strikes me most. The plot is intricate and quite unintelligible, now comic, now tragic, generally dull, but with innumerable episodes of pleasant interest. Each performer seems to himself of importance, which consoles him for not understanding the play in which he bears a part. Now and then come crises in the drama as a whole which make for apparent change of scheme, but the change affords no solution of the plot. We are witnessing one of these great scene-shifting changes now in the victories of Japan. The East is at last claiming her rights in the fields which the West had fancied was for her own occupation. At last the *wisdom* of the East has applied itself to practical affairs, and even in the realm of mere knowledge and facts, — the very chosen ground of the West, — displays an astonishing mastery.

How interesting it all is! how humiliating to our special national conceit!

I wonder if you have read Santayana's interesting

book, "The Life of Reason"? I have a profound distrust of most metaphysical speculation, and here and there in Santayana's work are arguments which seem to me needlessly metaphysical. But nothing could be better as a corrective of the barrenness of pure metaphysics than the general intent of Santayana's book, and the turning of his speculative enquiry to moral ends, — in other words to the uses of life. . . .

To Mrs. Eliot Norton

ASHFIELD, 14 July, 1905.

MY DEAR MARGARET, — . . . ——and her little girl came to us a week ago, and we are greatly enjoying their visit. I wish (as I have often said) that you and Tatoo [1] were here too. He and his cousin are different enough to set each other off and to get along well together. She is much interested, as he would be, in the various opportunities afforded by the barn, — the playing on the haymow, the feeding of the cows in the late afternoon, the riding on Betty the farmhorse's broad back, and the giving her a lump of sugar to pay for the ride. Denis had made for her out of two big boxes the most lovely barn that ever was, with real stalls and creatures (bought at the Falls) which move their heads in the stalls, and a hay loft with real hay in it, and other enchanting devices. I wish I could send one like it to Charles.

Have you had any novel lately as good as "The Magnetic North," or "The Sacred Flame" (or was the title "The Divine Fire"?)?

[1] Norton's little grandson.

With love from us all to you and the little boy, I am, as always,

Affectionately Yours,

C. E. NORTON.

To S. G. Ward

ASHFIELD, 13 September, 1905.

How has the summer gone with you? I hope that Swampscott has been pleasant and kind to you, and that you have enjoyed the neighbourhood of the sea. The sea is richer in suggestions to the imagination and the intellect, and in its appeal to sentiment than the everlasting hills. It does not minister to rest as the mountains do. Its superficial restlessness suits the restless American temperament. It is not surprising that the Western millionaire, who has lived half his life without one invigorating breath of salt air, is buying up our coast for his summer home.

But what interesting weeks these last have been! The ill-mannered Witte may boast of his skilful bluff, and of Russian triumph in the negotiations, but the victory — the diplomatic no less than the moral victory at Portsmouth — belongs to the silent and self-respectful and subtle Japanese. The giving up of the demand for compensation in money was no hasty stroke, but as long-considered as it was far-sighted. It was a piece of wisdom to spare the Russian pride from further humiliation. Howells, who has his summer home at Kittery Point, wrote to me a day or two since: "I have seen much of the unbottled diplomatists, with a growing aversion for both sides. Witte strikes me as a great, simple, if not single soul. The Japs are single, perhaps, but oh, never simple."

If you have not read Dicey's "Law and Opinion in England," let me commend it to you as well worth reading. It is able, fair-minded, and interesting as bringing out the significance and relation of a multitude of familiar facts, which for the most part have belonged to the lumber-room of the mind where unconcerning things are stored till some philosopher brings a parcel of them into order. . . .

To S. Weir Mitchell
                    SHADY HILL, 27 November, 1905.

You tell me what I had forgotten, that I spoke of football as the chief industry of the University of Pennsylvania, and to rebuke my wanton speech you send me a paper showing that "it is a centre of great mental activity." I have read this paper with attention and instruction, and shall henceforth be as little likely to speak disrespectfully of your University as of the Equator, — for I have learned among other things of the doing of which it has to boast during the past year, that it has discovered fifteen new gods, — no, "no less than sixteen new gods," that it has been compiling references to sea-sickness in Greek and Latin authors, that it is preparing an edition of the critical works of Dennis and of one or two other writers of equal importance, that it is continuing its investigations of the knee-jerk, and in brief is displaying an intellectual life of at least as high an order as the physical life which has won it its proud position in athletics! I am glad to scramble out of the pitfall into which my ignorance of these things precipitated me.

You choose a Middle English epithet for these glorious days, and promise me a letter before long written in Middle English! A letter from you in whatever dialect or tongue could not but be welcome, — but keep for my sake to that Modern English of which you are a past master. I feel toward Middle English as the scholar felt toward the Latin of the Middle Ages, when he translated the title of Ducange's invaluable *Glossarium Mediae et Infimae Latinitatis*.

No more! It is time to dress for dinner.

To S. Weir Mitchell

SHADY HILL, 22 December, 1905.

I write on the rebound that my thanks for your letter while my heart is still warm with the pleasure it gives me, and that my Christmas good wishes may reach you before the day itself has passed. How slowly Peace makes its way on earth! The song of the Angels has not lost its sweetness, but its tone is full of a deep sadness. Happy we who have a share in our own homes of the peace which is so scanty in the world! . . . Nowhere are peace and goodwill toward men, — no, that is rhetorical exaggeration, — but as George Sand says, *rien ne soulage comme la rhétorique*. So I bid dark thoughts vanish, and wish you most heartily a Merry Christmas and a Happy New Year.

I wonder if, now that you are passed three score and ten, you find as I do that the days seem to have fewer hours, and the hours fewer minutes than they had in earlier years. I lay out a day's work in the morning on the old scale, like this ————, and in the evening find I have accomplished something like this—. I take comfort in the thought that more or less is of little consequence now. I rejoice in the unabated power of work in a man like Howells, nearing the end of youth. What an incomparably sweet and delightful nature he was blessed with, and how faithful he has been to it! I never can cease to regret for his own sake that he had so late a coming into his rights as a novelist. He should have been born into the purple of the kingdom of good letters. Neither he nor Henry James has been as good as they would have been if they had been trained with some acquaintance in childhood with Homer and Virgil and the historic stream of imagination in literature. . . .

I am interrupted by the coming in of an interesting man, — Professor Ostwald of Berlin, and must finish hastily.

May we meet often in the coming year!

Yours always,

C. E. N.

Let me know if your wise men at the University discover more "new gods."

To S. G. Ward

SHADY HILL, 24 January, 1906.

I quarrel with myself for not writing more frequently to you, and following Sir Thomas Browne's advice, which I was reading this afternoon, I will "not call for many hour-glasses to justify" my failure.

Even as I write it, I see that the phrase out of its connection needs explanation. Sir Thomas means, don't
waste time in justifying yourself, for in so doing,
whether the justification be valid or not you commit a
new fault. Here is already a page wasted! . . .

I have just been reading two books which I am confident would be of interest to you if you have not
happened to get hold of them. Both are by Professor
Ker who holds the chair of English Literature in University College, London. He is an Oxford man, fellow of
All Souls, hardly middle-aged, but already one of the
best scholars in Europe in the field of the Dark and
early Middle Ages,—and not a pedant, but comparable
to Mackail in that union of culture with learning, of
good letters with good scholarship which is the boast
of the best English scholars (Jebb was another conspicuous instance), and which is seldom shared by the
Germans who are apt to be nothing but learned, or by
the French who are apt to subordinate learning to
pleasant easy literary style. But to go back to Ker, —
the first of his books, published two years ago, is called
"The Dark Ages" and is a capital survey of the intellectual life of that period. It is a small, compact volume of some 350 pages. His other book, published a
few months ago, a little larger in form but smaller in
number of pages, is called "Essays on Medieval
Literature" and is made up of half a dozen very pleasant essays originally published in the "Quarterly
Review" or some other periodical. One of the best of
them is an admirable study of Boccaccio and his
influence. A book of a very different sort, which I

dare say you have already had and found entertaining, is Captain Scott's remarkable narrative of the "Voyage of the Discovery," — one of the fine records of English pluck and intelligence.[1]

To S. G. Ward

SHADY HILL, 23 March, 1906.

Your late letter might put the youngest of us to shame. We none of us could hope to take the first prize in letter-writing were you in the competition. Did you learn in early life from that excellent little book of Mrs. Farrar's "The Youth's Letter-Writer"? As the other day I was passing the Farrar house with which you were once so familiar, I recalled that the first time I ever saw you was one Sunday morning as I was going to church with my mother. As we passed the gate she said to me, "There is young Mr. Ward going up the steps, to see the beautiful Miss Anna Barker." I suppose the little incident impressed itself on my memory, because the beautiful Miss Barker had been at our house and had made me, a boy of ten or twelve, captive by her charm. The gate and the steps remain as they were in those old days, but the house itself has been undergoing complete renovation and has been changed almost out of recognition. The lofty columns have been removed and the house built out over the piazza, increasing the size of the rooms by so much, and freeing the second story from the heavy overhanging brow which used to deprive it of sunlight.

---

[1] Continued in the record of heroism which in 1913 has profoundly moved the civilized world.

The College has bought the house and it has been thus remodelled and improved for its new occupants,[1] — cultivated, pleasant people worthy to come into the inheritance of its traditions. How sweet and primitive were those days! and how far away! You and I have lived as long as Methusaleh. . . .

To Goldwin Smith

ASHFIELD, 12 July, 1906.

MY DEAR GOLDWIN SMITH, — As I write your name the memory of your visit to us here more than forty years ago rises fresh and vivid in my mind. Those were interesting days. And how full of interest, — political, social, religious, moral, all the later years have been! I thank you for sending to me a copy of your recent volume, in which "in quest of light" you deal with the most fundamental interests of all. With many of your positions and conclusions I am in full sympathy, but I am a more complete agnostic than you, and I have less fear than you of the result on conduct of the weakening of belief in the divine origin and authority of Christianity. The motives for good-conduct and for refraining from ill presented by Christianity seem to me of an essentially selfish order, and, although their appeal to selfishness has been urged by priests and ecclesiastics generally, it does not appear to have been of much avail except with the ignorant masses of men. With them it is not likely, whatever changes take place in the creed of the comparatively small number of enlightened men, to lose its force. I

[1] Professor and Mrs. E. C. Moore.

believe that the motives which impel an intelligent man (who leaves God and Immortality out of his reckoning because inconceivable) to virtuous conduct, are the strongest which can be addressed to a human being, because they appeal directly to the highest qualities of his nature.

Your conception of "conscience" as a "faculty" (?) that bears testimony that is to be trusted to things of the spirit, in regard to which the reason is silent, has too much of the intuitional to be acceptable to a disciple of Locke and Hume.

But why dwell on differences? Here we are, old men, near the end of life, and awaiting the end without anxiety or a shadow of fear; perplexed indeed by the mighty mystery of existence and of the universe, and happy in the conviction that the chief lesson of life is that of love.

I hope that old age still continues kind to you, as kind at least as it is to me,—for, though my mental as well as my physical joints are not as limber as they once were, I still find pleasure in "cultivating my garden" and do not feel the grasshopper as a burden.

With kind and respectful regards to your wife, I am, as always,

Affectionately Yours,

C. E. NORTON.

While the evidences of Norton's freethinking have been made plain through the foregoing letters — written, many of them, it should be remembered, to men who shared his views — a few words must be added to his own statements in regard to his spiritual outlook on the world.

Briefly, for Norton, Montaigne's *que sais-je* said all. The definite affirmations of creed and dogma, whether founded in age-long observance and tradition, or in the profound needs of the heart, did not hold for Norton authority other than of man's invention. But the doctrine of the Church was all through his life, as his correspondence and his study of Dante show, matter with him of deep interest. This was natural; his inheritance, his intercourse with men, the times charged with discussion of such questions, conspired to it. Yet, as his brother-in-law has said of him, "the unvexed spirit of his agnosticism was rare." This "unvexed spirit" was, however, not due to an intellectual detachment in Norton, — averse though he was to speculation and religious emotion, as they may nourish sources of introspection; it sprang rather out of a preoccupation with the idea — lying, in his estimation, at the source of life — of the individual's responsibility to himself. And shift this responsibility you might not. For all seekers after Truth, the way was necessarily toward the heights crowned by "une dernière citadelle irréductible."

But character, sincerity, in whatever garb, — let it even have been all of dogma, — made an instant appeal to Norton's sympathies. Priest and prelate were among his friends, and broadly speaking — would they allow it? — he and they sought ends not dissimilar. If they approached life through the church portal, he made his appeal to youth through life itself. Cultivate every perception, refine the sense, "pensa che questo dì mai non raggiorna," obey the "new commandment": these precepts, vitalized by essential significance if applied to the conduct of life, were for Norton fundamental in importance, "these, and the wish to serve, to add something to the well-being of men."

To C. F. Adams

SHADY HILL, 25 January, 1907.

. . . I thank you for sending to me a copy of your address on General Lee. It is a thoroughly characteristic, and, consequently, a truly admirable performance, — thoughtful, vigorous, courageous, and full of important considerations presented for the first time. As I read it, I, more than once, found myself repeating the excellent phrase of Hosea Biglow, or, rather, of Parson Wilbur as reported by H. B., "I don't ollers agree with him, but by Time I *du* like a feller that aint a Feared." If I don't "ollers," I do "most gene'lly ollers" agree and applaud.

I am glad that Virginia was hospitable to you, and that the sun shone and that you enjoyed your visit there. You were doing a patriotic service and deserved the reward.

To S. Weir Mitchell

31 January, 1907.

. . . Why is it that the German race has from the beginning shown itself devoid of the sense of beauty in every art, and of the capacity for truly poetic imaginings? Compare "Faust" with any one of the greater

Shakespearean tragedies. It may, though I doubt, surpass them all in the region of the understanding, but there is more of poetic imagination in a single scene of "Hamlet" or "Macbeth" than in the whole play of the greatest of the Germans. When the reaction comes against the materialism of the present time and its mere intellectualism, as it will come in the course of ages, I do not believe that "Faust" will hold the same place in the regards of men which it seems to hold to-day.

What an interesting illustration Kipling affords of the poetic imagination working under difficulties! There is little to nourish or quicken the spiritual side of his nature, but he has done a better work for his time than any other man in treating through the poetic imagination the material conditions which surround us all; and with what magnificent success he has done it!

> "Confound Romance! . . . and all unseen
> Romance brought up the nine-fifteen."

And how splendid is "The Miracles": —

> "I sent a message to my dear —
> A thousand leagues and more to her —
> The dumb sea-levels thrilled to hear,
> And Lost Atlantis bore to her."

And what a marvel of expression and of picturesque presentation of the fates and fortunes of Englishmen is "The Song of the Banjo"?

His book, "Puck of Pook's Hill," has been lying on my table for the last two or three months unread, but I happened to open it the other day and came upon a little poem so charming, — such a nineteenth-century version of Herrick, — that it at once drew me to the reading of the whole, and the book is well worth reading. If it does not yet lie on your table, look at it the next time you go to your booksellers, and turn to page 123 and read the little poem,[1] and then I am sure you will carry the volume home.

I wish you would come to the celebration of the Longfellow centennial which we are to have here two or three weeks hence.[2] Longfellow deserves all that we can say in his praise. . . . Come if you can, and let us have a long talk together; but whether you come or not, hold me always as

Affectionately Yours,

C. E. NORTON.

Norton's pleasure and interest in helping youth to "find itself" was perhaps in no case more markedly shown than in his relation to his nephew, Francis Bullard. Stimulating, in a nature open to the appeal, a love of the arts, and critical discriminations, Norton never wearied of guiding those perceptions and discriminations by sympathy and suggestion. The almost matchless Bullard Collection of Turner prints, now through the too early death of their owner,[3] one of the treasures of the Boston Art Museum, is in a sense the record of intercourse between uncle and nephew — and a shared enthusiasm — happy for both in an eminent degree.

[1] Beginning
"Cities and Thrones and Powers
Stand in Time's Eye."
[2] At this celebration, in Sanders Theatre, Norton presided.
[3] Francis Bullard died in February, 1913.

To Francis Bullard

SHADY HILL, Monday, February, 1907.

Many thanks for your note and for the enclosures. If Mr. Mayer's word is to be trusted you are to be congratulated, for a first-rate impression of the "Knight and Death" is a precious possession. There is nothing to be compared with it in the whole range of German engraving.

Three hundred and fifty years ago prices were more moderate than they are now, — witness the following sentence, which I happened on to-day, written by a certain German, Johann Neudörfer, Nuremberg, 1546, — "und so einer alle seine [Albrecht Dürer's] gerissene und gestochene Kunst kaufen will, derer eine grosse Menge ist, kann er es unter 9 Gulden nicht wohl zu wegen bringen "!!

But don't bankrupt yourself lest Melancholia compel the Knight to fly.

One such acquisition as "The Lost Sailor," or the romantic "Raglan," ought to be enough for many months.

Your affectionate

UNCLE CHARLES.

To S. G. Ward

SHADY HILL, 4 February, 1907.

. . . Have you, by the way, seen Charles Adams's recent centennial discourse on Lee? It is a very striking and admirable performance. He has perhaps never written anything more masterly as a piece of literature, or more serviceable for the illumination and direction of public opinion. The tendency in him to extravagance and paradox which has been sometimes apparent, if it shows itself in this discourse at all, shows itself to the advantage of the end which he had in view.

I wonder if you would agree with me in thinking that many of the questions which occupied us fifty or sixty years ago and which seemed of prime importance then, — that many of the questions which have occupied men from the days of Plato till to-day, — have in recent years become seemingly of far less importance than they have been in the past. Were it not for the literary style which gives to Emerson's essays an indefinite permanence and, above all, were it not for the quality of the spirit that breathes through them, much in them would already seem antiquated and unimportant.

The last book that I read with much interest was the "Life of Leslie Stephen," of which I have spoken to you in a previous letter. If you have not seen it, I believe it would interest you also.

I dare say you read last year Lord Acton's lectures on modern history. They are worth reading, though they are the work rather of the scholar than of the philosopher, but a very great scholar so far as the accumulation of knowledge is concerned. If Acton had had a gift of narration proportioned to his power of acquisition, he would have made a great historian of the second order. His mind had been so shaped by the conditions under which he was born, and by his early training, that he could hardly have become a historian of the first rank. But he was one of those rare men who seem to be born with more knowledge than most scholars, however studious, can acquire; men with portentous memories holding every fact firm and in its due order, and requiring no effort to bring all their resources into immediate use. Acton could not perhaps like Macaulay have repeated the names of the Archbishops of Canterbury backwards from Victoria to the Conquest, but he could have told you the precise date of every fact even of secondary importance in the European history of the last thousand years. I never knew but one man who was his equal in the amount and variety of miscellaneous as well as scholarly knowledge which he possessed, and that was Mr. Ticknor's old friend in Paris, Comte Circourt. Acton's lectures are not easy reading, but you would find them of interest.

I have dictated this letter to you instead of writing it with my own hand because of a slight and transient weakness in one of my eyes which requires me to humour it for a few days. Let me have a good report from you before long.

Affectionately Yours,
C. E. NORTON.

To Francis Bullard

SHADY HILL, April, 1907.

I am much obliged to you for your pleasant letter written a month ago on board ship. . . .

You asked me for an interpretation of the symbolism in Albert Dürer's "Knight and Death." In a design which is so full of detail it is difficult to determine with confidence what the significance of many of its minor points may be, all the more difficult in the case of a German mystic like Dürer; but the main symbolism of the piece seems to me quite plain, and I care very little whether or not I can interpret the subordinate elements of the design precisely in accord with Dürer's intention in them; for his main intention is so plain that it could hardly be missed even by the most careless observer. It is the steadfastness of the valiant knight, armed against all the common dangers of life as he rides down through the valley, whether of the shadow of death, or any other shadow. All the symbols of death are around him, and more than the symbols of the devil; he is not afraid of them and looks neither to the right hand nor to the left, but goes on his way like Greatheart in the "Pilgrim's Progress," confident in his strength to meet and overcome whatever terrors of actual temptation or of the imagination may confront him. His steadfast strength is indicated not only by the expression of his countenance, but by his attitude, the grip of his hand on the bridle, by the vigour and spring of his horse, and by the trustful fidelity of the dog at the horse's heels. As for the rest of the detail, I give it over to you to ascribe to it whatever significance you like, but in the main we cannot be mistaken that it was Dürer's intention to give an image of the valiant man in his course through the perils of this world, perils by which we are all of us at some time or other beset. . . .

To C. F. Adams

CAMBRIDGE, 10 April, 1907.

I am sorry not to be at the meeting of the Overseers this morning, but prudence has kept me at home. But if, as you propose in the letter which I had the pleasure of receiving from you this morning, you have moved an adjournment of the meeting till the twenty-fourth, I shall not regret my absence to-day. Nor shall I regret to have the President present on occasion of such discussion as may arise on the motion which I propose to offer. It is possible to be entirely frank with Eliot because of his own frankness and simplicity of nature; and I would rather have him hear what is said at the meeting and give him the opportunity to make whatever remark he might choose upon it, than have him receive what might be an imperfect report of what was said. . . .

I share your pleasure in what Professor Moore wrote to you concerning your address on General Lee. I say I share it because I so fully sympathize with his sentiment in regard to the address, and because his account of reading it to his wife and children gives such a pleasant picture of domestic happiness and of a delightful old fashion of domestic education as cannot but warm the heart of an old man brought up in days when such pleasant relations and habits were more familiar than they are to-day. Professor Moore's account reminds me of what a namesake of his, Henry More, the poet and Platonist, tells in a dedication to his father of one of his books, some two hundred and fifty years ago, in which, as I remember, he recounts having had his ears tuned to poetry from his childhood by his father "entertaining us on winter nights with that incomparable poem, the Faëry Queen." I may not have his words exactly, but that is the substance of them, and the picture which the words gave me many years ago remains a pleasant one in the gallery of memory.

To Mrs. Huth Jackson [1]

SHADY HILL, 24 April, 1907.

. . . Such reading as I have done of late has been mainly of old and familiar books, but I have read one book recently, of which I shall send you a copy, that you may see what sort of youth it was that went from here at Harvard to fight our battles in the Civil War forty years ago. It is the "Life of Charles Lowell,"[2] a nephew of the poet, and commemorated by him in verses of peculiar tenderness. It has a universal interest because it is the life of a youth who had the true heroic qualities, — the qualities which distinguished the youth of Athens who still ride in their immortal beauty and gallantry in the Parthenon procession; the qualities which distinguished such a hero as Joinville; the qualities which belonged to Sir Philip Sidney, and which everywhere and in all ages have been the characteristics of the heroic youth. It is delightful to see them reappear in perennial freshness in this new country of ours, with its modern temper and ideals. It is pleasant to see now and then in such a country a link in the chain that binds the best in continuous sym-

[1] Daughter of Sir Mountstuart E. Grant-Duff.
[2] The *Life and Letters of Charles Russell Lowell*, by Edward Waldo Emerson, was published in 1907.

pathy from age to age. In spite of the fact that in this era of commercialism such types of character rarely manifest themselves, I believe, nevertheless, that they exist and that in time of need, such as will surely come before long, will be found ready to do their part in that fight for the good old cause in which the best men of each generation are always enlisted! . . .

It does not seem to me that of late the world is becoming a happier or pleasanter place in which to live, — but this is no season for pessimistic despondency. The Spring is more beautiful than ever, its recurrent miracle was never more wonderful, and never did Persia or Athens see such perfect roses as those which in these days of materialism America can show to any Hafiz or Anacreon.

Good-night!

Affectionately Yours,

C. E. NORTON.

To James Loeb [1]

SHADY HILL, 11 May, 1907.

MY DEAR LOEB, — . . . The great interest and value of your gifts and loans to the Museum [2] are properly

---

[1] The name of James Loeb, of the class of 1888 at Harvard, is so connected with Norton's that it should not be introduced without a special word. — As an undergraduate Mr. Loeb came much under Norton's influence in the classroom and at Shady Hill; and the dedication of his powers to scholarly ends and liberalities — such as the establishment of the "Loeb Classical Library" — speaks in a measure for that influence, among others. The passing years witnessed no change in the loyalty and devotion of pupil to teacher. Mr. Loeb has warmly supported and closely identified himself with the Archæological Institute; in 1901 he founded at Harvard the "Charles Eliot Norton Fellowship in Greek Studies"; in 1902 he gave to Norton the precious Chaucer portrait which he in turn bequeathed — in memory of Lowell and Child — to the University Library.

[2] The Fogg Museum at Harvard.

appreciated by the Committee. Your example is likely to be a powerful incentive to other graduates of the University interested in the promotion of the fine arts and who recognize the place which instruction in them ought to hold in any proper scheme of education.

Last night Professor Gilbert Murray delivered the last of a series of lectures upon Greek Poetry, which have been of unusual interest and have been attended with unusual success. You know his very remarkable translations from Euripides. The influence of his lectures has been altogether favourable to the promotion of the right sort of interest in classical literature. In this respect they have been not unlike the admirable course delivered by Professor Butcher two or three years since.[1] These two Englishmen have illustrated the worth of good English scholarship, exhibiting not merely thorough learning, but an admirable sense of the true ends to which learning should be devoted. It is a great pity that so many of our American scholars, old and young, have preferred the methods which lead only to the acquisition of facts often of no importance, to those which lead to the nobler cultivation of the intelligence and of the taste, and to the appreciation of the true ends of the study of language and of literature. . . .

[1] When Professor S. H. Butcher was at Harvard in 1904, he stayed for some time at Shady Hill. Norton, attracted by his remarkable qualities of mind and heart, parted with him, on his return to England, in terms that speak of mutual friendship, very unusual in its strong and quick growth. Both Professor Butcher and Professor Murray came to Harvard to deliver the course of lectures on the classics supported by the son of Norton's classmate, Professor Lane.

To Eliot Norton

SHADY HILL, 15 May, 1907.

You will be touched at hearing of Bernard's [1] death. He died yesterday afternoon, very quietly, without any considerable pain, and retaining his faculties to the last. He had been able to walk over here on one of the warm days of last week and had been greatly pleased to do so, and had been much satisfied with the condition of the cattle and the horse and the place in general. It had been a real pleasure to him to see Shady Hill once more and to see it in good order; and five or six days ago he had the pleasure of welcoming his son Charles, who has been, as you know, several years in Alaska. Charles had come home to stay, bringing his wife and his little daughter. This was a great happiness to Bernard, and it seemed as if, having satisfied himself that all was going well in his department here, and having enjoyed seeing his little granddaughter, and conscious of leaving his wife and Mary in good charge of her brothers, he was ready to die.

The funeral is to be on Friday, and if you can come on to it, we shall be truly glad to see you.

There is no other news here of interest. I hope that you three are well, and with love to you all, I am ever,

Your very affectionate father,

C. E. N.

[1] Bernard McGrath, an old servant of the Nortons', who had lived with them for forty-five years. He had come from Edgeworthstown to America; he recalled seeing " Miss Maria " [Edgeworth] in his boyhood; and many were his excellent Irish sayings quoted at Shady Hill.

To Miss Georgina Lowell

SHADY HILL, 20 May, 1907.

MY DEAR MISS LOWELL, — I return to you with many thanks the volume of Signor Wiel's *Versioni* which you were good enough to send to me. It has given me great pleasure, for the versions have such merit as to make them worth reading. But their very merit confirms my conviction that the transfusion of poetry from one tongue to another is a task of insurmountable difficulty. The translation may itself be a poem, but, however literal and exact in its rendering it may be, it will inevitably be a very different poem from the original. And so, skilful and happy as Signor Wiel often is in his renderings, his versions are apt to fail at the very point where the word of the original touches the imagination by verbal associations and suggestions which cannot be transferred. *Morire non puoi tu*, etc., can hardly thrill the most sensitive Italian reader, as "Thou wast not born for Death," etc., thrills even the common reader of the English verse. How completely different in the associations it summons and brings to bear on the fancy of the reader is

"Molest her ancient solitary reign,"

from

E lo molesti nel regal suo nido.

When Wordsworth proposed to translate Virgil into English verse, Coleridge wrote to him that he was undertaking an impossibility; and was he not correct? . . .

To Eliot Norton

SHADY HILL, 11 June, 1907.

. . . Your Uncle Darwin has left us this morning. I
am glad that he has so good a day for beginning his
return voyage; but what weather we have had! . . .

Mr. Howells was with us on Sunday, and seemed
better than I had expected, considering how poorly he
was during the greater part of the winter and spring.
Pleasant as he always is, he never was pleasanter, and
we had four or five hours of animated talk by which a
vast deal of ground was covered. His humour was delightful as of old. One quick bit of wit is worth preserving. I was speaking to him of Dr. James's new
book, and said that it was brilliant but not clear. "Like
his father," said Mr. Howells, "who wrote the Secret
of Swedenborg and kept it." . . .

To James Ford Rhodes

SHADY HILL, 17 June, 1907.

The chief charge I have to bring against old age is
summed up in Virgil's epithet *tarda*, "Tarda senectus."
As the days seem to grow shorter and to afford less
time for accomplishing the tasks that each of them
brings, so more time is required for the doing of these
tasks than of old, and the result is that the heap of things
undone grows higher from day to day, and one learns
only too readily to postpone till to-morrow the things
that may be done as well on one day as another. But

> To-morrow, and to-morrow, and to-morrow,
> Creeps in this petty pace from day to day,

still the postponable duty, however pleasant it may be, remains undone.

So it has been with the letter that I should have sent to you six months ago to thank you warmly for the gift of the last two volumes of your History, and to congratulate you cordially on the successful accomplishment of this part of your great task. Your work is such that you must never think it finished so long as life and power to work are left to you. 1877 is a good date for a halt, but not for a long stay. The tragic story which you are telling so well comes to a climax — as it were its third act — with the Spanish War; the breaking down of the Constitution, and the reversal of the traditional policy of the Republic. Act IV will be Roosevelt and autocracy. Act V will be who can say what? — at any rate something different from what the past has been.

You have twenty-five good years in which to continue the record, — and with the thoroughness of investigation, the amplitude of knowledge and the candour of judgment which give authority to your work.

You saw, perhaps, two months or more ago, a long letter in the "Nation" impugning your statements concerning Bancroft Davis and Caleb Cushing. Nothing has given me a sharper sense of our loss in Godkin's death. Had he been alive either the letter would never have appeared, or it would have been printed with a vigorous comment exposing its misstatements. The writer of it obviously trusted to the fact that few men cognizant of the actual facts in 1870

and '71 are now alive. The letter was in one respect
satisfactory, — it showed that Bancroft Davis was
ashamed of his record. If you have not seen Mr.
Rothschild's "Lincoln, Master of Men," let me commend it to you and have the pleasure of sending a copy
of it to you.

I hope that Mrs. Rhodes and you are well and are
having "a good time."

Let me repeat my thanks for your admirable book,
and believe me,

Very sincerely yours,

C. E. NORTON.

To W. L. Mackenzie King

SHADY HILL, 17 June, 1907.

I shall be greatly obliged to you if when you have
leisure you will give me some report of your work during the last four or five months. You may remember
that you sent me the draft of the Industrial Disputes
Investigation Act and at the same time the report of
the settlement of the strike at Lethbridge.

I was glad to see that the bill was shortly afterward
passed by your Parliament. But this information was
followed before long by the report in brief terms of
another serious strike among the coal-miners in the
Northwest and of your having been sent out to endeavour to settle it. Lord Grey was here just at that
time, but he had not then received any special information concerning the issue of the strike. He told me,
however, that he thought the Act was working well,
and that more than one strike had already been settled

satisfactorily under its provisions. I have great confidence that you were able to settle also satisfactorily, though perhaps with difficulty, the strike of the coalminers in the Northwest. Should this have been the case, and should no serious defects in the working of the law have become apparent, you are to be heartily congratulated in having devised the means for a settlement of industrial disputes.

If I am not wrong your bill was largely based upon the strike legislation of New Zealand. I should like much to have you tell me in what particulars it has seemed to you desirable to make changes. The matter is of such great importance to all our western communities that, if a satisfactory means has really been devised for the settlement of strikes, the benefit will not be confined to Canada and to New Zealand. But I fear it will be long before we shall be able to secure the passage of a similar law in the United States, however serviceable its working may prove to be. All labour questions are so intricately involved with the ambitions and interests of the politicians in both parties that it is vain to expect such legislation as might be secured in case the questions were treated simply upon their own merits by a body of rational men. But under the present régime industrial disputes are so likely to increase with disastrous effects that in the course of years some means of settling them other than now exists must be obtained, and then the example of the successful working of your experiment will have great force.

If you can without inconvenience send to me a brief statement of the working of the Act, accompanied by one or two copies of the Act itself, I think I can get these papers into the hands of one or two of the efficient shapers of public opinion in America. It is a great pity that so little attention is paid in the United States to the legislation and material development of Canada. . . .

To L. P. Jacks

SHADY HILL, 24 September, 1907.

I ought long since to have thanked you for your kind and cordial letter of the thirtieth of May. It would give me on many accounts great pleasure to comply with the request which it contained and to write for the "Hibbert Journal" some of the opinions which I ventured to express to you when I had the pleasure of seeing you in my study here. But it seems to me doubtful whether, considering the present attitude of the great body of liberal thinkers in matters of religion and the satisfactory progress which is making to greater and greater liberality, it would be desirable to express opinions such as mine. . . . I have no wish to make proselytes for my own opinions. If they be sound, the course of time will bring about their adoption so far as may be desirable. But I have no belief that such views as mine are likely within any reasonable period to be held by a considerable body of men. They make too great a break with the strongest and oldest traditions, and they seem, at least to those who are not able fully to understand them, to make too little account of sentiments and convictions essential to the moral life of the community. A few men in past generations

have held such opinions, and a few in the coming generations may hold them; but such men are likely always
to be in a very small minority.

But even if I had the disposition to set forth my
opinions at length for publication, I should be prevented from doing so just now by the fact that during
the past summer I was confined to my chamber for
many weeks by a slight but tedious illness, the worst
effect of which has been the diminution of the little
vitality which a man as near eighty years old as I is
likely to possess. I am gradually regaining my strength,
but it comes back slowly and not in a measure as
yet to authorize me to draw upon it for much serious
work.

You will, I am sure, follow with interest the proceedings of the International Council of Liberal Thinkers
assembled in Boston this week. It is, I believe, by far
the strongest assemblage of the kind which has ever
met, and embraces men of such different theological
opinion and of such varied learning and experience as
to afford the happiest augury for the relaxation of the
bonds of creed and for the union of Christians of whatever name, not merely in good will but in good works.
The expressions of mutual confidence and sympathy
of liberal and of orthodox are such as could not have
been heard twenty years ago. The old form, "in nec-
essariis unitas," is receiving a new interpretation, no
less than the clause, "in omnibus caritas." It is interesting to note the various elements in the proceedings
of the Council, and to see how, in spite of the lingering
of many superstitious ideas, the lines of division are

being obliterated between men inspired with the modern spirit. . . .

To S. Weir Mitchell

SHADY HILL, 13 November, 1907.

Your very welcome and kind letter of October 2d reached me an hour ago! Our excellent but sometimes careless postmistress at Ashfield seems to have held it back, as if it had been one of those fine pears that need ripening in the late autumn sun. . . .

Yes, I was in my chamber for six weeks during the summer. . . . But I have no complaint to make of old age. The days are still full of sunshine. I have not for many years cared how few they might be, and I find enough pleasure and entertainment and love in them to be content with them, — if only they may end before I become a burden.

I spent much of the time while I was on the bed with the poets, — the best of them, and there is no such company as they. And lately I have been reading with great satisfaction Horace Furness's volume of "Antony and Cleopatra." He is the only delightful commentator. I quarrel with him sometimes, but just as I would quarrel with any Shakespearian character. Not only his hand, but his heart as well, is subdued to what they have worked in so long, — and the subjection is ennobling. I am going to send to you, on the chance that you have not yet seen the little book, Macaulay's "Marginal Notes." They are enough to make a scholar envious, and those on Shakespeare especially quicken one's sympathies with their writer. Read them as if you and I were talking over them together.

Have you written no verses this summer? I see that you have published my favourite Ode.[1] Let me have another poem to keep with it.

Good-night! I offer my kindest regards to Mrs. Mitchell, and am

Affectionately yours,

C. E. NORTON.

[1] Dr. Mitchell's "Ode on a Lycian Tomb."

CHAPTER XIII

UNTO THE LAST

(1907–1908)

TO C. E. N.

"HIGH PASTURE"

Ashfield, November 16, 1907

Come up — come up: in the dim vale below
The autumn mist muffles the fading trees,
But on this keen hill-pasture, though the breeze
Has stretched the thwart boughs bare to meet the snow,
Night is not, autumn is not — but the flow
Of vast, ethereal and irradiate seas,
Poured from the far world's flaming boundaries
In waxing tides of unimagined glow.

And to that height illumined of the mind
He calls us still by the familiar way,
Leaving the sodden tracks of life behind,
Befogged in failure, chilled with love's decay —
Showing us, as the night-mists upward wind,
How on the heights is day and still more day.

EDITH WHARTON.

NORTON, the faithful observer of birthdays, was un-
prepared, when his own eightieth birthday arrived,
for the special expressions of affection that his friends
sent to him through many tokens: letter and flower
bearing the sign. Besides the sonnet from Mrs. Wharton, a sheaf of letters — written for publication in the
"Harvard Graduates' Magazine" — but previously
gathered together by its editor, Mr. W. R. Thayer,

into an exquisite little book and brought by him to Norton on November 16th, gave public voice, one may say, to a sentiment with personal limits that would be hard to fix.[1] President Eliot wrote of his cousin especially as a member of the college faculty, and said: "Thousands of Harvard students attribute to his influence lasting improvements in their modes of thought, their intellectual and moral interests, and their ideas of genuine success and true happiness. His work in the University and his training for it were both unique, and are not likely to be parallelled in the future." Mr. Howells, clothing his words in the friendship that covered the period of more than a generation, wrote: "For me he is of that golden prime which we Americans shall not see renewed in the course of many centuries. While he lives, Emerson and Hawthorne, Longfellow and Lowell, Whittier and Holmes, are not lost to the consciousness of any who knew them; the Cambridge, the Boston, the New England, the America which lived in them, has not yet passed away. He was not only the contemporary, the companion of those great men; he was their fellow citizen in those highest things in which we may be his if we will, for the hospitality of his welcome will not be wanting. Something Athenian, something Florentine, something essentially republican and democratic in the ideals common to them all has had its especial effect in him through that temperamental beneficence, that philanthropy in a peculiar sense, so characteristic of him. I suppose he never met a man without wishing to share

[1] Another kind deed of Norton's friends is recorded in Appendix E: "A Gift to Norton."

with him the grace of his learning, the charm of his wisdom, the light of his knowledge of the world; but this is poorly suggestive of the pervasive influence of his constant precept and example, which only those whose lives it shaped could duly witness of. The future is of better augury because of the past which unites with the present in him, and remains ours in what he has done and what he is."

Though the bodily restrictions of fourscore years were at hand to exact their toll, the spirit which the friends of Norton knew and loved in him shone steadfast to the end. There are no letters more filled with that spirit than those of the final year.

To James Loeb

SHADY HILL, 17 November, 1907.

I trust to your kindness to pardon me for dictating instead of writing an answer to your most kind letter of the fifteenth. I am so overwhelmed with the number of the friendly expressions that I received on my birthday that I am compelled to acknowledge them by means of the typewriter. But the typewritten word in this case is not less charged with my own feeling than if it were written by my own hand.

Your kind words and the very beautiful gift which accompanied them afforded to me as much pleasure as you could desire. I have often, when looking at the exquisite work of the Arretine potter, thought how fitting his design was for execution in one of the precious metals, and this bowl which you have sent to me seems only to enhance the beauty of his design. But I have not yet had the opportunity to study it thoroughly, for the lovely flowers which it contained when it reached me still hide many of its lines, and will for some days longer, I trust, prevent me by their beauty from becoming familiar with the beauty of the bowl itself.

I trust that Harvard's defeat yesterday will not discourage you from coming on to see the game of next week, and that we may have the pleasure of seeing you on Friday. Will you give us the pleasure of your company that evening at a domestic supper at seven o'clock? We should all be glad to greet you once more. . . . With warm regards from us all,

Your grateful and sincere old friend,

C. E. NORTON.

To Moorfield Storey

SHADY HILL, 22 November, 1907.

I find it difficult to tell you how deeply your letter on my eightieth birthday has touched me, how grateful I am to you for it, how highly I prize it as an expression of the personal regard of one whom I hold in special honour and respect, — and let me add affection. I cannot accept as correct the estimate which you and other friends place on my services to the community, but I am not sorry for it. On the contrary, it gives me a grave happiness as assurance of their sympathy with the principles which have guided my life and the ideals which I have cherished. Such a letter as yours would be ample reward for much greater achievement than mine has been. . . .

To C. F. Adams

SHADY HILL, 27 November, 1907.

The very kind and pleasant letter which you wrote to me ten days ago gave me great pleasure, and I should have thanked you for it before this time had I not been vainly striving to make head against a sea of letters which still threatens to engulf me. My arm is not as strong nor my hand as nimble as they once were. Old age with me is neither "unfriended" nor "melancholy" but it is "slow"; and, more than this, as the days of life grow fewer they seem to have fewer hours, and those hours shorter than of old.

Your reference to the late date in our lives of our closer association reminded me of a passage in "De Amicitia" which has often recurred to my mind in recent years, and which has a close application to our relations, expressed indeed in terms which might sound too sentimental in English, but which answer well enough under the decent veil of the Latin. It is Laelius who speaks: —

"Maxime quidem optandum est, ut cum æqualibus possis, quibuscum tanquam e carceribus emissus sis, cum iisdem ad calcem, ut dicitur, pervenire. Sed quoniam res humanæ fragiles caducæque sunt, semper aliqui anquirendi sunt, quos diligamus et a quibus diligamur."

This has been my good fortune, and I am glad to subscribe myself

Affectionately Yours,
CHARLES ELIOT NORTON.

To the Hon. W. Warren Vernon [1]

SHADY HILL, 1 January, 1908.

MY DEAR AND KIND FRIEND, — I cannot begin the new year better than by sending to you my best wishes that it may be a happy one for you, — happy in that sense which the word takes on as we draw toward the end of life, after sorrows have fallen upon us, the effect of which must be felt through all the years that follow them. But so long as our minds remain unclouded and our hearts retain their power of affection unchanged, life may still have much happiness for us, and among the best is that which we may receive from the good will of friends. So, as the new year begins, I count very confidently on the blessing of your friendship. The latest token of it has been giving me great pleasure during the past two or three weeks. It is just a month ago since you wrote my name in the first volume of the new edition of your "Purgatorio"; and since it came to me, I have gone over a good part of it with constant interest and increasing recognition of the improvement you have wrought in a work which seemed to afford little opportunity for improvement. I note with interest the change in your view of the nature of the sins for which Beatrice rebukes Dante before revealing herself to him unveiled in purgatory. I somewhat reluctantly came a good while ago to a similar conclusion to that at which you have arrived.

The thoughtful labour which you have bestowed upon

[1] This letter was the last in a long correspondence based upon a common devotion to the study of Dante.

your work is apparent upon almost every page. I congratulate you on the continued power of work. While I can hope to do little more myself, I can at least rejoice in the good work accomplished by those for whom I care.

A few days since, I had a kind and pleasant letter from our friend Canon Moore; . . . the shadow of his recent grief was still darkly clouding his life. I wish that he were able to devote more time to his favourite studies, for in them I believe he would find that occupation of thought and that steadying of the mind which is needful after a great calamity to bring one again into natural and healthy relations with life. No studies are better fitted to do this than studies of Dante.

During the past year old age has been making rapid advance upon me; but I have no quarrel with it, and this morning is full of sunshine. I am sorry not to write to you with my own hand, but I find writing now a slow and difficult task.

Let me end my letter as I began it, with every good wish for the new year for Mrs. Vernon and yourself, and assure you that I am, as always, your affectionate old (and aged) friend,

CHARLES ELIOT NORTON.

To Sidney Gunn
SHADY HILL, January 20, 1908.

DEAR MR. GUNN: — Among the many expressions of regard which came to me on my eightieth birthday, there was not one which gave me more pleasure than that which you, as representative of some three or four hundred students in various departments of our University, brought to me.

The terms of the Address, to which the signatures of these students are appended, touch me deeply. An old man can scarcely have a greater happiness than to be assured of the affection and the regard of the picked men of the younger generation of his contemporaries, and to know that the ideals which he has cherished are dear also to them.

I beg you to let the subscribers to the Address know of my grateful recognition of the honour they have done me, and of my sympathy with their interests, — at least to let them know this so far as it can easily be done. Pray accept my special thanks for your agency in the matter of the Address, and believe me, with cordial regard,

Sincerely yours,

CHARLES ELIOT NORTON.

To Sir Philip Burne-Jones

SHADY HILL, 7 March, 1908.

MY BELOVED AND FAITHFUL CHELA, — . . . I wish that instead of dictating a letter to you this morning, I could go in to a late breakfast with you, and see your pleasant quarters, and praise your new work, and hear from you all the family news up to to-day; or I wish that, transferred on a magic carpet, you could be here in this study which is so familiar to you and where you would be at once welcomed with joy not only by me but by Taffy of whom you used to be so fond! Taffy, like his master, has grown very old of late. He is now almost wholly deaf and pretty nearly blind; but he still retains his lively bark which was so soothing to your nerves, and he still delights in going out with me for the short walks which are all that I can accomplish, for during the past two or three months, old age has come upon me like an armed man in the night. And yet, with all other restrictions and discomforts and incapacities, I do not find the days of old age to be evil days, and I still take pleasure in living, and look forward to the coming spring with its annual miracle of revival with the assurance of as much delight in it as I ever took in the renewal of the earth. In it there are certain sights and sounds which I think give more poignant delight as one grows old and feels that it may be the last time that one shall see or hear them, than in the earlier days when one looked forward to their indefinite renewal. A red after-glow of sunset behind a row of pines, the murmur of the sea, the first twittering song of the birds in the morning, quicken in me the sense of the beauty and the charm of the external world as much as they ever did.

If you were to come in at the door at this moment, I should rise to welcome you as quickly as of old; but you would find me bent and my step tottering and my voice feebler than of old, but not so feeble but that it could welcome you with as much affection as ever. . . . Sally is greatly interested just now in the introductions to his old novels which our dear Henry James is writing. . . . I confess to finding his recent work not merely enigmatic in style but more enigmatic in character when compared with the ideals which his own nature suggests. . . .

To W. F. Melton [1]

DEAR MR. MELTON,— . . . I thank you for the verses which you were good enough to enclose to me, especially for the confidence you exhibited in sending them, in my sympathy with the emotion and sentiment which inspired them. They show the influence which Donne has had on your thought and style. I set great value on the verse of minor poets, not that it usually has much importance for others, but because of its worth to its writer. Their ranks are innumerable. Chaucer counted them as "many a thousand times twelve," and if that was their number in his day, it has vastly increased at the present time.

I cannot hold Lanier as much better than a minor poet and a minor critic, though he may have a high place among them. I doubt if Donne influenced Lanier in regard to indifference to the close sequence in verse of similar vowel sounds. The objection to this close sequence is apt to degenerate into a kind of pedantry. None of the greater poets altogether avoided it, although for the most part their ear and their sentiment prevented them from falling into disagreeable collocations of sound. Milton, one of the greatest masters of the happy arrangement of vowels in his verse, yet gives us occasionally such a verse as the following from

[1] Professor of English, in Emory College, Oxford, Georgia.

Lycidas: "That *sing*, and *singing, in* their glory move."
It is my impression that Donne hardly brings together
vowels of the same sound more frequently than many
of his contemporaries. There comes into my mind at
this moment a verse from one of Campion's most
imaginative lyrics, the delightful poem that begins,
"When thou must home to shades of underground," in
the course of which he writes, "White *I*ope, bl*i*the
Helen, and the rest." The felicitous arrangement of
vowel sounds in Gray's poems is one of the indications
of his poetic genius, and is one of the reasons why the
"Elegy in the Country Churchyard" is probably the
most widely known poem in English. To be a great
poet, one must have a good ear, and the poet who
exhibits it in his verse is not likely to be afraid at
times to admit a sequence in his verse of words of similar sound.

If you have not seen Mr. Pearsall Smith's "Life of
Sir Henry Wotton," let me commend it to you. It is as
a biography all that Gosse's "Life of Donne" is not,
and it contains much, besides its general interest, of
what will be of special interest to you in its report of
Wotton's relations to Donne. So far as I know, we
have had no better biography of any Italianate Englishman of the renaissance period. . . .

To Eliot Norton

SHADY HILL, 4 April, 1908.

. . . At last I am able to write to you in regard to
your essay on Lincoln.[1] I have read it with great

---

[1] *Lincoln, Lover of Mankind: an Essay;* New York, 1911.

interest and pleasure, and I think you present a striking view of one of the predominant features of his relations to other men. But I wish you had gone a little deeper into the psychology of the matter. General liking of other men is not properly a trait of character, but an exhibition of underlying traits. Such liking as Lincoln exhibited for other men had its main root in his sympathetic and social nature. Sympathy and sociability are two essential traits of character. These were both fostered in him by the conditions of his life, that is, by the political and social conditions of the people with whom he lived. The very rudeness of the state of society in the Middle West at the time of his youth, prevented the development in him of other traits which might have interfered with the full strength of these two predominant qualities.

You point out that there was nothing in him which prevented him from liking the coarse and vulgar. It was almost inevitable, considering how strong his sympathies were and how social his nature, that, while not lacking moral refinement and elevation, he should lack the finer fastidiousness of the most admirable character.

It is not a virtue to like men indiscriminately, though the liking may spring from a virtuous root. But Lincoln was a true child of the democracy that had grown up under American institutions, with the principle of equality ruling its moral convictions as well as its intellectual forces. It would have been a miracle, in view of the condition of his early life, had he acquired a discriminating taste in regard to relations with other men. The solidity of his moral nature saved him from the harm which his indiscriminating indifference to the qualities of his associates might easily have wrought in him. His sympathetic and social disposition, strong as it was, was not stronger than his moral sense, and the three together made him the man that he was.

The analogy which you point out between him and Sir Walter is very striking, and, so far as I know, is novel. But I think your discussion of it should be carried a little farther, in order to bring out the advantages which Sir Walter had in life, and which gave to his nature a charm which Lincoln's did not possess. "*True* gentleman," Tennyson calls Scott, and in that word lies the characteristic distinction between him and Lincoln. A gentleman is the result of high breeding, and it is no discredit to Lincoln that, born and bred as he was, he does not stand on the same level in this respect as Scott. I believe that as time goes on and the democracy reaches its full development, there may be just as complete gentlemen in the sense of high-bred men, as in any aristocracy with its long tradition. But a gentleman is not an immediate product of a new country, nor of a society starting on new principles like ours.

These are some of the reflections that your essay has brought me. If they strike you with force and modify in any respect your view, I would advise you to put aside the essay for some time and take it up again with fresh mind. But whether you do this or not, at any rate it seems to me desirable that you should modify it, so far at least as to indicate that you do not hold general liking of men to be in itself a trait of character, but recognize that it has its source in elemental principles of human nature. . . .

> With love to you and Margaret and the boy,
> Always affectionately yours,
> C. E. N.

To H. H. Furness

SHADY HILL, 8 April, 1908.

Not only be at ease about your address,[1] but take great satisfaction in it. It is worthy of you, and it is fit to charm any audience, were it all Childs and Kittredges, or all as ignorant of your theme as the average undergraduate. I am absolutely sincere in saying that I think it is admirably well fitted for the occasion. When you come to rewrite the passage about the commentators, pray say a word about what we owe to the generally overlooked, modest Theobald, and still more of what we owe to Coleridge in changing the tone of expression in regard to Shakespeare as well as in illuminating gleams of imaginative interpretation, and to such critics as Bradley in these late days. His work I hold in very high esteem. . . .

I am sorry for you with the prospect of two mighty speeches before the Phi Beta occasion. Fortunately the topics on which you have to speak are not very difficult. But I do not care to celebrate the man who, even more than Lincoln, might be called the first American,[2] — a man of the most superior intelligence and the very type of the complete materialist. . . .

[1] Norton had been reading in advance Dr. Furness's Phi Beta Kappa address, "On Shakespeare, 'Or, What You Will,'" delivered in Sanders Theatre, June 25, 1908.

[2] "I spoke my little piece on Franklin at the Philosophical Society's dinner," writes Furness to Norton on May 6th.

HORACE HOWARD FURNESS

To H. H. Furness

SHADY HILL, 5 May, 1908.

DEAR * HORACE: . . . Just before your letter reached me, I had dispatched a book [1] to you, which I think you will look over with interest. Its author, one of our younger professors, has more of that old-fashioned literary culture which you and I value, than most of the younger Germanized scholars of to-day. His essays show both wide reading and independent thought, and his conclusions are in the main such as you and I should approve. Culture in the true sense has been long out of fashion in the colleges, and I am sorry that —— in a recent address attempts a definition of culture which is not merely insufficient, but shows that he has no serious conception of the true significance of culture itself in respect to the civilization of the race. It is a great misfortune for us nationally that the tradition of culture is so weak and so limited. In this respect the advantage of England is great. But I hail such a book as Mr. Babbitt's as an indication of a possible turn in the tide of which another sign is the literary essays by Mr. Paul More from time to time in the "Nation."

I do not forget when I send you this little volume what you had told me of the number of books lying on your table unread and to be acknowledged. There is no way of dealing with the burden of such gifts but to acknowledge them with thanks at the moment, and

---

* In C. E. N.'s hand: "Dearest Horace: I am shy of dictating superlatives of sentiment. Add the 'est' to this." Almost all Norton's letters to friends, till the last year of his life, were in his own hand.

[1] *Literature and the American College*, by Irving Babbitt.

take no more concern in regard to them. It is not often that an author is so inconsiderate as the female professor of whom you told me, who wanted you to read her book before thanking her for it. I should give such an author but short shrift. You, however, are much more kind-hearted and gentle than I.

I must cut my letter short, for the close of my hour of dictation is at hand, and I have other letters to write of a sort which I wish could be spared. But, short or long, my letter is a token of unstinted affection.

To H. H. Furness

SHADY HILL, 12 May, 1908.

I had a letter from my boy Rupert yesterday in which he says: —

"I saw Dr. Furness last night, and gave him your message. He sent you his best love. At the dinner his talk was by all odds the best. It was reminiscent, but done with wonderful spirit and youthfulness, and he carried his audience away with him; and when he had finished there was unlimited applause."

I did not need to be informed that your speech was the best of the evening.[1] I knew it beforehand. And I am glad that this adventure of yours is happily terminated. You now have only one worry more before you, for you have only one more piece to speak; and this last will, I am sure, be the most successful of the three.

I fear that you never knew the delightful Tom Appleton. His memory is becoming faint, except in

[1] On May 9, 1908, Dr. Furness, introduced as the "Nestor of Harvard" at the dinner of the Associated Harvard Clubs in Philadelphia, gave some reminiscences of the college in 1854.

the hearts of a few old men like myself. This is the common fate, — the common fate of the man whose charm is specially social and whose wit is the wit of the dinner-table. Well, Tom, who was a true *bon-vivant*, intellectually as well as physically, [and] had a most cultivated sense of taste himself, used to say that we in New England suffer more in regard to that special sense from our Puritan tradition of the sinfulness of worldly delights, than in respect to any other of the senses. In Philadelphia and Baltimore that sense has had its rights more carefully preserved. Yet every now and then there has been an exceptional instance of delicacy of taste among these restrained New Englanders as, for instance, was Leverett Saltonstall's capacity of discrimination of sherries, about which there is a good story which I will tell you some day. All this is a preface to my thanks to you for the hominy which shall be cooked according to the receipt you sent me, and eaten with due thanks to the giver.

For the last two days we have been in full summer, and the leaves are rushing out at a breathless pace, poor misguided things to be eaten in their tender youth by the gypsy-moths or the elm-beetles, — the two pests which are destroying our finest trees.

Have I ever thanked you as I should for the framed photograph which arrived ten days ago, and which, when I look at it, gives me the feeling of sitting with you in your own study, you with a pipe, I with a cigar, and both of us enjoying one of those interludes of silence which are the tests and proof of the intimacy and interest of the conversation which has preceded them? Your study is rich with accumulated treasures. My only objection to it is the stairs which, at eighty years old, I should find hard to climb, but not so hard, indeed, as it is for me to get to the upper shelves of my own book-cases. Indeed, the ideal library should be a room of such extent that no book should be out of reach of the hand, and above the cases the walls should be covered with pictures and maps. When I build my own house, I will have a library at least one hundred feet long and half as many wide, and even then I am not sure that I should have room for all the books that I should want to keep in it. I am sending off a great many books in these days, books which my children will never want. Yesterday I picked out a large box full to go to that excellent, struggling institution, Tulane University at New Orleans. However many I may send away, I fear that I shall leave behind me too many.

Good-bye for to-day. With faithful affection (for yourself and for your dog!)

Your loving

C. E. N.

To S. Weir Mitchell

SHADY HILL, 22 May, 1908.

I thank you for sending to me a copy of your excellent address to the graduating class of nurses at the New York Hospital. It is a delightfully characteristic discourse, full of the wisdom of keen insight and long experience; full, too, of genial humour and of kindly view of humanity. The contrast which you draw be-

tween the conditions of the sick-room in charge of a
trained nurse and those which were familiar to us in our
earlier years, is very striking. Nowhere else has the
comfort of life been so much increased during the past
half century as in the sick-room, where comfort is
most needed.

In thinking of you, I often reflect on the happiness
that must attend you in the memory of the services
you have rendered to those who have most needed
human service and sympathy. The great and good
physician who has had a long career, has a happiness in
looking back over his life, which no other man can rival.
He at least has done positive good, relieved suffering,
restored strength and renewed hope. I congratulate
you affectionately on the blessing of such a retrospect.

I am sorry that such long intervals of silence should
prevail between us, but during the last four or five
months, old age has lighted on my shoulders like Sin-
bad the Sailor's old man of the mountain, and I have
found it difficult in carrying this load to accomplish the
pleasanter tasks of life. I have been well, but every
day have gone a little further down hill, till now my
knees are feeble, and I cannot walk far, and my hands
refuse to do their commonest duties. But my eyes are
still good and my hearing is not much impaired. Days,
though they often bring me weariness, have not ceased
to bring me also delights. It seems to me that I never
enjoyed the beauty and wonder of the spring more than
I have this year. The glory of this lilac week is more
glorious than ever, and I join with my old friend
Grant-Duff in celebrating the praises of St. Busbequius

(as he called the worthy Busbecq) for bringing the lilac into Europe, one of the most precious gifts of the East to the West. Last Sunday the apple orchards were in perfection. It is the bridal moment of the year.

I have every reason to be grateful to old age for not cutting off my liking for the things which I have liked during the earlier part of life, and for not dulling my heart. I find as much pleasure in books as ever, and I have as much love for old friends as I had in foregone days.

I hope that you keep well, and with faithful regards to you and to Mrs. Mitchell, I am,

Your affectionate friend,

CHARLES ELIOT NORTON.

To W. F. Melton

SHADY HILL, 25 May, 1908.

Your letter of three or four days ago gave me much pleasure. . . .

I am greatly interested to learn that you are on a warm trail of some of Donne's manuscripts. If the manuscripts actually exist, are they not probably of some of his sermons? It is not unlikely that these may still exist in some small ecclesiastical library. You remember the remarkable story of Grosart's finding the manuscript of George Herbert's poems in the Williams Library in London. Such a discovery makes another of a similar kind seem not improbable; so I hope all your anticipations of an interesting find may be justified.

I am much obliged to you for sending to me Profes-

sor Belden's review of your book. I return it herewith.
So far as I am able to judge, it seems to me judicious
and appreciative. . . . I think it contains a desirable
warning, lest you should press the essential points of
your theory too hard. I find it in vain to get up other
than a languid interest in all these questions of metre,
accent, arsis, thesis, stress and the like. They seem to
me to deal with the outer shell, and in the case of a poet
of the second class to have very little importance in
literary or æsthetic respects. In the case of a poet like
Milton, a great master of language, or of Dante, diction
and form are essential portions of their poetry; but I
doubt if any one will read the poetry of George Herbert
with deeper appreciation and greater pleasure, because
of knowing that this or that piece is unique in its
metre, or if any one will get a stronger impression of
Donne's being in some respect the first poet of his time,
from becoming skilled in all the peculiarities of his
versification. The charm of the rose is not increased
by our knowing to what class and order of plants it belongs, and the "violets dim, but sweeter than the lids
of Juno's eyes," are not rooted in iamb and trochee.
No, verse is one thing and poetry is another, and the
man who devotes himself to the study of versification
is not likely to be the best lover of the poets. I do not
question the value of such work as yours upon Donne,
and I admire the industry and the acuteness of intelligence which it exhibits; but it seems to me to have little
more relation to the great qualities of Donne's poetry,
to all that gives it real charm, than the study of the
bones of the skeleton has to a portrait by Titian or

Tintoretto. It may be of interest from the scientific point of view, linguistic or historic, not from the poetic. But I will not repeat what I have practically said a long while ago to you.

It is not likely that I shall leave Cambridge before the middle of July, and I may possibly not leave it at all this summer. . . . Old age has taken from me so much of my strength that I am not always down-stairs ready for a visit before noon. But I shall be glad to see you whenever you come. . . .

In the spring of 1908, Norton decided, on the advice of his physician, that instead of going to Ashfield as usual, the summer should be spent at Shady Hill: — this was to acknowledge his failing strength, and there could not but be sad recognitions in the acknowledgment. Yet the summer was not without its pleasures. Twice during the earlier part of it, Norton went with his eldest daughter for a few days at a time to Manchester, to stay with his sister-in-law, Miss Sedgwick, and there, reading and smoking on a pleasant piazza within sight of the sea, the old Newport days were recalled: —

> "Gleich einer alten, halb-verklungnen Sage
> Kommt erste Lieb' und Freundschaft mit herauf."

At Shady Hill the familiar order of the day remained unchanged till early in September, when illness confined Norton to the room he was not to leave again. Though the passing weeks brought steady failure of bodily strength, there was no loss of mental clearness: — letters were still dictated, books read, directions sent to Ashfield about Academy matters, and interest taken in University affairs. And still old delights, though touched with the pathos of mortality, remained vivid. The beloved little granddaughter's presence from time to time in the house yet held for him the happiness it had always given, and even when he was not able to see her, the child's voice floating upstairs brought the smile that did not fail, though illness increased: so, too, the return of his youngest son from Europe in September brought a real pleasure. And flowers that filled the room were enjoyed with such constant reference to their loveliness that what had ever been to Norton "so wondrous sweet and fair" clearly had lost none of its charm.

To Miss Gaskell

SHADY HILL, 24 July, 1908.

DEAREST META, — Such a letter as yours deserves an instant response which I make to-day with my heart and wish that I could do so with my hand also. . . . Indeed, it is only in this feebleness of the muscles and the resultant slowness of action that old age fails to treat me with rather unusual kindness. It brings me neither pains nor aches, and it does not diminish my enjoyment of the things which I have enjoyed during my long preceding life. Indeed, it rather seems to enhance that enjoyment, from the sense, as each pleasure recurs and passes, that it may be for the last time for me, since

"To-morrow I may be
Myself with yesterday's seven thousand years."

We gave up going to the hills and to our summer home at Ashfield this summer mainly on my account, because it seemed well for me to avoid the journey and the risks of being ill at a distance from our old home. We find it comfortable and pleasant here, in spite of an unusually hot season, and we lead quiet lives with little society, for our Cambridge neighbours are almost all fled to the hills or the seashore, and we seem here almost as retired from the busy world as we should be in our little Ashfield village.

Your letter carried my thoughts back to the happy days of fifty years ago when we first met. What delightful days those were! I cannot believe that the charm of Rome is as great as it was then, and yet my dear old friend Howells who has just returned from a long stay there and made me a delightful visit yesterday afternoon, has fallen under the spell of its charm as completely as if it were the same delightful Rome that we knew so well before it had become the prey of the scientific archæologist, the modern representative of the Goth, so far as the destruction of beauty is concerned. I send you the last of a series of letters which Howells has been publishing from week to week during the past months. It will recall to you some of the pleasant places which were once so familiar to us. Howells' wide and ready sympathies and his quick perceptions, make his descriptions of whatever place may be his theme among the best that have been written. Do you know his recent books on England published a year or two ago? If not, let me send them to you. You will find them extremely pleasant reading.

His temper and spirit exhibit themselves in his rare
humour and perhaps his still rarer tenderness of
perception.

One of our near neighbours and friends, the brother
of Henry James, and hardly less eminent than he,
though in a very different field, is in England this year,
and I wish that you might fall in with him. I had a
letter from him last week in which he speaks of Oxford
where he has lately been, to deliver a series of con-
troversial metaphysical lectures. After being at Oxford, he went to Durham to receive an honorary degree,
and then came down to the Lakes for a period of rest
and quiet. He says: —

"The whole scene at Durham was tremendously
impressive. It was so unlike Oxford, so much more
American in its personnel in a way, yet nestling in the
very bosom of those mediæval stage properties and
ecclesiastical principalities suggestions. Oxford is all
spread out in length and breadth, Durham concentrated in depth and thickness. There is a great deal of
flummery about Oxford, but I think, if I were an
Oxonian, in spite of my radicalism generally, I might
vote against all change there. It is an absolutely
unique fruit of human endeavour, and, like the cathedrals, can never to the end of time be reproduced. Let
other places of learning come in for all the improvements. The world can afford to keep her only Oxford
unreformed. I know that this is a superficial judgment
in both ways, for Oxford does manage to keep the best
of a utilitarian spirit and at the same time preserve
lots of her flummery unchanged. On the whole, it is a

thoroughly democratic place, so far as aristocracy in the strict sense goes."

He says in a later part of his letter: — "England seems to have got itself into a magnificently fine state of civilization, especially in regard to the cheery and wholesome tone of manners, improved, as this is getting to be, by the greater infusion of the democratic temper. Everything here seems about twice as good as the corresponding thing with us. But" (and here comes out his invincible Americanism) "I suspect we have the bigger eventual destiny after all, and, give us a thousand years, and we may catch up in many details."

James is an unusually delightful person, fresh, animated, with active and vigorous intelligence, often irrational, but all the more interesting for being so. He is the most independent and the most popular of metaphysicians and psychologists, and, as you know, is the great protagonist of the new doctrine of pragmatism which is worth to my mind just about as much as the systems of metaphysical speculation which have preceded it. James's spirit and temper do good to whoever comes within their range; and it is as much through their affections as through their intellects that his disciples are attracted to him. It shows how sweet his nature is, that he can get on with me who am absolutely a skeptic in regard to every metaphysical system and as to the value of every inquiry into the unknowable. . . .

I hope the suffragettes will give you no further annoyance. Their recent course of brawling can have done little to promote the cause which they profess to have at heart. It hinders, indeed, the adoption of the moderate measures which are all that a wise policy would promote. I fear that the present administration is not confident enough of its hold on the country, to resist the clamour which the suffragettes keep up so loudly. . . .

With love to Julia as well as to yourself, my dear Meta, I am, and, so long as I shall have consciousness, shall remain,

Your affectionate old friend,

CHARLES ELIOT NORTON.

To H. H. Furness

SHADY HILL, 28 July, 1908.

DEAREST HORACE, — You shall not go on your cruise in the treacherous southern waters without a Godspeed and blessing from me. I wish I were to be with you to sail over that Spanish Main which was once more interesting than it is to-day, once, when it was the sea-field of adventurers, men who, whatever their faults and crimes may have been, had at least vigour which would make them dear to our president, and which makes their lives entertaining in these days when the same seas are given over to "United Fruit Companies" and the like. One of my earliest memories is of the trial in Boston of a gang of Spanish pirates who had been marauding in those seas and making them dangerous for peaceful commerce. There are no such disturbers of the peace left. Captain Marryat's tales, which used to be the delight of boyhood, seem now as remote as the Middle Ages. The world has taken an immense stride in the direction of prose during your and my lifetime, and a purely utilitarian world is much less entertaining at least than one in which there was more demand on courage and more possibility of adventure. The *terra incognita* of our maps seventy years ago stimulated the imagination far more than the excellent maps of our United States surveyors and our geographical magazines. The *terra incognita* left room at least in which the imagination might roam at will, keeping us in touch with Sir John Mandeville. Exact and universal knowledge has no doubt its blessings, but are they comparable to the blessings of a moderate ignorance? Science is accumulating fact on fact wherever it ranges, building up heaps of useless information, but not enlarging human faculties or the scope of human vision. I do not see but that the accumulation of fact may go on till we have pyramids of it that surpass those of the Egyptians, but stand, like those, in a desolate desert; all which might be interpreted, but would be falsely interpreted, as the reflection of an old man comparing the pleasant times of youth with the duller days of age. But Donne is right in his verse (which I dare say I have cited to you before, for it is a favourite of mine) in which he speaks of "those unconcerning things, matters of fact"; and the world is more full of those unconcerning things now than it was eighty years ago, and is likely to grow fuller and fuller of them the longer it lasts. They do not provide soil for the gardens of the mind. So we must fall back more and more on the poets, and it will be the poets of Greece and of England who will supply the spiritual nourishment which we chiefly need.

But why write all this to you just as you are starting for your delightful summer voyage, following the wake of the old Spanish prows? I wish I were to be with you, but, wherever you may be, my blessing will follow you, and I shall wait for news of you with eagerness.

Ever yours, with love,

C. E. N.

To H. H. Furness

SHADY HILL, September 3, 1908.

Though dictated this word, it carries you my love as warm and fresh from my heart, as if written by my own hand. Your notes are delightful and have given me as much pleasure as you could desire. I have been reading "Hamlet," and am this morning wondering what his precise meaning was in saying — "and a man's life, is no more than to say one." In my own case that "one," both in the present and in memory, stands before an almost infinite number of cyphers. Long or brief as it may be, it is the happier for the thought of you.

Your loving

CHARLES.

P.S. I add a postscript to tell you a story which flashed into my memory this morning, and which may amuse Weir Mitchell when you see him. (Give him my love.) When old Jerry Mason, a famous lawyer in Boston of the Daniel Webster period, was lying on his death-bed, his daughter and the doctor thinking him asleep engaged in a low conversation together by a window across the room. When the doctor had gone he roused himself and said to his daughter, "Jane, what was the doctor saying to you?" "Ah! nothing, Father, nothing," was her reply. "In what precise terms did he say nothing, my dear?" instantly came the old cross-examiner's inquiry. This has not been brought to mind by my own experience!

To H. H. Furness

SHADY HILL, 17 September, 1908.

You never received a letter so delightful as the one which I have wished to send you every day for the past ten days; but wishes are poor things in the best case and especially when not seconded by powers capable of fulfilling them. Meanwhile you have been doing the best possible for me. Your notes have been admirable tonics, and you gave me one truly happy evening when one of my boys read aloud to me your Phi Beta discourse and I lay on my *chaise longue* smoking one of your "Romeo and Juliet" cigars. I know nothing better that it would be possible to say of your address than that it is worthy of you, — charming in its general tone, and alike subtle and profound in its criticism. I found myself either already in entire agreement with you or brought into agreement by your words, except in one instance where it seemed to me that you hardly allowed for an alternative which I believe exists in the interpretation of those words of Lady Macbeth against the common interpretation of which you protest so vigorously. When she says, "That which hath made

them drunk, hath made me bold," there seems to me
nothing strange in her speech, and no reason for inter-
preting it as if it meant that she had taken anything
more of wine than would serve as a tonic and not as an
intoxicant. There is nothing strange or unpleasant to
me in the thought of her taking a cup of wine as a
transient and temporary expedient, not to deaden her
faculties or to heighten her resolve, but simply to put
the instant fire in her veins which should render her
hand as steady in its accomplishment as her purpose
was determined. On the other hand, your exculpation
of the poor Ophelia, slandered by the imputations of
the commentators, seems to me altogether satisfactory.

I agree with your boys in being glad that you did not
have the chance to see and feel a West India hurricane.
Even the sight of cows and chickens carried through
the air would not make up for the horror of such an
extravagant exhibition of the powers of nature. I do
not like these noisy, violent convulsions of such uncon-
trollable forces. I feel as old Dr. Popkin did in regard
to the character of the Greek tragedies, — "They are
too horrible." He liked to see, as he said, everybody
peaceful and happy, and I like to see Nature in her calm
and beautiful moods rather than in her passionate
excesses. I have even seen some storms in New England when the glare of the lightnings and the crash of
the thunders were far beyond the limit of enjoyment.
I like much better to think of you safe, peaceful and
content at home, than exposed to the furies of the
tropical storm. . . .

As for myself, I am regaining health from day to

day slowly, but as fast as the wintry blood of old age permits; and, however wearisome the days may be as one to-morrow follows another without apparent change, I console myself with the philosophy of the old New Hampshire woman of whom Howells reports (I may, by the way, have told you this story before) that finding her in her home in one of the low valleys of New Hampshire where the surrounding mountains made the days short, he said to her, "Don't you find the winters long and dreary here, so shut in as you are?" "Oh, yes," she replied, "they are long and dreary, but they are only a day at a time": in which lies an admirable philosophy.

I read but little. After skimming the newspaper, I turn to Shakespeare, and yesterday and to-day I have been living in the Forest of Arden, finding the best of company with Jaques and Touchstone. What a wonder! I say to myself, and how absolutely exceptional are the range and quality of the work that makes the Shakespearean miracle!

No more to-day but love and gratitude for all you are and have been and are to be to

Your faithful friend,

CHARLES E. N.

To James Ford Rhodes

SHADY HILL, 21 September, 1908.

I have just read your paper on Godkin with such pleasure that I venture to tell you of it. Your estimate of him and of his influence seems to me admirable, and it must give the greatest pleasure to all to whom he was dear. I am writing to you from the sick-bed to which I have been confined for the past five weeks, and will not attempt in my present condition to express anything more than my cordial appreciation of your work and my entire satisfaction with it. There are one or two points upon which, when I grow stronger, I should be glad to talk with you, but they are such as would only serve to complete not to change the portrait which you have drawn. May I beg you to have this study of his life and influence printed separately, just as it stands, or, still better, with some enlargement? . . .

With grateful recognition of the service that you have rendered not only to Godkin's memory and to the cause of clear thought, but also to the causes which he maintained, and with hearty congratulations to you on the accomplishment of so valuable a contribution to the history of the past forty years, I remain,

Cordially and faithfully yours,
CHARLES ELIOT NORTON.

To H. H. Furness

SHADY HILL, October 8, 1908.

Since I am not the son of an ordained clergyman I have not your privilege of profane swearing, and I have never found it a privilege of such worth that I have cared to invade your prerogatives. There are so few profane ejaculations, even of the Elizabethan time, that are kindled by the fire of passion, or glowing with the harmless lambent flame of humour. But even the most scrupulously mannered man might well be pardoned an occasional "damn," as innocent as one of

Marjorie Fleming's, at finding all his muscular strength as completely evaporated as the sparkle of a glass of champagne, left to waste on the convivial dinner-table. But truly I have no reason for complaint, for I suffer from no pain, and all my wants are prevented by the loving kindness of children, or friends. Even before Mr. Spooner's famous "fish"[1] is half-warmed in my heart, some attendant "Abra" is present ere I speak her name, to complete the warming and serve it up for me.

But enough of trifling. The end cannot be far off and although few men have more to leave than I, I am neither reluctant, nor sentimentally sorry to leave it. If this should happen to be my last note to you, let it take to you the needless assurance that your love for me has been one of the chief blessings of recent years, and will continue to be so as long as any beat lasts in the heart, or consciousness in the mind of your loving old friend,

C. E. NORTON.

P.S. I hope yet to send to Sir Theodore Martin an acknowledgement of his kindness, and of the honour he has done me in giving me a copy of his interesting paper on Francesca da Rimini. How he puts me to shame! Good-bye once more, with love.

To H. H. Furness

SHADY HILL, October 13, 1908.

DEAREST HORACE, — Your last words to me are almost too sacred to be spoken of through a third per-

---

[1] "We all know, my friends, what it is to have a half-warmed fish [half-formed wish] in our hearts ": a slip of the tongue which delighted Norton.

son. . . . As I was having read to me the other night, a bit of the new and excellent biography of Aldrich,[1] I could not but feel the extravagance of his demand that the readers of the poets "should bring as much beauty as they (the poets) sing"; and then at once I felt how true this was of such a friendship as you give me, and how all your words of love are rather the image of yourself than of me; — and as I thought further and was happy in what you said, Dante's words came to me,

"Lo tuo ver dir m'incuora
Buona umiltà."

My last note was written to you on a day when it seemed I had taken a longer step downwards than usual, and I had a hope the end might be nearer than it now seems likely to be. I have but an infinitesimal remnant of muscular strength, but that remnant seems to have infinitesimal divisions, and neither I nor the doctors can guess when the end of these may be reached.

Meanwhile you may think of me as without pain, as surrounded by comforts, and as rich in blessings.

No more words between us as if our lives were not yet to be long.

Your loving and grateful   C. E. N.

To C. F. Adams

SHADY HILL, 14 October, 1908.

DEAR MR. ADAMS: —

"The breezy call of incense-breathing Morn,
The swallow twittering from the straw-built shed,
The cock's shrill clarion, or the echoing horn,
No more shall rouse them from their lowly bed."

[1] Ferris Greenslet's *Life of Thomas Bailey Aldrich* appeared in 1908.

Your cheerful call comes too late. I wish I could take part with you, as you propose, in the celebration of Milton's birthday by our Historical Society and by the University. The idea is altogether one according to my own mind. But I have been laid up now for two months with illness which, though not severe at any time and not causing me any considerable pain, yet has diminished my strength and is gradually sapping it till at last there is so little left that I have to depend upon others for help in the performance of acts which used to seem purely automatic. I regret my present condition more when obliged to refuse to do what I should like, as in such a case as this. A good deal depends on ———'s reply to you. If he should take up your proposal actively, he would interest the whole English Department in it without difficulty, and success would be practically secured. If his reply should be lukewarm, please let me know, for I might possibly be able to raise by a few degrees the temperature which it marked.

Meanwhile I follow with unbated interest those of your varied activities concerning which the papers afford us information. I hope you are not going away this winter from Boston. Your departure at any time leaves Boston deprived of one of its high motive forces.

I hope that age has not begun to undermine even the least of your defences. That those whom the gods love die young, is by no means universally true; but the Historical Society at least affords several examples of the fact that the gods do not like to be bored, and so are quite ready to prolong the lives of some men whose death might occasionally be felt as a relief to the long-suffering members of the societies or communities to which they belong. There is no need to be more particular.

With kindest regards and cordial good wishes,

Very sincerely yours,

C. E. NORTON.

per S. Norton.

DEAR MR. ADAMS, — This letter comes to you alas! not signed by my father, as he is more ill than you would gather from it. His mind is wonderfully active and absolutely clear, but the body is very weak — and he has been losing strength the past week. Your letter gave him pleasure. I add this word, as I think you would like to know about him.

Believe me

Yours sincerely,

SARA NORTON.

The autumn day drew onward; the tulip-tree by Norton's window dropped its golden leaves; the evening mists had grown heavier. Early on October 21, after a few hours of unconsciousness, with all his children near him, Norton died.

In Ashfield, on that day at noon, the village bells were tolled.

THE END

WORDS OF A CONTEMPORARY

WHEN intercourse between Norton and Arthur Sedgwick began in 1861 — shortly before they became brothers-in-law — neither would have considered himself the contemporary of the other, for Mr. Sedgwick was then sixteen years old and Mr. Norton thirty-four. But when a close relation continues for forty-seven years, the terms defining it may undergo important changes. The man who has known another for so long a period acquires most of the attributes of a contemporary. Not the least valuable of these is the capacity, and the authority, to say certain things which lie beyond the province of such representatives of a younger generation as the compilers of this biography. It is fortunate, therefore, that some reminiscences of Mr. Sedgwick, embodied in a long letter to Miss Sara Norton, are available for inclusion here.

To your father in 1861, I must have been little more than a mere school-boy. The steps by which he became my infallible adviser and friend, and by which I was made to feel almost as much at home at Shady Hill as if it had been my father's house, I cannot now recall. The process was imperceptible and gentle, and I mention the fact chiefly because it illustrated a trait in him which was very characteristic. He was not only a man of strong family affections, but took a deep and active interest in young people, which afterwards made it seem as if he had always been destined for success and distinction as a teacher. But at this time everything seemed to point to a different career for him.

I was strongly attracted to him, and during the whole time that I was in college, and afterwards, while I was in the army, while in the Law School, and while practising law in Boston, I was under his influence. I looked up to him as to a mature and exceptionally wise, good, and able man, while he had the art, by openness and an affectionate disposition, to make the distance in years between us seem much less than it was. So that for many years, while he replaced my father, he at the same time seemed like an elder brother. All this he made so natural that I did not at the time perceive the trouble he must have given himself to gain my confidence. Now that I am coming to the end of my life, and look back at this period of it, I see what an unusual piece of good fortune it was to have acquired, by the chance of my sister's marriage, so kind and so constant and so valuable a friend. Kindness and constancy were always characteristic of him, and he was drawn, as I have said, to young men by a sympathy which had its roots in an inborn capacity and desire to help and guide. This trait, always known to those who were closest to him, became apparent to every one when, in later years, he came to teach in the University, and when the hold which he established upon the affection and attention of his classes was seen by everybody.

When we removed to Cambridge, we lived first at the other end of the town from Shady Hill, near Elm-

wood, but the near relation between the two house-
holds drew us nearer, and after occupying for a couple
of years Dr. Palfrey's house, — then almost connected
with Shady Hill by the charming avenue of pines
planted, I think, by your grandfather for his walk to
Divinity Hall, — my aunts finally, in 1864, established
themselves in the place on the Shady Hill property
made for them by your father and bought by them,
and now owned by my sister.

At this time life in Cambridge was very simple and
very pleasant, and Shady Hill was perhaps its pleasantest house. I remember being struck long afterwards by an old friend of his referring to him as a man
"remarkably masterful"; and so no doubt with age,
and as he felt his powers develop and his authority
increase, he became. Indeed, no one can understand
his life who does not remember that the authority of
the Puritan Church was in his blood, and that his
father in his day had been lately one of the most distinguished spokesmen for the Unitarian faith in New
England. But at this time what struck me as a shy and
boyish stranger was chiefly his cultivation, his accurate
knowledge, his intense feeling for everything beautiful
and fine, whether in life or art, his general desire to
share with others and to learn from others. Looking
back now I see that at this time he was still young and
unsophisticated. In his later life, when he had incurred
a good deal of enmity on account of his pronounced
and intrepid stand against Imperialism, his critics
derived satisfaction from imputing to a littleness in
him his relations with friends who were men of con-

spicuous distinction in the world, and whose names were in fact household words. But in reality, those who knew him were aware that these friendships had their source and foundation in the best qualities of his character, — his admiration for whatever was worth admiring, his desire for constant self-improvement, his zeal for the best intellectual companionship. He was the last person in the world to desire to shine by reflected light. Of himself he thought very modestly. Vanity was incompatible with his character. An unaffected seriousness of temper and purpose was its basis.

Like all men who are conscientious about their work, he took the most careful pains with everything he did,[1] leaving no stone unturned to avoid inaccuracy and error, and even all looseness of expression. He detested exaggeration. This made his style sometimes seem laboured, and affected his letters and conversation. But it was as far removed as possible from that preciseness of speech, tone, and style which affectation sometimes produces. If he had a constant and dominant motive always acting upon his will, it was a zeal for well-doing which led him to self-disparagement.

"I never care for anything I do," he says in a letter which I have before me — meaning that it was the *object in view* he cared about, and not his own connection with it. And this was very true.

His dislike of exaggeration was a part of his Puritan

---

[1] It was a family recognition at Shady Hill, referred to often with a smile, that no one was so particular about the doing-up of a parcel; no one would take more pains about such a matter, if necessary, than the master of the house. — *Editors' note.*

inheritance, though it was also connected with his
delicacy of taste, in letters and art. So far as it was the
latter, it was derived from that eye and ear for the
"golden mean" which has always been the life of what
is classic and immortal. So far as it was the former, it
was derived from a strong moral and religious worship
of truth. He not only avoided it himself, but could
not forbear reprobating it in others. But with the exaggeration of humour he had the strongest sympathy,
and in this he was neither Puritan nor classic, but a
genuine American. Lowell found his suggestions with
regard to the "Biglow Papers" worthy of attention,
and later on I was surprised to find how much he enjoyed "David Harum."

Through him I enjoyed for many years — indeed
for most of my life — the acquaintance of his friends
and intimates in Cambridge, and I think it may be
said that they were simply the men best worth knowing
in the world in which he lived, and that they liked him
because they felt him to be one of them. Men as different from one another as Lowell, Longfellow, Howells, Godkin, and Curtis, all recognized him as a man
competent to criticize their work. Friendship which
can stand the test of candour is very rare, and very
true. His success in making and retaining friends
among those whom he criticized to their faces, and
greatly and openly admired at the same time, was due
to their perception and love of a curious simplicity of
character in him, careless of and blind to suspicion
which it knew to be unwarranted.

The behaviour of the *mens conscia recti* is very difficult for the sophisticated world to follow or believe in. Sometimes it is to friends only that it is possible. To the end, I think, he could never understand why it should be thought peculiar for rectitude to be naïf. Conventions of a thousand sorts he had no objection to, and willingly adopted, but simplicity of heart and spirit he cultivated. In consequence of this his expressions of opinion were often not merely unexpected, but very surprising to others. I remember a conversation in which J. L. Motley and his diplomatic career were under discussion. He thought highly of Motley's talents, but one thing damned him — "he was not wholly simple." In the case of a man of the world, a diplomat and a historian, it seemed at the first blush strange that he should produce such a criticism as a comprehensive and vital condemnation. But Motley was not devoid of vanity; and throughout life his critic's eyes were fixed on simplicity as a final test of character.

Fidelity to the tasks which ideals imposed was stanchly embedded in Norton's character. The idea of his being unfaithful to anybody, or to any idea once conceived and adopted as a duty, was something that never entered the head of anybody who knew him well. When I first knew him, religion was a part of his life. As he became more sceptical, he found his consolation in holding fast to morality. He was fond of maintaining that Politics was a branch of Ethics, and what attracted him most to Ruskin and the Pre-Raphaelites was their beautiful dream of a marriage between morality and art.

By education and early association he belonged to

the Harvard College which preceded the University. In the latter he taught later on. The prescribed curriculum of our day — for it had not changed much down to the time of the war — had one great advantage, that it made a solidarity or freemasonry of knowledge among the graduates, which in the modern system must be very much lost. All graduates possessed a common fund of learning and training which, as far as it went, represented what was expected to be known by those who called themselves educated men — what had been handed down in the modern world as the summary of necessary human knowledge. And what was taught was taught accurately. Slovenly students there were who scraped through, but such a type as a slovenly teacher was to me almost unknown. To be a professor at Harvard under the old system was to be a "master of those who know." In this, Child, Lowell, Gray, Gurney, Longfellow, Lane, Torrey, Goodwin, Peirce — all the members of the Faculty — resembled each other. They were not merely specialists, but belonged to the old fraternity of scholars to none of whom any branch of learning was alien. The atmosphere in which they lived was almost entirely academic. The idea of a college as a place primarily for distinction in sport, or even primarily for "vocational" objects, would have filled them with aversion.

The Cambridge of Lowell's earlier days has been preserved by him in a delightful paper. Down to the time of the war, and for several years more, it retained much that recalled the earlier stage. There was still an innocent simplicity and freedom of manners between the sexes which existed, perhaps, nowhere in the world outside of New England. It was somewhat as if, the lesson of Puritanism having been learned, there was no longer any reason for restraint. Instead of our being, as our forefathers had insisted, naturally depraved and prone to evil, we were really, if allowed to be happy, virtuous. The feeling of the indefinite perfectibility of the individual through training and education was nowhere more likely to take hold of the imagination than in a seat of learning and the community connected with it; and one of the traits which I recall as most marked in your father's early manhood, in the daily life of himself and his mother and sisters, was a cheerful and generous optimism founded on the new faith in humanity which democracy was spreading. In New England a severe Puritanism had bred a hardy, self-respecting, self-disciplined, simple race, which longed, not for forbidden fruit, but for release from a strait-jacket.

It has often been pointed out that the democracy of New England was a natural outgrowth of the equality of the prevailing material conditions. This view, however, can easily be pressed too far. There has never yet been any actual equality of condition between the lives of the well-to-do and cultivated and the lives of those who support themselves by daily manual labour. The equality that existed, and, for the time, seemed sometimes to have killed envy on the one side and arrogance on the other, was the equality of burdens and opportunity and generous hope and ambition, spiritual as well as material. The town meeting of that day was still a

meeting of the owners of the land which made up the
town; the members of the church, or churches where
there were more than one, were these same townsmen.
There were no large numbers of property-holders
absentees during half the year. Taxation was equal
and unfelt. Pauperism was nearly unknown. The mill
hands of Lowell were American families who read the
"Atlantic Monthly" and the "Tribune." It was a
community and government the success of which
seemed to prove that the ideal state as imagined by the
yet unborn Socialist — to every one according to his
need, from every one according to his ability — had
actually been incarnated by sturdy, democratic individualism. And there were none so rich as to suggest
the question how much riches one ought to be allowed
to have, and there were none so poor as to be without
hope in the world.

The eager and enthusiastic optimism of the New
England of that day was as different as possible from
the gross material optimism of a later generation. It
produced Emerson and the Transcendentalists on the
one hand, Dr. Channing on the other; it produced an
order in which Lowell, Longfellow, and Holmes were
men of the world. The basis of its existence could not
be denied or disproved. Even those sceptical critics
who knew that the regeneration of the world had not
yet been accomplished, could neither deny nor argue
away the fact of the happiness existing throughout the
contented community. They could only insist that
so much self-contentment, so exuberantly expressed,
was tiresome, as indeed it no doubt was to many

observers. Carlyle, irritated by it, protested that Americans bored him.

How did this state of things affect your father? I should say, from my recollections and from comparing them with later impressions, that while he was too distinctly a scholar and critic to be carried away by it, his whole youth and early manhood derived a buoyancy and glow from it that never left him throughout his life. It was this buoyancy which enabled him to share the feelings of the young and innocent, and it made him prone always to reserve a corner of his mind for a belief in some not impossible Utopia. To him who had grown up in the New England Arcadia, Utopia could never seem wholly a dream. Those who profited, as so many hundreds did, by his sympathy and instruction and advice in his later life, generally had little idea how much they owed to the remarkable qualities of his early intellectual, moral, and social inheritance.

The turn given to his mind and character by the war was important, and the events of it led to consequences which were even more so. It was not that the outward circumstances of his life in Cambridge were much changed. The field of conflict was very far off, and even the drill of the undergraduates in companies and their garrisoning the old Arsenal, near the Washington Elm, to defend it against enemies who never appeared, did not make it much closer. But in the world of thought and feeling it was a cataclysm. Your father would, I think, had his health permitted, have gone to the war, and in doing so he would have taken up arms against some of his best friends, with whom he not only had no quarrel, but was on terms of the most cordial intimacy. Southerners had always been fond of sending their sons to Harvard, and Northern and Southern society had had a common meeting-ground during half the year at Newport; the Middletons of South Carolina were among the best friends of the Shady Hill household. The long civil dissension over slavery had been bad enough, but civil war kills friendship; or at any rate for the time paralyzes it; and that it was civil war, over the long-forbidden subject now in every one's mouth, was the terrible fact at the outset of the struggle that stared all in the face. For years, in what had been the most peaceful and contented community in the world, war was to rage and not to stop until the North had subjugated the South. As this at first incredible prospect unrolled itself to view, it became out of the question to think any longer in the terms of the old American life.

Critical and conservative by temper as he was, your father had from the very first a clear conception of the gravity of the impending conflict, but though he always cultivated a dislike for enthusiasm as a state of mind necessarily involving exaggeration, he was born an enthusiast for right over wrong, for truth over error. In his eagerness to do his part, he soon found the direction in which his powers were of most avail; and where under other circumstances he might have become only a man of letters, he became and remained as well a moulder of opinion, and through those whose opinion he moulded, of that of the public. This is one of the things generally overlooked in his career. As a Dante scholar and translator of Dante he would have been distinguished; that he should have been an efficient moulder of opinion, through the Loyal Publication Society, through the editors of the "Atlantic," through the "North American Review" and as one of the founders of the "Nation," and collaborator and stanch supporter of its creator for long years against both "candid friends" and implacable enemies, then as the organizer and director of the annual open debate at Ashfield, and finally, as one of the most conspicuous leaders of the remnant that stood out against the Spanish War and Imperialism, would have been a career by itself. That he should have combined the two and been distinguished in both is what marks him as having displayed powers beyond those of ordinary men.

It was in fact his own life that was his masterpiece. From the time when he first felt within him the scholar's inspiration (Rowse's portrait is to my mind very characteristic of him in his earlier period) to the time when he retired because his work was done, he trained himself incessantly to do the best that could be done with the faculties that nature had given him; and that not for profit nor display nor fame, but for those he loved, and the common good, and for duty's sake.

Of those now alive, very few know that to him was in great part, if not chiefly, due the existence of Memorial Hall. After the end of the war the feeling that there should be some proper, perpetual memorial to graduates of Harvard who had died in it, was wide-spread, but there was no agreement as to what form it should take. A large body of graduates were in favour of giving it a military and triumphal character — of a trophy of some sort — and they had the advantage of being led by a graduate much beloved and respected, both in Boston and Cambridge, by all those graduates who had gone to the war or supported it — John Ropes. But for a physical disqualification, he would have been in the thick of the war. As it was, in addition to being very successful in civil life as a lawyer, he was an accomplished military critic and writer, and was wrapped up in the affairs of the Twentieth Massachusetts (a regiment almost entirely officered from Harvard College, and three times, I think, virtually destroyed in successive campaigns); every year he dined with the association of officers, an adopted father or brother of the regiment. His military turn and his devotion to the cause of the Union, and his persuasiveness and skill in argument, made him a formidable antagonist. The view of the other party, led, as I remember, by your father, was that the memorial should be one which did not suggest victory or triumph in war, but the sacrifice of life for a cause wholly disconnected with ordinary warfare, and above it, and that the memorial should be avowedly dedicated to the uses of peace and the objects of the university which had sent out its young men to give their lives for their country and Freedom. The struggle between the forces naturally produced much feeling, and for the time, bitterness; and the part played in it by your father was most important. His view prevailed. I suppose that to-day few would maintain that a military trophy would have been the proper memorial.

For gifts, he had a wonderful memory, the old indomitable Puritan will, and a faculty for order and method (he was, as I have said, sedulously accurate) which, devoted to other ends, might have brought him great success in business or public affairs. He had also a peculiar delicacy of taste which pointed him out as fitted for a critic, and a turn for exposition and inculcation, which made him a gifted teacher; while his affection for his pupils made him beloved and revered at the same time. He knew how to make himself feared, though this power he rarely exercised, I think, consciously. He put great restraint on a natural gift for a peculiarly mordant sarcasm, inherited, I believe, from his father. This, however, seldom earned him enemies, partly because it was not often indulged in, and partly perhaps because it was rarely sardonic. It always had in it a wit which even a victim might enjoy. It is difficult to give instances which reproduce the effect, but I remember two which struck me at the time as very characteristic. He was to begin a lecture before a large class, in which he wished to say something about the ideal imported by the word "gentleman." He began with a very conciliatory gravity, "None of you, probably, has ever seen a gentleman." On another occasion, at the height of the Republican split over Blaine and his moral unfitness for the presidency, he was arguing the matter with an eminent supporter of Blaine (he was as combative on a moral point as any divine could have been over a dogma); the advocate of

Blaine emphatically insisted that the specific facts involving lack of integrity on Blaine's part did not in any way affect his merits as a candidate. "That," said Norton, "gives me your gauge." In this case there was an estrangement.

As editor with Lowell of the "North American," he gave that publication a new lease of life. The modern idea of an editor as a mere agent for the dissemination of readable papers on all sides of all subjects, however inconsistent with each other or with his own opinions, would have been intolerable to him ; the object he had in view was a publication for which he was willing to be responsible, with a wide range of topics and discussion, but always with the idea of advancing what he believed to be the truth. It was the adherence to this plan — the tradition of editorship, once almost universal — which gave the periodical press of fifty years ago a weight for which no sensationalism and no amount of contributors' names can ever make up. When the publication spoke, it spoke for itself; with the combined force of all the brains and character and repute behind it.

A genuine editorial faculty includes the power to estimate capacity in others — to see in advance what sort of work a man can do. To him chiefly was due the selection of Godkin as editor of the "Nation." The "Nation" was a continuation and completion of the work of moulding opinion which had its beginning in the Loyal Publication Society. That your father should have given the stanch support he did to the editor he picked out and established, was natural. What was remarkable was that he should have divined the extraordinary, hitherto untested capacity of Godkin for the task. On the latter's death in 1902, he wrote me a letter containing a passage which was not only very good as an estimate, but is interesting because part of what he says of his friend's influence might have been said by Godkin of him: —

CAMBRIDGE, Mass., 22 May, 1902.

... The news reached us yesterday afternoon of Godkin's death. I feel deeply the sorrow that it brings to his wife; but, except for her sorrow, there is no reason to regret it. Indeed, those of us who cared most for him can only have hoped during the last two years that his life would not be prolonged. But how much of our own past life he takes with him, and what an interesting chapter for us both is closed by his death! The services that he has rendered to the country are greater than the people generally will recognize. All the strongest evil forces of the time have been against his efforts and against the fair recognition of their importance and value. No man has opposed a more vigorous and effective resistance to those forces; but they were too strong to be overcome. A great part of his influence has had no external manifestation. Many men who have openly opposed it were nevertheless greatly affected by it, and many of his most bitter enemies in the press were more or less consciously, even at the time when they were attacking him, exhibiting the good effect which his work had had upon them. He did more than any one else to improve the character of editorial writing throughout the country, and although he could not prevent the popular newspaper press from lowering itself to the standards of the ignorant and the unprincipled, yet he succeeded in setting an example of what the newspaper press should be, and of raising the level of a great number of the daily newspapers, so that, on the whole, in a wide view of the press of to-day as compared with the press of forty years ago when he began his work, the improvement which is mainly due to him is notable. He was taken from work at a time fortunate for himself, and he may be called *felix opportunitate mortis.* . . .

There was, during his lifetime at Shady Hill and at Ashfield, more pleasant conversation of an original sort than it had been my fortune to know of in any other house. Of your father's share in it it would be difficult to give any one, who had never heard him, a fair idea. He belonged to a generation in which much attention was still given to conversation and much importance attached to excellence in it. Lowell, R. H. Dana, and Curtis seemed born talkers; so, in their different ways, were Godkin, Gurney, Chauncey Wright, and Child. Conversation with them was in the best American manner, which is, or at that day was, somewhat but not entirely that of English talkers, and many thought better. A subject taken up was discussed, a story of interest told at length in full detail. Both he and his friends had many "short stories," told instead of being written, and now lost forever, which made the tradition of the talk of *raconteurs* of an earlier day live again. The newspapers do these things for us now, but in doing it they kill conversation, just as with their simultaneous and ubiquitous news they leave us little for our letters.

Conversation can be general and at the same time individual, and there are always those who are ready to listen. Your father had always willing listeners, and he was a good listener himself. His extraordinarily retentive and active memory furnished his mind with a store on which he could draw at will. A long narrative once heard, he could reproduce years later with every detail. He had the hospitable host's knack of suggesting topics which promoted conversation. A modern trait is a dislike to be "drawn out." This may come from shyness, or it may come from a consciousness of there being nothing on which to draw. At any rate, people who had plenty of conversation used to like it. With young people, and on his own subject, he was always interesting.

His letters speak for themselves. His style, to my mind, was cultivated, but not in the least an imitation of any one. It was peculiar to him — I remember no correspondence in the least like it.

An art allied to that of conversation, which was natural to him, he developed in his lectures, but nothing could better show his perseverance in perfecting himself than that he made himself late in life a successful speaker. At Ashfield he became not only host, but manager and protagonist of the speaking. I had known him during most of my life. I had not thought of him as an orator, and to my surprise, I found that he had become a very successful speaker. He had evidently

made a study of it, so that when I heard him for the
first time after a long absence, it seemed as natural as
if he had been doing it always; at these Ashfield dinners, to which all of the leading men of the country
were invited, and to which many came, I felt most
distinctly what his "masterfulness" meant, and was
not sorry that I still had left some of my youthful awe
of him.

In Ashfield, his figure, and that of George Curtis,
will always remain in my memory. Both of them came
as strangers and remained as townsmen. His public
work as a townsman and host at the annual dinner is
common property; his private life always recalled
Cambridge and Shady Hill. One of the most hospitable
of men, his doors were always open; his interest in
everything never flagged. When he first went there it
was a much more remote place than it is now, and one
of my earliest recollections of it is of the long twelve-
mile and three-hour drive from South Deerfield to Ashfield in the mail stage at the close of the day, then the
only way of getting there, and of talks with strangers
by the way, in which your father took the lead, and
developed a range of subjects and a scope also, which
were often rather surprising to his auditors, to whom
conversation was an unknown art.

Trolleys and railroads have made it difficult now to
find any real country in New England. Within their
reach it is in great part urban, or what is often worse,
suburban. Ashfield had been picked out by him for a
summer place as one of the hill-towns of western Massachusetts, in which the rural life, vanishing from Cam-

bridge, still lingered on. Like every one else, he had an ideal of occupation in leisure, though it did not generally give him much liberty from work. It was a moderate ideal — indeed, the old classical ideal of a pleasant home in a smiling country, with books, friends, children, dogs, horses, fields, and a garden and trees. He remembered such a one in his youth, and attained it in his age.

APPENDICES

APPENDIX A

(From Ruskin's *Præterita*, III, 2 and 3.)

IT chanced so, one day, when we were going from Vevay to Geneva. It was hot on the deck, and we all went down into the little cabin, which the waves from the paddle wheels rushed past the windows of, in lovely wild masses of green and silver. There was no one in the cabin but ourselves (that is to say, papa, mamma, old Anne, and me), and a family whom we supposed, rightly, to be American, of the best sort. A mother with three daughters, and her son, — he in charge of them all, perhaps of five or six and twenty; his sisters younger; the mother just old enough to *be* their mother; all of them quietly and gracefully cheerful. There was the cabin table between us, covered with the usual Swiss news about nothing, and an old caricature book or two. The waves went on rushing by; neither of the groups talked, but I noticed that from time to time the young American cast somewhat keen, though entirely courteous, looks of scrutiny at my father and mother.

In a few minutes after I had begun to notice these looks, he rose, with the sweetest quiet smile I ever saw on any face (unless, perhaps, a nun's, when she has some grave kindness to do), crossed to our side of the cabin, and addressing himself to my father, said, with a true expression of great gladness, and of frank trust that his joy would be understood, that he knew who we were, was most thankful to have met us, and that he prayed permission to introduce his mother and sisters to us.[1]

[1] See Norton's letter to S. C. Cockerell, *ante*, p. 210. — *Editors' note.*

The bright eyes, the melodious voice, the perfect manner, the simple, but acutely flattering, words, won my father in an instant. The New Englander sat down beside us, his mother and sisters seeming at once also to change the steamer's cabin into a reception room in their own home. The rest of the time till we reached Geneva passed too quickly; we arranged to meet in a day or two again, at St. Martin's.

And thus I became possessed of my second friend, after Dr. John Brown; and of my first real tutor, Charles Eliot Norton.

The meeting at St. Martin's with Norton and his family was a very happy one. Entirely sensible and amiable, all of them; with the farther elasticity and acuteness of the American intellect, and no taint of American ways. Charles himself, a man of the highest natural gifts, in their kind; observant and critical rather than imaginative, but with an all-pervading sympathy and sensibility, absolutely free from envy, ambition, or covetousness:[1] a scholar from his cradle, nor only now a *man* of the world, but a *gentleman* of the world, whom the highest born and best bred of every nation, from the Red Indian to the White Austrian, would recognize in a moment, as of their caste.

In every branch of classical literature he was my superior; knew old English writers better than I, — much more, old French; and had active fellowship and close friendship with the then really progressive leaders of thought in his own country, Longfellow, Lowell, and Emerson.

All the sympathy, and all the critical subtlety, of his mind had been given, not only to the reading, but to the trial and following out of the whole theory of "Modern

---

[1] I mean, covetousness of beautiful things, the only sort that is possible to people like Charles Norton or me. He gave me his best Greek "Fortune," a precious little piece of flying marble, with her feet on the world, engraved with hexagonal tracery like a honeycomb. We both love its honey — but best, given by each other.

Painters "; so that, as I said, it was a real joy for him to meet me, and a very bright and singular one for both of us, when I knocked at his door in the Hôtel du Mont Blanc at five in the morning; and led him, as the roselight flushed the highest snow, up the winding path among the mountain meadows of Sallenches.

I can see them at this moment, those mountain meadows, if I rise from my writing-table, and open the old barred valves of the corner windows of the Hôtel Bellevue; — yes, and there is the very path we climbed that day together, apparently unchanged. But on what seemed then the everlasting hills, beyond which the dawn rose cloudless, and on the heaven in which it rose, and on all that we that day knew, of human mind and virtue, — how great the change, and sorrowful, I cannot measure, and, in this place, I will not speak.

That morning gave to me, I said, my first tutor; [1] for Dr. John Brown, however far above me in general power, and in the knowledge proper to his own profession, yet in the simplicity of his affection liked everything I wrote, for what was true in it, however imperfectly or faultfully expressed; but Norton saw all my weaknesses, measured all my narrownesses, and, from the first, took serenely, and as it seemed of necessity, a kind of paternal authority over me, and a right of guidance, — though the younger of the two, — and always admitting my full power in its own kind; nor only admitting, but in the prettiest way praising and stimulating. It was almost impossible for him to speak to any one he cared for, without some side-flash of witty compliment; and to me, his infinitely varied and loving praise became a constant motive to exertion, and aid in effort: yet he never allowed in me the slightest violation of the laws, either of good writing, or social prudence, without instant blame, or warning.

I was entirely conscious of his rectorial power, and affec-

---

[1] Gordon was only my master in Greek, and in common sense; he never criticized my books, and, I suppose, rarely read them.

tionately submissive to it; so that he might have done anything with me, but for the unhappy difference in our innate,
and unchangeable, political faiths.

Since that day at Sallenches it has become a matter of the
most curious speculation to me, what sort of soul Charles
Norton would have become, if he had had the blessing to be
born an English Tory, or a Scotch Jacobite, or a French
Gentilhomme, or a Savoyard Count. I think I should have
liked him best to have been a Savoyard Count; say, Lord of
the very Tower of Sallenches, a quarter of a mile above me
at the opening of the glen, — habitable yet, and inhabited;
it is half hidden by its climbing grapes. Then, to have read
the "Fioretti di San Francesco," (which *he* found out, New
Englander though he was, before I did), in earliest boyhood;
then to have been brought into instructively grievous collision with Commerce, Liberty, and Evangelicalism at
Geneva; then to have learned Political Economy from
Carlyle and me; and finally devoted himself to write the
History of the Bishops of Sion! What a grand, happy, consistent creature he would have been, — while now he is
hopelessly out of gear and place, over in the States there,
as a runaway star dropped into Purgatory; and twenty times
more a slave than the blackest nigger he ever set his white
scholars to fight the South for; because all the faculties a
black has may be fully developed by a good master (see Miss
Edgeworth's story of the grateful Negro),[1] — while only
about the thirtieth or fortieth part of Charles Norton's
effective contents and capacity are beneficially spent in the
dilution of the hot lava, and fructification of the hot ashes,
of American character; — which are overwhelming, borne
now on volcanic air, — the life of Scotland, England,
France, and Italy. . . .

[1] I showed the valley of Chamouni, and the "Pierre-a-Bot" above
Neuchatel, to Mrs. Beecher Stowe and her pretty little daughter Georgie,
— when Georgie was about sixteen, and would n't let me say a word against
Uncle Tom: howbeit, that story of the Grateful Negro, Robinson Crusoe,
and Othello, contain, any of the three, more, alike worldly and heavenly,
wisdom than would furnish three "Uncle Tom's Cabins."

APPENDIX B

"What we love, we live; and if we truly assimilate the principles of ideal art, we may unconsciously and gradually incorporate into ourselves its truth, order, proportion and simplicity."

J. R. LOWELL.

"Poi chi pinge figura
Se non può esser lei, non la può porre."

(From Norton's Commonplace Book.)

IN a subject like the study of the Fine Arts the range is so wide, the possibility of linking æsthetic and ethical suggestion so natural, so inevitable for a mind like Norton's, that, as we have seen, his appeal to youth, made with strong conviction in his University courses, was both impressive and effectual. As Mr. Woodberry, with just discrimination, has said of Norton's teaching: "He found the significance of art very much in its presentation of historic phases of the moral character of a people, or the civic conditions at an epoch, — not so much in its absolute beauty, *per se;* indeed, he seemed to me always unsatisfied with beauty as an end in itself, and restless till he could give it an intellectual value or moral relation."

From a pupil who graduated at Harvard in the final year of Norton's service as an active Professor (1898), and who preserved his notes of the lectures in "Fine Arts IV," we catch an echo, as it were, even through condensed phrase and reported word, of Norton's voice in the class-room. The art of the Greeks and its relation to modern life; their virile sanity; the value of their principle of moderation in all things; the moral influence of beauty; the enrichment of life through poetry — in its widest application; the need of the cultivation of true simplicity; — these and other "counsels of perfection," together with a mass of definite fact, were outlined in the course. The notes upon its conclusion, and some points touched on earlier, give so clear an impression of the effect the course was intended to produce that they are here reproduced as set down by the pupil:—

No man is solitary on earth — he is an infinite complex of conditions made for him by others. He cannot escape, if he would. Must be hammered into greater nobility to be full-grown.

The love of the beautiful is the best possession that a man who wants to lead a moral life can have. It is purifying, uplifting, ennobling, encouraging.

There is no ideal that is not founded in reality.

The Greeks were the first to succeed in expressing their ideals in visual form. Parthenon — perfect representation of ideals of that time. Doric column most vitalized bit of architecture man has put his soul into.

History ought not to be read with dull acceptance, but with intelligence and quickened imagination. Our minds should not be merely quiescent receptacles.

There is such a lack of nobility in human nature that the advance of others is trying to the average man.

Gladness and gravity of life. Don't indulge in foolish cynicism.

Culture — true discipline of mind.

Too much erudition kills life. There are many German corpses.

The imaginative poets are the true realists.

Such sentences run through the notebook, and its last words are:

Reverence thyself. Make the best of thyself. Train thyself in the service of others. Seek not happiness — but find it. Young man, here you have tasted heavenly food (then with a smile) at least, the bread of angels has been set before you. You are about to go out into the world, where the crowd will be eager for material gains. Let not your eyes be

clouded by the dust of the world. Hold fast to the ideals of
your youth. Though men call them illusions, they are the
most enduring realities after all.

Walter Scott — that gallant gentleman, when on his
death-bed, said to his son: "My son, be a good man." In
that threadbare truism — I fain would believe it is not
wholly threadbare — lies the whole moral law. The last
and best thing I can say to each one of you is, — be a
good man.

To these notes are added two letters. The first came to
Norton, during the last year of his life, from a former pupil
of whose name and personality he had no recollection. The
second, from a Japanese, also a former pupil of Norton's,
requires no comment.

My dear Mr. Norton, —

For a long time, at the end of each academic year, I have
wished to send you a word to acknowledge how much I owe
you, and I have refrained because I knew that you were constantly receiving such tribute from those whose success in
life lends value to what they say; but perhaps once in a life-
time it may be permitted to yield to this instinct, which I
trust is not unconscious egotism, but the wish to acknowledge a great debt.

I speak only the bare truth, when I say that in these thirty
years I have not looked at a gorgeous sunset, or listened to
exquisite music, or read a worthy book, without thinking of
you, and by that thought expanding immeasurably within
me the joy and delight which you taught us to derive from all
beauty and nobility.

That I could have enjoyed more if I had diligently obeyed
you when in college, or if I had followed since the lines you
laid down for us, does not alter the fact that all the most
genuine pleasure I have had in thirty years I owe to your
teaching and to the constant thought of you.

I beg you not to try to identify me, but only to think of me as one of that great number of men scattered over this world, whose names and faces are wholly unknown to you, who rejoice inwardly when they think of you and of the life you have led, and who find in that recollection a solace and refreshing that never fails them.

I am, Sir, with profound respect and gratitude,

Your obedient servant,

26 August, 1908.

DEAR MISS NORTON, —

I thank you very much for your kind remembrance of me — the very act of remembrance as well as the token of it.

I at once read through the book [1] and felt as if I was again at his study at the Shady Hill silently looking at his kind face.

I have lived nearly fifty long years but not been fortunate enough to see another like him. And when I think of it the sense of loneliness steals into me.

But I have no doubt that, no less than his published works and the part of his life which was a more or less public property, his less known spoken words of instruction and deeds of kindness that touched men's mind and heart though difficult to trace are still working and will long work their part in this world of ours. . . .

KAGOSHIMA KEN, TOKIO,
Feb. 19, 1913.

[1] Addresses by Edward W. Emerson and W. F. Harris before the Archæological Institute in memory of Charles Eliot Norton.

APPENDIX C

CONCERNING THE ACADEMY DINNERS IN ASHFIELD

In 1901, Norton, replying to a critic who had objected to the frank utterances at the Academy Dinner in regard to the Philippine question wrote:—

"I have no wish to offend the feelings of my good friends of the town and the neighbourhood. But I have from the first, almost for a quarter of a century now, aimed to make the Dinners an occasion to connect the life of this little community with the larger life of the country, to quicken its sense of the close relation of its permanent interests with those of the nation at large, and to lift it out of the rut of merely local affairs.

"Following the bright example of Mr. Curtis I have tried to inform and deepen the spirit of true patriotism, that spirit which is inspired with love of country not so much for what that country is, as for what that country may be, if its people be true to the principles of its constitution and faithful to the ideals to which they profess allegiance. One of those principles is that of freedom of speech, and our dinner platform has always been one of independent thought and free speech. The speakers have by no means always been of my own way of thinking. Within the last three years you have heard the Rev. Dr. Moxom eloquently and vigorously celebrating the glory of war, the Rev. Dr. Plumb not less ardently defending, on the ground, as he asserted of Christian principles, our subjugation of the Filipinos, and President Hall rebuking the honest words spoken in condemnation of the President who is mainly responsible for the war with Spain and all its miserable consequences. Mistaken as I hold the sentiments of these gentlemen to be, I was yet glad of their utterance as an illustration of the freedom which our Dinners encourage, and I am proud to believe that these Dinners are

recognized by the community at large as occasions when
men may be heard who do not hesitate to express opinions
however temporarily unpopular, and are not to be silenced
by any clamour of the press or of the crowd. . . .

"Should I continue to preside over the Dinners I shall not
cease to speak my mind freely in regard to national affairs in
which we, little and few as we are, have a part; nor shall I
cease to invite as speakers, men of eminence whose views
may not be in accordance with those of the majority of the
nation, or of the people of the town. Here, at least, the principles which the minority hold as sacred, shall be maintained."

A PARTIAL LIST OF THE SPEAKERS

George William Curtis.
President G. Stanley Hall.
The Rev. John W. Chadwick.
The Rev. J. B. Harrison.
The Rev. Charles G. Ames.
Charles P. Cranch.
James Russell Lowell.
Charles Dudley Warner.
William Dean Howells.
George W. Cable.
President Carter (Williams Col-
lege).
President Seeley (Smith College)
Booker T. Washington.
The Hon. Joseph H. Choate.
The Hon. E. J. Phelps.
Dr. Robert Collyer.
Edward Atkinson.
Henry S. Prichett.
William Garrott Brown.

Nathaniel S. Shaler.
William James.
Josiah Royce.
Richard H. Dana.
Wayne MacVeagh.
Franklin MacVeagh.
Sherman S. Rogers.
Gov. William E. Russell.
Gov. D. H. Chamberlain.
President T. C. Mendenhall
(Worcester Polytechnic Insti-
tute).
The Rev. Philip Moxom.
The Rev. Robert E. Jones.
Col. William G. Rice.
Charles S. Hamlin.
Moorfield Storey.
Edwin Burritt Smith.
Sir Frederick Pollock.

On the walls of the Ashfield Town Hall where the Academy Dinners were held are two bronze tablets, with the
following inscriptions engraved upon them: —

IN GRATEFUL AND AFFECTIONATE REMEMBRANCE
OF
GEORGE WILLIAM CURTIS
AND AS A MEMORIAL OF HIS PRESENCE AND SPEECH
ON MANY OCCASIONS IN THIS HALL
THIS TABLET IS SET UP BY
THE CURTIS CLUB OF ASHFIELD
MDCCCXCVI

THIS TABLET IS ERECTED IN LOVING MEMORY
OF
CHARLES ELIOT NORTON
AND OF HIS
LONG AND CONSTANT FRIENDSHIP
FOR THIS TOWN
BY
CITIZENS OF ASHFIELD
MDCCCCIX

APPENDIX D

PROFESSOR NORTON, SENATOR HOAR, AND THE WAR WITH SPAIN

WITHOUT the text of Senator Hoar's words about his classmate, and of the correspondence that ensued, it is impossible fully to understand Norton's position at the time of the Spanish War.

At the sixth annual session of the Clark University Summer School (on July 13, 1898), Senator Hoar discussed "Americanism and American Honour"; in the course of his speech he said, according to the printed report: "I see that Professor Norton of Harvard is quoted as telling the youth of the University that it is characteristic of the American people to be trifling. . . . The professor, a little later, gives us his opinion that the war is unjust and dishonest, and advises the youth who look to him for counsel that it is not their duty to enter it. The trouble with Professor Norton, who thinks his countrymen are lacking in a sense of honour, is that there are two things he cannot in the least comprehend — he cannot comprehend his countrymen, and he cannot comprehend honour."

On July 15 Norton wrote from Ashfield to Senator Hoar: —

"You have seen fit, disregarding our almost lifelong relations of friendliness, to make a public attack on me of verbal severity, but of such a nature as relieves me from all necessity of self-defense. Having the intention of making an attack of this sort, it might have been expected that you would be careful to make sure of its grounds. This, however, was not the case. You assail me for words which you say you have seen quoted as addressed by me to 'the youth of the university' where you and I were classmates more than fifty years ago. If you saw them thus quoted, you were led into error. No such words were addressed by me to the youth of the university. They are garbled sentences from an account in a Western newspaper of an interview with me, dishonourably obtained and incorrectly reported.

"I did say to the youth of the university that this war with Spain was 'inglorious'; that for the accomplishment of the ends which, as a nation, we proposed to seek by its means, it was 'needless' and consequently 'criminal'; that every American held his life at the service of his country, but that they should carefully consider whether the best use they could make of themselves in her service was to enlist in such a war. I see no reason to change these opinions and this advice."

On July 18, Senator Hoar replied: —

"I have your letter of 15th July. I am sorry that what you say does not seem to impose upon me any necessity for either apology or regret. The utterances attributed to you, which I quoted, were printed in many of the newspapers of the country for a long time without being disavowed. It seems impossible that a man who does not entertain such sentiments, in substance, should fail to disavow them, if he have any care or respect for the opinions of his countrymen.

"But whether they were literally reported or not, they are in general accord, I am sorry to say, with the sentiments I am constantly in the habit of hearing of as coming from you, both in public utterances and private speech, and of the style with which I used to be not unfamiliar when I occasionally met you. All lovers of Harvard, and all lovers of the country, have felt for a long time that your relation to the University made your influence bad for the college and bad for the youth of the country. It was high time that somebody should say what I have said. I could easily, from my own memory, and from the report of persons who have met you on social occasions, point out many utterances quite as deserving of severe reproof as those to which I have adverted.

"I am afraid that the habit of bitter and sneering speech about persons and public affairs has so grown upon you that you do not yourself know, always, what you say. At any rate, there are plenty of persons who will be able to judge of the matter. I should be sorry to do you any injustice. Indeed, it is not in anybody's power to do you injustice, but yourself."

To these letters a word may be added: when Senator Hoar and Mr. Norton met, several years later, the relation of earlier days was in a measure renewed.

APPENDIX E

A GIFT TO NORTON

MANY as were the expressions of friendship and kindness which came to Norton during the latter years of his life, none touched him more deeply than the gift made to him in 1905, when the rare and interesting books from his library were bought by friends, and given to the Library of Harvard University.

The names (581) of those who had joined in the gift, were inlaid in a volume, beautifully bound, and bearing the following words of dedication:

TO

CHARLES ELIOT NORTON

FROM

HIS PUPILS ASSOCIATES AND FRIENDS

IN APPRECIATION

OF HIS SERVICES TO HARVARD UNIVERSITY

DURING MANY YEARS

IN ADMIRATION

OF HIS LIFELONG DEVOTION TO HIGH IDEALS

IN LETTERS ART AND CIVIC DUTY

IN GRATITUDE

FOR HIS HOSPITALITY COUNSEL FRIENDSHIP

INSPIRATION.

Felice te, che sì parli a tua posta!

MDCCCCV

APPENDIX F

BIBLIOGRAPHY [1]

I

PUBLICATIONS RELATING TO DANTE

The New Life of Dante. *Atlantic Monthly*, Jan., Feb., March, 1859.
Also published separately, considerably enlarged, with additional translations and original matter, with the title: The New Life of Dante; an essay with translations. Cambridge, 1859. (100 copies.)

A Review of a Translation into Italian of the Commentary by Benvenuto da Imola on the Divina Commedia. *Atlantic Monthly*, May, 1861.
Also issued separately. Cambridge, 1861. (50 copies.)

On the Original Portraits of Dante. Cambridge, 1865. (50 copies.)
[On the Original portraits of Dante. Translated into Japanese by T. Funahashi.] *Aoyama Review*, Dec. 30, 1893.

Dante and his latest English Translators. *North American Review*, April, 1866.

The New Life of Dante Alighieri. Translated by C. E. N. Boston, 1867.
Also Boston, 1892; and Cambridge, 1892. (Large paper ed. 250 copies.)
The "Sonnets" as here translated were also republished as Sonnets from the Vita Nuova of Dante. Translated by C. E. N. Brookline, Mass., 1906. (Privately printed, 30 copies.)

The Divine Comedy of Dante Alighieri. Translated by C. E. N. Boston, etc., 1891–92. 3 vols.
Also Cambridge, 1892. 3 vols. (Large paper ed. 250 copies.)
Revised edition. Boston, etc., 1902. 3 vols.

Dean Plumptre's Translation of the Divine Comedy. *Nation*, Feb. 3, 1897.

Dante. (*In* The Warner Classics, selected from the Introductory Studies included in the Library of the World's Best Literature. N.Y., 1897. Vol. 3.)

The Purport of the Divine Comedy. *Roma Letteraria*, 10 aprile, 1899.

[1] Prepared by Mr. David Heald of the Harvard University Library.

[Dante; an Essay. Translated into Japanese by En Kashiwai. With an appendix containing a translation of chapters II and III of Dinsmore's Aids to the study of Dante. Tokio, 1906.] Note on the Vocabulary of the Vita Nuova. (*In* Dante Society, Cambridge, Mass.; 25th annual report, 1907.)

II

OTHER WRITINGS

Five Christmas Hymns. [Edited by C. E. N.] Cambridge, 1852.

Dwellings and Schools for the Poor. *North American Review*, April, 1852.

Considerations on some recent Social Theories. Boston, 1853.

A Book of Hymns for Young Persons. [Edited by C. E. N.] Cambridge, 1854.

The Manchester Exhibition. *Atlantic Monthly*, Nov., 1857.

The Indian Revolt. *Atlantic Monthly*, Dec., 1857.

The Catacombs of Rome. *Atlantic Monthly*, March, April, May, June, July, 1858.

Letters relating to a Collection of Pictures made by J. J. Jarves. Cambridge, 1859. (Privately printed.)

Despotism in India. *North American Review*, April, 1859.

Model Lodging-Houses in Boston. *Atlantic Monthly*, June, 1860.

Pasquin and Pasquinades. *Atlantic Monthly*, Oct., 1860.

Notes of Travel and Study in Italy. Boston, 1860.

A portion of these notes appeared in *The Crayon* during 1856.

Original Memorials of Mrs. Piozzi. *Atlantic Monthly*, May, 1861.

The Advantages of Defeat. *Atlantic Monthly*, Sept., 1861.

Journal of a Privateersman. [Edited by C. E. N.] *Atlantic Monthly*, Sept., Oct., 1861.

Alexis de Tocqueville. *Atlantic Monthly*, Nov., 1861.

The Soldier of the Good Cause. Boston, 1861. (American Unitarian Association. Tracts, Army Series, No. 2.)

Arthur Hugh Clough. *Atlantic Monthly*, April, 1862.

The North American Review. [Edited by J. R. Lowell and C. E. N. 1863–68.]

Immorality in Politics. *North American Review*, Jan., 1864.

St. Louis and Joinville. *North American Review*, April, 1864.

Goldwin Smith. *North American Review*, Oct., 1864.

Abraham Lincoln. *North American Review*, Jan., 1865.

America and England. *North American Review*, April, 1865.

American Political Ideas. *North American Review*, Oct., 1865.

The President's Message. *North American Review*, Jan., 1866.

Harvard Memorial Biographies [a Review]. *North American Review*, Oct., 1866.
The Work of the Sanitary Commission. *North American Review*, Jan., 1867.
Religious Liberty. *North American Review*, April, 1867.
Arthur Hugh Clough. *North American Review*, Oct., 1867.
Charles Dickens. *North American Review*, April, 1868.
The Church and Religion. *North American Review*, April, 1868.
John Hookham Frere. *North American Review*, July, 1868.
The Poverty of England. *North American Review*, July, 1869.
The Holbein Madonna. [London, 1872.] (Privately printed.)
A list of the drawings, engravings, and etchings by Turner, and from his designs, shown in connection with Mr. Norton's Lectures on Turner and his work, at the Parker Memorial Hall, Boston, April 23–May 5, 1874. Cambridge, 1874.
Catalogue of the plates of Turner's Liber Studiorum, with an introduction and notes. Cambridge, 1874.
Philosophical Discussions by Chauncey Wright. With a Biographical Sketch of the Author by C. E. N. N.Y., 1877.
The Dimensions and Proportions of the Temple of Zeus at Olympia. *American Academy of Arts and Sciences, Proceedings*, May–Nov., 1877.
Venice and St. Mark's. *Atlantic Monthly*, Feb., 1878.
Florence, and St. Mary of the Flower. *Atlantic Monthly*, Nov., Dec., 1878.
List of the Principal Books relating to the Life and Works of Michelangelo; with notes. *Harvard College Library Bulletin*, Nos. 7–11. 1878–79.
   Republished as no. 3 of the Bibliographical Contributions of the Library of Harvard University, 1879.
Notes of Drawings by Mr. Ruskin placed on exhibition at the Museum of Fine Arts, Boston, February, 1880. Cambridge, 1879.
Historical Studies of Church Building in the Middle Ages: Venice, Siena, Florence. N.Y., 1880.
The Greek Play at Harvard. *Atlantic Monthly*, July, 1881.
Address [at the Celebration of the Two Hundredth Anniversary of the Building of the Old Meeting-house at Hingham, August 8, 1881.] (*In* The commemorative services of the First parish in Hingham, on the two hundredth anniversary of the building of its meeting-house. Hingham, 1882.)
   Also published separately, Cambridge, 1882.
The Correspondence of Thomas Carlyle and Ralph Waldo Emerson, 1834-1872. [Edited by C. E. N.] Boston, 1883. 2 vols.

The same. Supplementary letters. Boston, 1886.
The first American classical Archæologist [J. I. Middleton].
American Journal of Archæology, Jan., 1885.
Early Letters of Thomas Carlyle. Edited by C. E. N. London, etc.,
1886. 2 vols.
Correspondence between Goethe and Carlyle. Edited by C. E. N.
London, etc., 1887.
Reminiscences by Thomas Carlyle. Edited by C. E. N. London,
etc., 1887. 2 vols.
Letters of Thomas Carlyle, 1826–1836. Edited by C. E. N.
London, etc., 1889.
The Intellectual Life of America. *New Princeton Review,* Nov.,
1888.
A Definition of the Fine Arts. *Forum,* March, 1889.
The Lack of Old Homes in America. *Scribner's Magazine,* May,
1889.
Rawdon Brown and the Gravestone of "Banished Norfolk."
Atlantic Monthly, June, 1889.
The Building of the Church of St.-Denis. *Harper's Magazine,* Oct.,
1889.
The Building of the Cathedral at Chartres. *Harper's Magazine,*
Nov., 1889.
James Russell Lowell. *Harper's Magazine,* May, 1893.
The Letters of James Russell Lowell. *Harper's Magazine,* Sept.,
1893.
The Heart of Oak Books, edited by C. E. N. Boston, 1894–95.
6 vols.
"A collection of traditional rhymes and stories for children."
Letters of James Russell Lowell. Edited by C. E. N. N.Y., 1894.
2 vols.
Harvard. (*In* Four American Universities: Harvard, Yale, Prince-
ton, Columbia. N.Y., 1895.)
The Educational Value of the History of the Fine Arts. *Educa-
tional Review,* April, 1895.
The Poems of John Donne, from the Text of the Edition of 1633
revised by James Russell Lowell. With the various readings of
the other editions of the seventeenth century, and with a preface,
and introduction, and notes by C. E. N. N.Y. The Club. 1895.
2 vols.
Some Aspects of Civilization in America. *Forum,* Feb., 1896.
The Poems of Mrs. Anne Bradstreet (1612–1672); together with
her Prose Remains. With an introduction by C. E. N. [N.Y.]
The Duodecimos. 1897. (144 copies.)

APPENDICES 465

The Text of Donne's Poems. *Harvard Studies and Notes in Philology and Literature*, vol. 5. 1897.

Francis James Child. *American Academy of Arts and Sciences, Proceedings*, July, 1897.

Two Note Books of Thomas Carlyle, from 23d March, 1822, to 16th May, 1832. Edited by C. E. N. N.Y. The Grolier Club. 1891. (390 copies.)

Il Pesceballo, opera in one act. Italian words by Francis James Child. English version by James Russell Lowell. Chicago. The Caxton Club. 1899. (210 copies.)
Contains an introduction by C. E. N.

Rudyard Kipling; a Biographical Sketch. New York, 1899. (100 copies.)
"This sketch was written for the new popular edition of his writings."

The Work of the Archæological Institute of America; an Address at the opening of the first general meeting of the Institute, held at New Haven, Dec. 27–29, 1899. *American Journal of Archæology.* Jan.–Mar., 1900.

The Life and Character of George William Curtis. (*In* Memorials of two friends, James Russell Lowell: 1819–1891, George William Curtis: 1824–1892. N. Y., 1902. (Privately printed, 50 copies.)

The Poet Gray as a Naturalist, with Selections from his Notes on the Systema Naturae of Linnæus and Facsimiles of some of his Drawings. Boston, 1903. (500 copies.)

Letters of John Ruskin to Charles Eliot Norton. [Edited by C. E. N.] Boston, etc., 1904. 2 vols.
First published in part, in *Atlantic Monthly*, May, June, July, Aug., Sept., 1904.

The Love Poems of John Donne. Selected and edited by C. E. N. Boston, 1905. (535 copies.)

Reminiscences of Old Cambridge. *Cambridge Historical Society, Publications*, I, 1906.

The New Humanistic Type. *Printing Art*, Jan., 1906.

Henry Wadsworth Longfellow; a Sketch of his Life by C. E. N., together with Longfellow's Chief Biographical Poems. Boston, etc., 1907.

INDEX

Throughout the Index the initial N., standing by itself, represents C. E. Norton. In some other cases initials and familiar abbreviations are used where there is no possibility of mistake.

Aaron Burr Legion, **2,** 321.

Abbeville, Church of, **1,** 310.

Abbot, Ezra, co-editor with N. of A. Norton's works, **1,** 82, 83.

Abolitionists, labours of, less damaging to slavery than course of slave states, **1,** 217.

Acland, Sir H. W., **1,** 174, 175, 176, 177, 501.

Acton, John, Lord, his position at Rome, **1,** 379 and *n.;* his death, **2,** 325; his lectures on modern history, 370; his vast knowledge, 371; **1,** 381, 382, **2,** 294.

Acton, Lady, **1,** 381, 382.

Adams, Charles F., **1,** his opinions worthy of confidence, **1,** 233; dissatisfied with Lincoln, but a strong ally of Seward, 233; **2,** 60.

Adams, Charles F., Jr., his life of Dana, **1,** 98*n.;* quoted, **2,** 278; on methods of dealing with labour disputes, 331 and *n.;* his address on R. E. Lee praised by N., 366, 369, 370, 373; his letter on N.'s 80th birthday, 391; letter of Sara Norton to, 423. *Letters to,* **2,** 366, 373, 391, 421.

Adams, John, **1,** 10*n.*

Adams, John Quincy, **1,** 10*n.,* 399.

Adams, Nehemiah, his views on slavery, **1,** 121.

Addison, Joseph, Forster's copy of his *Letters from Italy,* **1,** 321.

Adirondack Club, **1,** 183*n.,* 191, 192.

Æschylus, **1,** 101, **2,** 34.

Agassiz, Louis, and the *Origin of Species,* **1,** 202; admires McClellan, 260; his death, **2,** 36*n.;* Lowell's poem on, 36, 42; **1,** 129, 183*n.,* 191, 446, **2,** 39.

Agnew, Joan, the prime minister of Ruskin's household, **1,** 355, 358, 363. *And see* Severn, Mrs. Joan.

Agnostics, timidity of, **2,** 216.

Agra, **1,** 35.

Aitken, Mary, Carlyle's niece, **1,** 322; marries Alex. Carlyle, **2,** 117. *And see* Carlyle, Mrs. Mary (Aitken).

Akers, Benjamin R., **1,** 154.

Alabama, terrorism in, **1,** 212.

Alabama (cruiser), destruction of, **1,** 271.

Alban Hills, the, **1,** 157.

Alcibiades, **2,** 343.

Alcott, A. Bronson, the potato-and-apple evangelist, **2,** 113; **1,** 88.

Aldrich, Thomas Bailey, **2,** 20, 421.

Alembert, Jean B. d', **1,** 464.

Alexander, James, **2,** 68.

Alexandria, Egypt, **1,** 35.

Allen, J. H., **2,** 289.

Allingham, William, **1,** 423 and *n.,* 429, 440, 464, 466, **2,** 52.

Allston, Washington, **2,** 316.

Amberley, Lady, **1,** 493.

Ambleside, home of the Cloughs at, **1,** 148.

America, and Europe, contrast between, **1,** 178; lack of thought in, N.'s lecture on, **2,** 186. *And see* United States.

American archæology, **2,** 111, 112.

American ideals, **2,** 262.

American invasion of Europe, **1,** 136, 137.

American Journal of Archæology, **2,** 99*n.*

American patriotism, spirit of, **2,** 263.

American Unitarian Association, publishes N.'s *Soldier of the Good Cause,* **1,** 221.

492; his moral influence unimpaired, 492; N.'s feeling toward, 492, 493; Mrs. N.'s regard for, 492; Carlyle on his relations with Mrs. Taylor, 498; disapproves of George Eliot's union with Lewes, 498; cause of his breach with Carlyle, 499, 500; marries Mrs. Taylor, 500; on the study of art, **2**, 4, 5; his *Autobiography*, 18; his experience of love, 18, 19; C. Wright's memoir of, 22 and *n.*; **1**, 344, 353, **2**, 174.

Mill, Mrs. John S. *See* Taylor, Mrs.

Millais, John E., **1**, 174.

Mills, Charles H., *letter to*, **1**, 55.

Milman, Henry H., *Life of Horace*, **1**, 31, 34; his notes on Gibbon, 34; 45.

Milnes, Richard M., **1**, 71.

Milton, John, quoted, apropos of Lincoln, **1**, 243; Lowell's essay on his *Areopagitica*, **2**, 203; *Paradise Lost*, 330; Lycidas, quoted, 397; **1**, 32, 101, 102, 460, **2**, 338, 407, 422.

Milton (ship), N. sails for India on, **1**, 28; her voyage, 31, 32.

"Minor poets," verse of, valued by N., **2**, 396.

Minot, Dr. Francis, **2**, 131.

Mirabeau, Comte de, his correspondence with La Marck, **1**, 94; N.'s view of his character, 94, 95; his death, 95.

Mississippi, terrorism in, **1**, 212.

Missouri, question of emancipation in, **1**, 184.

Missouri Compromise, proposed repeal of, **1**, 105; repealed, 111.

"Missouri Legislature" of Kansas, calls Lecompton convention, **1**, 187.

Missourians in Kansas, **1**, 131.

Mitchell, S. Weir, his 70th birthday, **2**, 339, 340; his *Ode on a Lycian Tomb*, 386; his address to graduating nurses, 405; his services to his fellows, 405; 415. *Letters to*, 339, 358, 359, 366, 385, 404.

Mitford, Mary R., **1**, 71.

Model Lodging-Houses in Boston, described by N., **1**, 203–206.

Molière, Poquelin de, *Tartuffe*, **1**,

312; Brunetière's lecture on, **2**, 253.

Molly Maguire troubles, riots following, **2**, 69.

Monitor, the, **1**, 254.

Monroe, James, Pres. U.S., **1**, 399.

Mont Blanc, **1**, 145.

Montaigne, Michel de, quoted, **2**, 216; 365.

Montaperti, battle of, **1**, 401.

Monte Generoso, **2**, 155.

Moody, William V., **2**, 226, 227.

Moonshees, **1**, 43.

Moore, Charles, *letter to*, **2**, 345 and *n.*

Moore, Prof. E. C., **2**, 363 and *n.*

Moore, Canon, **2**, 393.

More, Henry, **2**, 373, 374.

More, Paul Elmer, **2**, 401.

Morecambe Bay, **2**, 148.

Morley, John, N.'s judgment of, **1**, 432; a worthy disciple of Mill, 432; gets into Parliament, **2**, 144; visits Boston, 349; **1**, 351, 431, 448, **2**, 142, 294.

Morris, William, his character, **1**, 310, 470; N.'s first meeting with, 342; and Burne-Jones, 344, 345, 346; his first poems the extremest expression of Pre-Raphaelitism, 345; his *Earthly Paradise*, 346, 403, 404 and *n.*; lofty character of his work, 348; N.'s attachment to, 348; *Lovers of Gudrun*, 404; his travels, 489, 490; what his genius lacked, **2**, 286; **1**, 422*n.*, 436, 445, 448, 450, **2**, 351.

Morris, William, Life of, **2**, 285.

Morrison, J. Cotter, **1**, 449 and *n.*

Morse, Edward S., *letter to*, **2**, 343.

Motley, J. Lothrop, contributes to first number of *Atlantic*, **1**, 186; his letters discussed, **2**, 190, 191; N.'s estimate of, 430; **1**, 189, 223, 224, 272, **2**, 108, 231.

Motley, J. L., Correspondence of, **2**, 190, 191.

Müller, Max, Emerson on, **1**, 513; 493, 501.

Munro, Hugh A. J., his *Lucretius*, **1**, 289.

Muratori, A. L. A., **1**, 396, **2**, 83.

Murphy, Thomas, collector of N.Y., **1**, 414.

[1] For references to the particulars of Norton's intercourse with his friends and others and of comments upon their characters and works; and to the many subjects to which he referred in his letters, see under the appropriate entries.

quaintance with Italy, 61; advantage of the approach *via* India, 61; his experiences in Paris, 1850, 61–68; his first meeting with G. W. Curtis, 68; his experiences in England, 1850, 68–71; social life in London, 70, 71; again on the Continent, 72*ff.*; on his lack of knowledge, 72; in Florence, 73*ff.*; intercourse with the Brownings, 73; again in Paris, 79, 80; his sister's marriage, 80; the fruits of his journey, 80.

Engaged in East India trade, 81; his business career brought to an end by 1855, 82; his *Five Christmas Hymns*, 82; on his father's death, edits certain of his works, 82, 83; his biographical sketch of his father, quoted, 83–85; his *Considerations of Some Recent Social Theories*, 85; life at Newport and Shady Hill, friendships, literary and social interests, and interest in public affairs, 85–135.

In Europe in 1855–57, 136–177; notes changes in Paris, 141; journal of an expedition in Southern Italy, 144, 145; beginning of his devotion to Dante, 144; his views on Italian politics, 160, 161; and on Catholicism, 166; his letters from Venice, 169; on the contrast between America and Europe, 178; his *Notes of Study and Travel in Italy*, 137, 154, 179.

His literary labours, 1857–1861, 179, 180; contributes to the *Atlantic*, 179; publishes his translation of the *Vita Nuova*, 179; loses MSS. for first numbers of *Atlantic*, 182, 189; on affairs in Kansas (1857), 183, 184, 185, 186–188, 190; on the hard times of 1857, 184, 185; on the condition of Mexico, 190, 191; Seward his choice for President, 194, 232; describes the Boston Model Lodging-Houses, 204–206; deplores the prevailing "looseness and avoidance of thought," etc., 208; on the prospect and consequences of secession, 211–213, 216, 217; on the attitude of the North, 212, 213; believes that the solution

of slavery will be found in the present troubles, 214; on the lack of interest in literature, 214; no time for timid counsels, 215; a nominal union not worth preserving, 215, 216; deems civil war "a remote possibility" (Feb. '61), 217, 218; his changing opinions of Lincoln, 218, 219, 228, 232, 242, 243, 245, 246, 252, 253, 255, 258, 263; on the proposed 13th Amendment, 219; significance of his letters during the war, 221; with Lowell, becomes editor of the *North American Review*, 221, 266, 268; describes the founding and work of the Loyal Publication Society, 221–223, 259, 260; marries Susan R. Sedgwick, 224; continues to live at Shady Hill, 225; lectures at Lowell Institute on *Characteristics of the Twelfth Century*, 225, 226; his letters to Curtis mark the course of his life for 42 years, 226, 227.

Anticipates collision between North and South (Apr. 10, '61), 228; on the problems of the new administration, 229; disapproves of Sumner's talk, 232, 233; on the effect of the attack on Sumter, 234; on the N.Y. papers, 238; on the prospects of the war, 241, 244, 255, 256, 270, 271, 272, 277; hopes for change in the Cabinet, 241, 242; rejoices in the Emancipation Proclamation, 256, 257; on the elections of 1862, 258; one of the founders of the Union Club, 261; on Democrats and Republicans, 262; on the elections of 1863, 265; does full justice to Lincoln, 266, 267, 271, 282; beginning of his friendship with L. Stephen, 266, 267; makes his summer home in Ashfield, 268, 269, 270; sees the beginning of the end, 277, 278; on lack of good sense among Republicans, 278; on Lincoln's reëlection, 282; on Lee's surrender, 282; his patriotic services after the war, 283; assists in founding the *Nation*, 283; Godkin ascribes success of the *Nation* to him, 283, 284; his

on *Church Building in the Middle Ages*, 56; looks for a break-up of old parties (1876), 65; on his children's interest in Raphael and Holbein, 78; is conscious of growing old, 79; on the depressing state of public affairs (1878), 80, 81; on the new parties, 81; reading on the Renaissance, 84; his identification with the concerns of Ashfield, 87–89; his mother's death, 90, 91, 92, 93; his relations with her, 91; bound to the U. S. by duty to her and to his children, 91; where would his life be better? 91, 92.

The wide reach of his industry, 94 *ff.*; publishes his translation of the *Divine Comedy*, 104; his untiring revision of the translation, 104; his erudition, his scorn of loose thinking, etc., 106; the proposed Independent Republican movement of 1880, 109; his *Church Building in the Middle Ages*, 109, 110, 111; his uncertain health, 114; on Froude's handling of the Carlyle biographical material, and his various publications, 119, 120, 135, 136, 139, 143, 146, 170, 174, 178, 183; on natural beauty, 122; commemoration at Hingham, 125; one of the Faculty Committee on the Regulation of Athletic Sports, 134; undertakes to edit the Emerson-Carlyle correspondence, 137, 139, 143, 173, 174; letters from Emerson and Carlyle thereon, 137, 138; on the literature of the 19th century, 140; his practice of reading aloud, 140, 141.

In England and Italy for his health in 1883, 148*ff.*; crosses the Simplon, 152; travelling in northern Italy, 152*ff.*; on the ills caused by the progress of democracy in Europe, 156; on changes in Cambridge, 158; again in England in 1884, 159*ff.*; represents Harvard at the Tercentenary of Emmanuel College, 159, 160–162, 163; receives honorary degree from Cambridge 160–162; on Emmanuel's service to Americans, 163; on the campaign of 1884, 165; on various

phases of "democracy," 166, 239, 242, 243, 244; on pessimism, and the out-and-out pessimist, 167, 168; on the needless rubs and worries of life, 177; entertains students on Christmas Eve, 178; is a society worth saving that has lost its fastidiousness? 179, 180; on the paucity of "literature," 181; on the men of letters of his time, 181, 182; his solitariness, 182; on life and its significance, 182, 183; writes on the *Lack of Thought in America*, 186; dislikes winter, 186; one's *best* always falls short of one's ideal, 188, 189; is indifferent to everything but love for his fellows, 189; on the "killing out" of society by modern materialism, 193, 194; constant extension of his friendships in the younger generation, 195, 196; his connection with the Tavern Club, 196–198; edits the *Heart-of-Oak Books*, 199 and *n.*; reflections aroused by the meeting of the G.A.R. in Boston, 199, 200; on the unimportance of time in friendship, 200, 201; on the twofold aspect of Italy, 207, 208; on the Catholic Church, 208, 209; on the delusive consolations of religion, 211; human nature in presidential campaigns, 214; on agnosticism, 215, 216; on the character of the American people, and their standards, 219, 220; on the teaching of Philosophy, etc., in Japan from Western textbooks, 222, 223; on the effect of victory over China on Japanese ideals, 223; his openness to the modern appeal in literature and art, 226; his dislike of insincerity in art, 226; his interest in beautiful engraving, 227; his ideas on modern illustration, 227; on beauty, 230; on the temptations of the summer days, 231, 232; his *Some Aspects of Civilization in America*, 238, 241; on the depressing state of public affairs, 241, 243, 244, 270, 273; on the warlike aspect of affairs, 242; has lived in the most interesting period of history, 242, 244,

The Riverside Press
CAMBRIDGE . MASSACHUSETTS
U . S . A